the

BEST

is yet to

COME

First Print Edition, 2023
Printed in China

Publishing Services: Jodi Cowles, Brandon Janous, and Rachael Mitchell, Blue Hat Publishing
Cover Design & Interior Layout: Tim Marshall, Blue Hat Publishing
Author Photograph: Amanda Gargano, Paint the Stars Photography
All other photos courtesy of Steve Healy

ISBN (print): 978-1-962674-00-3
ISBN (ebook): 978-1-962674-01-0

BLUE HAT
PUBLISHING
BOISE · KNOXVILLE · NASHVILLE · SEATTLE
WWW.BLUEHATPUBLISHING.COM

STEVE HEALY

the BEST *is yet to* COME

52 REFLECTIONS ON WHAT SHE TAUGHT ME

CONTENTS

To our children, Bailey, Rian, and Everett.
You are the best of us, and your mom is so proud of you.
I love you. I want to be just like you when I grow up.

INTRODUCTION

Thursday, July 14, 2022

AFTERMATH

I can't believe it's been a month since you left. One whole month without you.

What has followed has been a month spent releasing you. A month spent remembering you and reeling about losing you. All while starting to remove your tangible presence from the life we built together. I'm grateful…but gutted at the same time.

I'm so relieved you aren't suffering anymore, but I miss holding your hand.

I'm thankful for all the time we had, but I miss talking to my friend.

I'm so happy you are in Glory, but what remains of me down here is pretty busted up.

Most of all, I'm infuriated.

I'm infuriated that this disease, this pestilence, this hateful curse of cancer robs not only me but our kids, and everyone else for that matter, of you, continuing to show all of us the things Jesus had revealed to you in the countless quiet hours you spent with Him. It seemed like you were just getting started. It ended way too soon. It's just not right…

So, I've decided to do something about it.

I've decided to do my best to honor you and our King by ensuring the precious principles you learned in solitude that daily set your frame, hands, feet, speech, and heart are passed along.

Your death will not be the end of your ministry.

The banner has not fallen. Your flag has not been captured…

It's been passed on, and I will do what I can to see that His guidon keeps moving forward.

I know I have an enemy that will war against me as he did you. But this is far too important, and this is far from over.

So, I'll be back soon...I'm gathering all the things you taught me along the way. The profound truths Jesus graciously taught you.

Your death was untimely. But the wisdom He gave you was eternal. It is worth cherishing. It is worth communicating.

It is worth it because He is worthy.

This is the post I wrote one month following the passing of my wife, Nicole Healy.

Nik died on June 14th, 2022, after a nearly 3-year battle with rectal cancer. Nik died one week prior to her 40th birthday.

As her husband and as a pastor, I had the bittersweet responsibility of overseeing and conducting her funeral. When the time came to eulogize my beloved wife, I said,: "...Nik was loyal, caring, tender, humble, selfless, and keenly self-aware. She loved her family, her friends, the beach, Christmas, eating crabs, drinking good wine, celebrating her children, and making others feel awkward with her affinity to flip the bird at those who dared to try and take her photograph. She was funny, loving, quietly bold, and rooted everything in her faith in Christ. She was an ever-present help to those in need. She was a woman of integrity, character, and action. She was faithful and never went to bed without holding my hand. Though she spoke little, her words carried great weight and were infused with deep wisdom. The more one learned about her, the more impressive she became. She was accountable and bore her scars with grace. She was loved dearly and will be missed deeply."

Her funeral was attended by hundreds. The viewing the evening before amassed thousands. By the time of this writing, the streamed version of her service has been viewed more than 5,000 times on YouTube and 17,000 times on Facebook.

Nik's "popularity," for lack of a better word, came in part due to my role and position at our church. Much to the surprise of all of us in leadership, Jesus has grown our once small, simple little church into a mighty movement of God. Lighthouse Church, situated just outside of Baltimore, Maryland, is the home to thousands of Jesus-followers who pursue God with a daily ferocity that I find inspiring. As a member of the teaching team there, Nikki's story quickly spread far and wide throughout our greater community.

Approximately a year and a half before her passing, a gentleman who works at the local Baltimore Christian Radio Station, 95.1 Bright FM, learned of Nikki's ordeal. What would follow would be a 10-part podcast during season 3 of the aptly named "Long Story Short," in which David Paul (the podcast owner and creator) chronicled what would be Nik's last year here on Earth. This would make Nik even more "cancer famous" than before (a term Nikki may have dubbed personally, rolled her eyes over, and snickered about constantly). Because of this podcast, our extensive church family, and our former military life, this naturally resulted in us having friends and acquaintances literally all over the globe; Nik had a monumental impact for God's kingdom.

Few could believe it. Her own father told me just days before her memorial service, "Who could have ever imagined? Quiet, reserved, Nikki. That she would put herself out there like she did, and as a result, all these people were affected..."

I was not being argumentative, but I disagreed. I responded, "I did." You see, what people got to witness, albeit for a brief time, I saw every day of my adult life. Nik and I got married at 21 and 22, respectively. We had a child within the first year of our marriage. We were babies having babies. My 10-year career in the Navy took us all over the country, resulting in many nights, weeks, and months apart. Our time together these last several years in ministry and in misery (i.e., her diagnosis and subsequent treatments) galvanized us. We lived a lifetime together in our 18-year marriage. We grew up together. We learned together. We cried together. We fought together. We lost together, and we won together.

Through it all, two things remained constant.

First was Jesus. In good times and in bad times. In sickness and in health. In richer and in poorer. He was always there. Even in our early years together, when we weren't pursuing Him, he was pursuing us. Left unto ourselves, both Nik and I would have never become the couple we were or the individuals he molded us into being.

Second, Nik's unrelenting commitment to keep moving forward. Nikki had righteous indignation for stagnation. In her economy, you were either growing or you were slipping. Climbing or falling. Putting in the hard work or taking the easy path. So, when the time came for much to be made of Christ through Nikki's story, it was no surprise to me that so many stood in awe of this quiet woman's bold faith.

But when the story was told, the last episode released, the final arrangements were made, and my children and I spread her ashes in the ocean tide, a single thought refused to leave my mind: this can't be the end.

Despite the circumstances, I had begun to make peace with Nikki's departure upon her passing. She was in so much pain for so long that I was actually grateful and relieved that she did not have to endure anymore. No more treatment. No more hospitals. No more appointments. No more pain. No more fighting. No more suffering. She was finally at rest, at peace in heaven. Despite the hole in my heart and the loss of my person, I could find some solace in the fact that she was now in the presence of the great I AM.

What I could not reconcile, what I could not place, was that all the wisdom He had put in her would slip away. All the deep knowledge obtained through a lifetime of experiences wrought with the deepest joys and loneliest sorrows was now left to be slowly forgotten over the passing of time as the anecdotes and memories of this incredible woman of God inevitably would fade. Even for me.

It wasn't right. It couldn't be the end. There were things left to be said. There were lessons yet to be taught. The things He taught Nik. The things she selflessly wanted to pass along as quickly as she received them.

What has followed is this: my attempt to pass on, as chronicled within these pages, the principles my wife walked out and taught to anyone wise enough to pay attention. They are worth learning. They are worth pursuing. If taken seriously and done well, I genuinely believe the next year of your life could be one of the most formative ones you will ever have. You will come out on the other side changed. A better spouse, a better parent, a better friend, and more in love with Jesus than you ever have been before.

Now I understand that's quite a claim. I am fully aware that I may not be the most objective judge as I am ghostwriting and purveying the wisdom of my late wife, but I stand by it all the same. So, take me up on my challenge. If you aren't a better human being a year from now than where you started, look me up; I'll extend my hand, apologize earnestly, and buy you a beer.

Until then…Godspeed.

HOW TO USE THIS DEVOTIONAL

Throughout my life in pursuing Jesus, I have read many devotionals. As a pastor, I am aware of a great many more. Due to Nik's 3-year public fight with cancer, she received approximately 86,438 devotionals mailed to our home directly – a slight exaggeration, of course. That said, we often joked that a devotional was part of the "Standard Cancer Care Package," as we affectionately called them around our home. Blanket. Fuzzy socks. Coloring book. Gift card. Devotional. All standard issue. The occasional candle was also included, and I have drawers of them in my home. Should we ever lose power, illuminating our home will not be an issue.

People are incredible. They rally and do what they can. Our experience was many didn't know what to do, or what to say, for that matter – so they would send us the words of another in the form of devotional books.

In all my experience with this genre of literature, I noticed that, for the most part, they all followed a relatively predictable pattern. Each day, a concept was covered. A portion of Scripture was highlighted. And a charge was given. One powerful, dynamic thought to be contemplated for however long that day's schedule allowed. Perhaps a place to take a few notes. Only to close the book, go about the day, and return tomorrow to a new piece of profundity.

This isn't that kind of devotional.

I can be a little thick-headed, and sometimes, it takes a minute for me to partly comprehend a subject, let alone begin to put it into practice. The speed with which the world is moving only worsens my natural predisposition. I can easily be distracted or pulled off-topic due to competing priorities. So, it was my regular experience to read a good, God-honoring concept during my morning prayer time, and totally forgot all about it by the time the lunch hour hit on that day…let alone allow the truth to which I was exposed to actually transform me.

To be clear, I don't blame any author for my shortcomings. Many of the devotionals I have read over the years have been really, really good. They were well thought out, challenging, and (if applied) extremely edifying. The problem lies with me. I needed more time to marinate in a topic. Moving from one topic to another day in and day out ultimately resulted in me checking the box that I was spending time with Jesus but seeing no real heart change. No sanctification. No real growth. I was lying to myself. If I was going to grow and gain perspective, if I was going to be able to traverse "the desert" (explained more in "Concept 1"), then I was going to do that which I have never done before to get that which I never had – a full-year committed to becoming more like Jesus. And that was going to take time.

And I don't think I am the only one.

So, this devotional is likely different from any other devotional you have done. Instead of concentrating on a single concept daily, you will spend an entire week on one single idea. Each week in the same rhythm. Pondering, assessing, planning, and exercising a unique practice.

HERE'S HOW IT WORKS:

On **MONDAY**, a concept is introduced. A brief anecdote about the woman who inspired this book and how I saw Jesus move in her life by putting these concepts into practice. Mondays are simply to get you thinking. Think about the week's topic and reflect upon the concept's application and activity in your life (or lack thereof). Candidly, it's also an opportunity for me to tell you about my wife in my attempt to communicate to you why I even wrote this in the first place. I think by getting to know her, you'll like her. If you think it silly and superfluous to our aim – tough. This is my book. Go ahead and write your own.

On **TUESDAY**, you will read a portion of Scripture that pertains to the concept. It could be a biblical narrative. It could be a psalm or proverb. Regardless, read over it several times. If so compelled, crack open your Bible and read it in the translation that works best for you. Study the context, and if you are so bold, break out a commentary and see what someone a lot more intelligent than this author has to say about it. But at a minimum, read it a few times over. Read it slowly. Allow God's truth to penetrate your mind and your heart. After that, read through the guided prayer. Ask Jesus to meet with you this week as you prepare to grow in the highlighted area. Proclaim to commit to the process of finding what the activity of the forthcoming days will reveal.

On **WEDNESDAY**, **THURSDAY**, and **FRIDAY**, you should be doing some real heavy lifting mentally. You will assess the concept's current application and/or presence in your life (Wednesday – "Assessment"). Then, you will lay out a plan to improve this area of potential growth (Thursday – "Battle Plan"). Lastly, you will identify and commit to removing all possible excuses that could hold you back. You will commit to the process (Friday – "Gut Check").

Each of these days, you will be given a set of 5 thought-provoking questions in order to help you along the way. You don't need to answer all 5 every week. Answer the pertinent ones. If you feel God may be asking you a different question than those proposed, write it down. God still speaks, and I guarantee His questions are better than mine. He knows you; He knows what He wants you to ponder, plan, and remove.

On **SATURDAY**, the rubber meets the road. You will take your first steps toward applying all that Jesus has revealed to you. Some weeks, the first step will be easy and come without much effort. On other weeks, taking that first step may push you so far out of your comfort zone that you may wonder if you can muster the fortitude necessary to move an inch off dead-center. Whatever the week holds, easy or difficult, a walk in the park or a heart-wrenching step of obedience, this is the most critical part of the week. Enlightenment without action is merely head knowledge. God doesn't give you the download to stay still. He wants you to move. After all, faith without works is dead (James 2:26).

Finally, on **SUNDAY**, you will sabbath. You will rest and reflect on all the work you did and all the work Jesus did in you that week. Take a long walk. Sit in silence for a while. Process what happened. You might laugh. You might cry. You might feel like you conquered a giant. You might feel like you failed. You may feel like you finally accomplished something you never felt possible. You might feel like you just started the process, regardless of where you find yourself. Take it to Jesus and, in light of what you learned and did, begin to discern what might be next. Just be sure to spend time thanking Him for all He is doing in you.

Then, you will repeat that process again the following week. 52 times in total. 52 opportunities to get better – to become more like Jesus.

Some concepts you will work through will be unique to that week and that week alone during your year-long journey. Others you will return to later in the year to examine from another angle, akin to turning a gemstone over in your hand, looking at the variety of the nuanced aspects within that greater idea itself. Regardless of whether you examine a topic once or multiple times, the work you will do will be extensive.

To that end, a few last closing comments…

You are going to need a good journal and a good pen. This is work. For this to have any hope of any lasting effect, you will need to write things down. Thoughts that you need to wrestle with. Demons you need to face.

Blind spots that have been revealed. Victories you are going to want to remember and return to one day.

Every day, write things down. Don't let the lessons learned be relegated to memory. They will slip away with time, and you're not going to want to lose a single scrap of what you thought, what you committed to, what you did, and how you saw God show up.

Finally, this work will be tough and there will be plenty of opportunities to quit. Don't. The reason my wife finished well is that she never quit. She did the work every day. Even on the day she died. Because she did the work, this planet is literally a better place. The Kingdom of God grew because she refused to quit growing, learning, and trusting in Jesus.

Now it's your turn.

I'm praying for you, friend. I'm cheering for you. As is the Host of Heaven. The baton is now firmly in your hand.

Time to run.

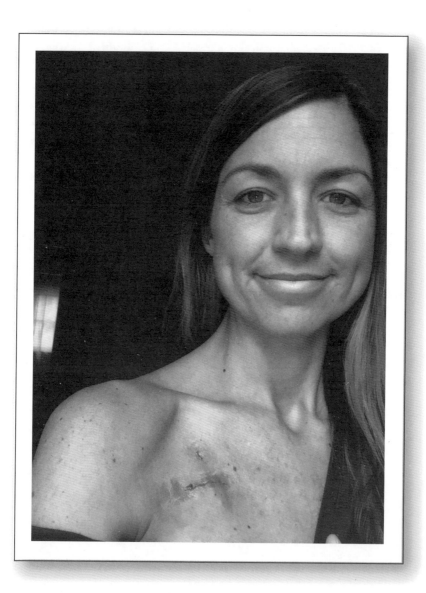

MOVING FORWARD

MONDAY: What She Taught Me

"Be brave. Set boundaries. Stand up for yourself. Love JESUS. And take lots of vacations." - My first "What She Taught Me" Instagram post on July 18, 2022 (52 weeks of weekly lesson postings would follow.)

In the days and weeks following Nik's passing, I watched as countless people, some that knew Nik well and some that never even met her, repost, share, and exclaim her final encouragement and counsel.

An anthem. A battle cry. A simple charge to serve us and the lives we lead that tend to be filled with so much chaos, strife, striving, and the tendency to misappropriate our priorities.

It was the greatest privilege of my life to stand by her side and for her to show me all that Jesus was showing her.

It's my job now to see that work continued.

Some are simple. Some seem silly. At first glance, some are downright offensive. They have shaped who I am, how I perceive things, and in no small way, why I love Jesus so much.

Each week, I'll share one.

One that I am pondering and wrestling with as I process the loss of my person. To paraphrase an incredible mind I am gleaning from these days: "You don't walk out of the valley (trauma) and into the promised land (new beginning)... instead you walk out of the valley, into the desert (processing), and HOPE, one day perhaps, to walk into the promised land - but do know this - as painful and lonely as it may be, there is no hope for a promised land without first going through the desert." - Jordan Peterson

I lost my person in the valley. Now I enter my desert without her.

I enter this place with no expectations, assumptions, or timeline as to when/if I'll pass through it…but if I am to pass through…this is part of that process.

So, I'm gonna start walking and, like my brave wife, try my best to be as real about it as possible in the attempt to help others along the way.

Just like she did.

I'm taking the grace God gives me, the hope Jesus promises me, and the instructions Nik left me.

TUESDAY: *Commitment*

"The LORD had said to Abram, 'Go from your country, your people, and your father's household to the land I will show you'…So Abram went, as the LORD had told him; and Lot went with him. Abram was seventy-five years old when he set out from Harran."- Genesis 12:1,4

"Have I not commanded you? Be strong and courageous. Do not be afraid; do not be discouraged, for the LORD, your God will be with you wherever you go." - Joshua 1:9

LORD, I am not called to stay here. If You had completed Your work in me, I would be at home in heaven with You. Obviously, then, there is more for me to do down here.

I do not know where You will lead me, but I trust You, and I know wherever it is, it is for Your glory and my good. I am choosing to be obedient and follow Your leading. No matter how hard it gets, please give me the grace to always remember that in following You, the best is yet to come.

Amen.

WEDNESDAY: *Assessment*

1. In what aspect of my life have I grown overly comfortable? Do I consider growth important? Do my actions validate this belief?
2. Where am I being challenged to grow?
3. What am I carrying that I am being called to lay down? Am I reticent to lay it down? If so, why?
4. What am I being called to pick up that I have neglected or abdicated to someone else? Am I reticent to pick it up? If so, why?
5. Am I being disobedient and refusing to move forward? If so, why?

THURSDAY: *Battle Plan*

1. What is the first step of obedience in the area God desires for me to grow?
2. Who do I need to take with me or hold me accountable? Why are they the right choice for this task?
3. What does accountability look like, practically speaking?
4. Do I have the necessary time to make this happen? If not, what can I do to make time?
5. Do I have the necessary skill(s) to make this happen? If not, what can I do to acquire the necessary skill(s)?

FRIDAY: *Gut Check*

1. Am I going to do what's necessary? If so, how, and when?
2. What is a measurable assessment of whether or not I have started this process?
3. What does moving forward look like in 30, 60, or 90 days from now? 6 months? Or one year? Am I willing to keep at it, no matter what?

4. Do I believe God will be with me throughout this process, even if I don't always feel like He is? If not, why not?
5. What am I going to do when this work gets hard?

SATURDAY: Baby Steps

I have been a gym rat for most of my life. Dating all the way back to the early days of high school, I have spent most of my days in the weight room. I love it. But after Nik's initial diagnosis, all of that came to a screeching halt. Some of it for good reason. Prioritizing her care meant a lot of rearranging of my schedule. Most, if not all of the margin was taken out of it.

But there were some bad reasons in there too. I lost my motivation. I lost my drive. It just didn't seem to matter anymore. And little by little, bit by bit, I got more and more out of shape, unhealthy, and sick.

One of the first things Nik commissioned me to do upon her passing was to start taking care of myself again. Her words, written in her hand, telling me it was time to start moving forward and to start taking back ground I had lost. Thankfully, I listened. And little by little, bit by bit, I started to find myself again. I got back in shape. I started to get healthy. And I was no longer sick. I did it for myself. I did it for my kids. I did it because Nik told me to. She always did know best.

Now its your turn. It's time for you to take your first step forward.

So do it. Do the first thing you must do to move forward. Confess. Forgive. Have the conversation. Cry. Whatever the first thing you know you must do, take a measurable step toward it. If you can take another step, do it, but take at least one step forward. Today.

When you have done it. Write it down. Write down everything you did, everything you were feeling, everything that was said, and everything that was left unsaid. Write down the date and time. Write down what the weather was like. Write down where it happened and who was there. Crystallize this moment. Return to it often. This is your starting place. You had the courage to begin. Sometimes you will feel like you don't have the courage to continue. Use this moment in those times. You did it once. You can do it again.

Choose today to move forward.

SUNDAY: *Reflect and Rest*

Father God, where are You calling me to move forward? What practical steps did I take this week to be obedient to Your command for me to move forward? What is/are the next practical step(s)?

Father God, thank You for meeting me in this place. Thank You, God for loving me just as I am, yet loving me so much more that You refuse to leave me where You found me.

LORD, I know You are beckoning me to move forward to take the next step in becoming more like Your Son, Jesus. I want to want to take those steps. I want to want to have the same desires as Your heart.

Yet I know at times I will not. I know at times I will falter. I know at times I will be frozen by my fears and inadequacies.

Father, in those times, allow me to feel Your loving presence all around me. Grant me the courage to be brave. For I know if I am brave and choose what You have for me, my life will be a life that brings You glory and me much joy.

Thank You Father in advance for going before me. I love You, Lord. Amen.

BE AUTHENTIC

MONDAY: What She Taught Me

"I don't know how to do this! I mean, rectal cancer! How gross! How embarrassing!" - Nik's private conversation with me following her initial diagnosis in early October 2019

These were the words Nik sobbingly exclaimed when she was finally diagnosed in October of 2019. I think there were a few F-bombs in there, too, honestly.

She was trying to find her footing. She was trying to find her way forward. She was looking for help. And she wasn't talking to me…She was talking to Him.

Often I think I can only go to God in my Sunday best. He will only be pleased with me if my report card warrants it. My lack of piety will result in a lack of His presence.

Nik showed me that Jesus wants all of me. The good and the bad. In my praising and in my questioning. My shouts of gratitude and my shrieks of grief.

In every circumstance, He desires to guide me and lead me…but that can only happen if I am brutally honest with Him.

Only by exercising authenticity do we allow Him to do the heart work necessary to become better. To ascend higher.

So come to Him.

Raw and real. Ecstatic or angry. Penitent or pissed-off. Come broken. Come joyful. Come radiant. Come crushed.

Just come.

Come as you are.

Don't let the devil, this world, or your doubt keep you away.

He is bigger than all of that. And if you do, He promises to help you.

More incredible than that, He will make you more like Himself.

Be authentic.

TUESDAY: Commitment

"Hear me, Lord, and answer me, for I am poor and needy. Guard my life, for I am faithful to you; save your servant who trusts in you. You are my God; have mercy on me, Lord, for I call to you all day long. Bring joy to your servant, Lord, for I put my trust in you. You, Lord, are forgiving and good, abounding in love to all who call to you. Hear my prayer, Lord; listen to my cry for mercy. When I am in distress, I call to you, because you answer me."
- Psalm 86:1-7

Lord, for far too long, I have not been genuine with You. My prayer life is prone to be cursory, repetitive, simplistic, and sporadic. I am hesitant to come to you when I need You the most. I am slow to return to You when I have failed. I avoid You when I am hurt and confused by Your plan. You desire intimacy with me, yet I refuse to reciprocate for so many reasons.

Forgive me, Lord. I recognize that avoiding You or marginalizing our relationship only prolongs my pain and takes me from where You would look to grow me. I repent today. No longer will I avoid our relationship. No longer will I keep it shallow and lacking authenticity. I will come to You when I am joyful. I will come to You when I am sad. I will come to You in questioning. I will come to You in my anger, even in the long seasons of silence. In the seasons of waiting, I will still come.

You are my Father, and I am Your child. My relationship with You determines who I am, how I think, what I do, and where I ultimately will be.

Thank You, Father, for desiring a relationship with me.
Amen.

WEDNESDAY: Assessment

1. How often do I genuinely spend time with God? Do I prioritize this time? If not, why not?
2. Do I have a prayer life? If so, what does it look like?
3. How do I honestly view God? Why?
4. How do I honestly think God views me? Why?
5. What reasons, obstacles, and paradigms have kept me from being honest with God?

THURSDAY: Battle Plan

1. What is the first step in improving my relationship with Jesus and making it more genuine?
2. What do I need to say, confess, or confront God about to move forward in our relationship? Am I hesitant to do so? If so, why?
3. Do I have the necessary time blocked out in my schedule to spend time with Him? If not, how do I make time?
4. How often am I willing to intentionally spend time with God? What does that practically look like?
5. What priorities must I realign to make this happen?

FRIDAY: Gut Check

1. Am I willing to finally get real with God?
2. What is a measurable assessment of whether or not I have started this process?
3. Am I willing to do what is necessary should my honesty with God result in the need for further confession or action on my part that may involve others?
4. Do I trust God will see me through this process? If not, why not?

5. Do I truly believe God wants what is best for me and will guide me in establishing an authentic relationship with Him? If not, why not?

SATURDAY: Baby Steps

It's time. No matter the depth of your relationship with God the Father, Jesus, and the Holy Spirit, there is always more. If we understood His true nature, we would never leave our prayer rooms. We would give anything and everything to be in His presence perpetually. Today God is calling you to take that first step to go deeper with Him.

So, take that first step. If you already have an established prayer life and your times with Jesus are sweet, there is still more He desires for you. Retreat with Him. Ask Him to take your relationship further. If you have relegated your relationship to droning repetitive prayers, own that, confess that, stop that, and start having a genuine conversation. If you don't read His Word daily, start. If you're angry at Him, tell Him, He already knows anyway. If you're confused, hurting, lost, or scared, cry out to Him, and He will meet you in that place. You may not have a mountain-top moment with Him for some time. You may have to wait. But this is certain: you will never have one if you don't start the process. Your life will always be a subpar version of the one He ultimately has for you unless you have an ever-growing relationship with Him.

So, start.

Mark the day down. Write down what you talked to Him about. Write down whether He responded or not. Write down if He gave you the next step in your journey or if you need to stay where you are for a moment. Do it again tomorrow and the next day after that, and the next day after that. After a year, go back and read what you wrote. Look at what He has brought you through. Thank Him. But for now, just start the real conversation.

SUNDAY: *Reflect and Rest*

Jesus, what did I learn when I got honest about our relationship? Where do I want to continue in practice? What do I need to alter or purge? What do I need to do to make this a discipline of my life?

King Jesus, thank You for reminding me this week that You desire an authentically real relationship with me. Thank You for reminding me that You desire for our conversations to be frequent and honest. Thank You for reminding me that You left the hallowed corridors of heaven to make all of this possible. Thank You for reminding me that You do not desire to be distant and far off from me. Thank You for reminding me that You do not want me to be distant and far off from You either. Thank You for meeting me where I am and calling me into more with You.

Lord, I pray this is the start of a deeper and more genuine relationship with You. And I know all of this is possible because of the price You so loving paid for it. I will not take that for granted again.

Thank You, Jesus. I love You, Lord.

Amen.

READ THE ROOM

MONDAY: *What She Taught Me*

"You know, Steve, you never know what the person standing next to you in the grocery store is enduring." - Nik's remark just prior to receiving her first chemo treatment in late October 2019

Despite all her admirable qualities, due to her deep self & situational awareness that could arguably categorize her as an empath, Nik had little tolerance for others who lacked either the forethought or selflessness required in a delicate situation.

Equally so, she was often moved to tears when a person stepped into another's quagmire and rendered the comfort that could only come from a genuine human connection and the desire to ease another's pain.

When the actions of another left her dumbfounded, I would explain to her over and over again that she should never be surprised when an individual acted as they always had, good or bad, in accordance with their character.

She never got that. To Nik, there was always the right thing to do. And if you didn't know what that was, it was your job to figure it out and do it. Being a decent human requires it.

Make time for the phone call to wish a happy birthday. Send "thank you" notes often. Grieve with those who are hurting. Be intentional in listening rather than looking for an opportunity to respond.

I am not a natural empath. I often speak too quickly. I should write more "thank you" notes. I should call upon others to check in on them rather than connect only when I have an agenda. But I'm working on it. Walking with Nik these last few years taught me the importance of slowing down and trying to view the world through the perspective of others. To rejoice with them. To lament with them. To be a comfort to them.

Our interactions with one another are so meaningful. They best reflect how we view His most precious creation, our fellow man.

Life is hard, on everyone. One of the most significant ways we can show God's love toward others is to slow down and pay attention to what is being said and, sometimes, more importantly, what is not. To step outside ourselves and put the needs of others in front of our own. It can be challenging. It takes work. But it is important. Slow down. Look for clues and context. It honors people. It honors God.

Read the room.

TUESDAY: Commitment

… "The Teacher is here," she (Martha) said, "and is asking for you." When Mary heard this, she got up quickly and went to him. Now Jesus had not yet entered the village but was still at the place where Martha had met him. When the Jews who had been with Mary in the house, comforting her, noticed how quickly she got up and went out, they followed her, supposing she was going to the tomb to mourn there. When Mary reached the place where Jesus was and saw him, she fell at his feet and said, "Lord, if you had been here, my brother would not have died." When Jesus saw her weeping, and the Jews who had come along with her also weeping, he was deeply moved in spirit and troubled. "Where have you laid him?" he asked. "Come and see, Lord," they replied. Jesus wept. - John 11:28-35

"Now the earth was formless and empty, darkness was over the surface of the deep, and the Spirit of God was hovering over the waters." - Genesis 1:2

"'Come now, let us settle the matter,' says the Lord. 'Though your sins are like scarlet, they shall be as white as snow; though they are red as crimson, they shall be like wool.'" - Isaiah 1:18

Lord, I need to slow down. I admit that I move too quickly when it comes to interacting with others. I am quick to speak. I am quick to judge. I am quick to assume or dismiss. Seldom do I take the time necessary to better understand the situation and circumstances before speaking into them.

Lord, despite Your omnipotence, Your Word proves that you always relate with Your creation before reacting to it. Your face hovered above the waters before You spoke order out of chaos. You let Job rant before providing Your perspective. You wept with empathy before You acted miraculously.

Lord, I know You want me to have a heart for Your people, so remove the scales from my eyes to see them as You do. For Your Glory, God.

Amen.

WEDNESDAY: Assessment

1. In general, how do I view others? Am I cynical, overly critical, or jaded?
2. Do I tend to operate under many assumptions, or do I seek clarity before speaking or acting? Would those closest to me agree with my assessment?
3. Do I actively try to see things from another's perspective? Do I tend to think of myself as someone who sees/interprets things rightly? Conversely, am I circumspect about my perspective?
4. Am I motivated out of a desire to be proven right or to instead make a difference? Do I tend to be a help, or do I desire to make my point, have my way, or get what I desire?
5. Do others enjoy my presence and company? Do I add value to others?

THURSDAY: Battle Plan

1. Who have I intentionally or unintentionally wounded due to my negligence, selfishness, or myopic perspective? What do I need to confess to God to ask for forgiveness?
2. Who has intentionally or unintentionally wounded me in action, word, or deed due to negligence, selfishness, or a myopic perspective? What bitterness has this created in me that I need to confess?
3. After confessing to God, who is the first person I need to talk to, forgive, or apologize to concerning this confession?
4. How can I facilitate this interaction? Do I write to them? Call them? Can I do this face-to-face? When is the best time to do this?
5. Who else do I need to repeat this process with?

FRIDAY: Gut Check

1. Am I actually going to commit to honoring others while still honoring myself? What changes do I need to make to make this happen?
2. Do I believe I am worthy of healthy relationships? Do I believe others are as well?
3. Am I a selfish person? If so, why?
4. Am I willing to be selfless? If not, why not?
5. What does elevating the needs of others look like practically today? Tomorrow? Over the next month? Over the next year? Am I willing to commit to this process?

SATURDAY: Baby Steps

Being selfish is easy. So is being a doormat. The default position for most of us is to tend to gravitate toward either extreme. Many of us either speak and act in a way that is primarily self-serving or self-gratifying. Many of us overly compensate for the selfishness of others and fail to establish healthy boundaries, conversations, and/or activities, ultimately devaluing ourselves while endorsing toxic and harmful behavior.

Narrow is the path (Matthew 17:13-14). The cycle needs to be broken for the sake of others and for ourselves. Today is your day to start that process. Actively look for areas to enter another's world that will help them while honoring yourself. Who among you is hurting? Who among you is celebrating? Who among you needs a shoulder to cry upon? Who among you can you join in laughter? Where can you put the needs of others above your own that will make a genuine impact, either great or small, that will bring God glory? Now go do it.

At the end of the day, journal the event. Write down what happened. If you bought a homeless person a meal, write down what it was. If you called your elderly relative just to check in, write down what you talked about. If you played catch with your teenage son, write down where you did it and how he responded to the gesture.

Write it down to remember it. Not to pat yourself on the back but to view it through the eyes of the other individual. If it went well, celebrate it. If it went poorly, commit to improving the next time.

Take the first step towards loving humanity well. Then tomorrow, take another.

SUNDAY: Reflect and Rest

Holy Spirit, what did I learn this week when I honestly assessed my interactions with others? What mindset and activity must I be mindful of regarding my relational interactions? What areas of relational health come naturally and which do I need to be intentional in developing?

Wonderful Counselor, thank You for the time we spent together this week. Thank You for opening my eyes, lifting my gaze, and seeing others as they truly are – beautiful and busted – just like me.

Thank You for reminding of the need to be gracious, patient, kind, and long-suffering. And that while dealing with people can be difficult, I am reminded this week, that I am a "people" too. As such, I am called to extend the same love that You so generously extend to me. Thank You, Jesus, for charging me to love others well.

Amen.

Things to Keep doing —

Kids scrapbooks until graduation
- All photos get downloaded on
costcophoto costc.com

Each kid has a book I've periodically
written in — they are on the bottom
shelf at my to night stand. Please
keep writing (until) ~~they~~ ~~become~~
you see fit — Tell them about
themselves

Hug them and tell them I love
them

Find someone that makes you laugh
Try to be happy

Just in case God is real ☺ make
sure you tell the kids — I expect
to see them in Heaven.

Take a job that makes you feel
fulfilled and productive

Buy everyone new socks, underwear + undershirts
every 6 m. Throw away gross Stuff

Order everett clothes for the next season
a few months ahead b/c they sell out
Old Navy + Walmart, — when older H can pick

DO THE WORK

MONDAY: What She Taught Me

"Hug them and tell them I love them…and just in case God is real ● make sure you tell the kids I expect to see them in heaven."
- Scrapbook list left to me by Nik entitled "Things to Keep Doing" in June 2022

Nikki spent her final months writing goodbyes and directions to those closest to her. All to be disseminated after her passing: Her last words, final instructions, encouragements, and guidance.

She left the kids and me a lot. On top of her journals, I got four "final letters." The kids each got a more sizable stack. Each is unique to the occasion for which she wrote. One is to be opened on the first day of the 5th grade. One is to be opened at the age of 21. One for the first real breakup. One to open after having a baby. One to tell me what to do next.

She did the work.

Despite what she was enduring, despite what she was facing, Nik fixed her eyes like flint on the task at hand, to love her people all the way to the end. To show us the way forward. To live well. To live on purpose.

To be clear, she didn't do it out of some innate part of herself, some superhuman characteristic that was distinctive to her. She did it because she loved Jesus, and that's what she saw Him do.

Despite what He was facing, despite the inevitable pain and endured suffering, He knew He would endure. In the end, Jesus took the time necessary to reassure those closest to Him. A time that seemingly should have been spent seeking reassurance for Himself.

While everyone was looking to hold on to what they had, He told them of the place He was going to prepare for them. He reminded them of what it was they were to do in the meantime, between here and heaven.

Jesus did the work.

In a world that screams for autonomy and recognition, there is nothing more precious and profound than coming across a person who is committed to doing the work. To fulfill the greatest commandments, to love God and people, despite the cost. To keep the main thing the main thing in everything.

So simple yet so difficult at times. Not complicated but so easily crowded out. However, if done correctly, if done well, it has an impact that cannot be overstated.

I know…because she did it for us.

Do the work.

TUESDAY: Commitment

"Do not let your hearts be troubled. You believe in God; believe also in me. My Father's house has many rooms; if that were not so, would I have told you that I am going there to prepare a place for you? And if I go and prepare a place for you, I will come back and take you to be with me that you also may be where I am." - John 14:1-3

"For the Son of Man did not come to be served, but to serve, and to give his life as a ransom for many." - Mark 10:45

Lord, I can be lazy. I tend to seek out the path of least resistance rather than do the hard thing. Sometimes I do it simply out of habit. Sometimes I do it unintentionally. But sometimes, I do it because it's self-serving. Sometimes I do it and know I should take a different path, I need to do the work. Lord, please forgive me. Please give me eyes to see, ears to hear, and a heart that is bent towards serving You and serving others, even when it comes at a cost to me, even when I am hurting, even when I have an excuse not to. Help me, Lord. Help me be more like You.
Amen.

WEDNESDAY: Assessment

1. In assessing my overall health (Spiritual, Mental, Emotional, Physical, Financial, and Relational), what area(s) are weak, immature, or underdeveloped? How has this affected my ability to lead myself and others?
2. Am I a steady person? Am I easily affected by circumstances?
3. Can I provide comfort, or do I add to uncertainty in a crisis?
4. Where do I seek refuge in difficult times? From what or from whom do I derive my comfort?
5. Do I lead well despite my circumstances? What behaviors do I model? Am I a selfish leader or a servant leader?

THURSDAY: Battle Plan

1. How can I become more grounded in difficult times? What does "doing the work" in this regard mean?
2. What specific disciplines can I put in place to continue to develop myself as a Christ-follower and leader to serve others better?
3. How do I create time in my schedule to prioritize this?
4. What can I do to get the necessary resources to mature me?
5. Who have I led poorly and need to seek forgiveness from? For what do I specifically need to apologize? What concrete steps can I take to ensure I break this pattern?

FRIDAY: Gut Check

1. What excuse or distraction do I need to remove from my life today to be better poised to lead myself and others better?
2. Practically, what does removing the excuse and distraction look like?
3. Am I willing to commit to the process of becoming a better servant leader? Who can hold me accountable?

4. How can I trust God in this process?
5. Am I willing to do the work despite what it may cost me personally? If so, how? If not, why not?

SATURDAY: Baby Steps

It's time to start doing the work. It's time to take the first step. Pick a workout routine and commit to it. Read a book instead of playing a game on your phone. Talk to your kids about something meaningful. Ask her out. Say you're sorry. Speak to the elephant in the room. Just start. Start doing the hard work and commit to continue to do it.

It'll probably get harder before it gets easier. Worse yet, it might become mundane. But stick to it. Keep a record of how often you are keeping at it. Mark it on the calendar. Write down milestones. Today is the first. Write down, "Today, I started to do the hard work." Tomorrow, do some more, then write down, "Today I did the work." See how many days you can stack up in a row. But for today, just start.

SUNDAY: Reflect and Rest

Jesus, what is the primary area of my life that requires significant work? What did I learn about myself this week in this regard? What am I going to do about it moving forward?

Lord Jesus, thank you for speaking to me this week. Thank You for showing me the area(s) I need to put in some hard work. I trust you will continue to come beside me and develop me in this way. I trust you will provide the relationships and resources necessary to help me. I know it will not be easy. I know it will take time. Important things always do. But I am encouraged to know that You are with me and will guide me throughout this process.

Please, Jesus, keep me from becoming overly discouraged when I fail or falter. Give me the fortitude to get up and try again. Please give me the courage to commit to continuing to do the work again and again and again.

Thank You, Lord.

Amen.

Jesus-

Thank you for dying on the cross - Thank you for forgiveness. And mercy. Thank you for walking with me during this time. And through all seasons of my life. I see your protection and grace many times.

I know I am not promised an easy life - or a long life

So please give me the ability

LEARN HOW TO BE ALONE

MONDAY: What She Taught Me

"Jesus, thank You for dying on the cross. Thank You for forgiveness and mercy. Thank You for walking with me during this time…" - An excerpt from Nikki's journal in July 2020

Nik didn't always like being alone. She didn't like where her head would go when the distractions were removed. When the noise wasn't there. When her world slowed down just enough that she could think.

The first time she had to face her reality alone came the day she was diagnosed, lying in an MRI machine. Alone with nothing but the diagnosis and the devil to whisper: "What now…" and "What if…"

She came out of that tube sobbing and heaving. In the silence, she got really scared.

After that, she resolved that she needed to learn the art of solitude. And not just tolerate it. To learn to expect it and embrace it. Not to resent it but rather use it to renew her resolve.

Because that's what Jesus did.

Jesus would often retreat into seclusion. To spend time meditating upon the things His Father had said to Him, His Son in whom He was well pleased. Jesus liked being alone.

Jesus triumphed at Golgotha because of His quiet preparation in the Garden.

Nik pursued this practice. In her suffering, she learned how to seek Jesus in the silence. Despite the pain, she discovered how to petition the Father in the quiet. Amidst chaos and confusion, to discern how to plead to the Spirit for comfort while completely alone. Whether praying privately in a hospital awaiting a procedure, worshipping in her bed following treatment, meditating by a pool, or resting quietly on a shoreline. She determined to drown out the screams of the devil with the whispers of her Creator.

In the end, she loved being alone.

Recently, a fellow widower called to check up on me. I told him I was scared to be alone, like "alone alone," without my person. He laughed, then said, "It'll be like that for a while...You'll be alone, and you'll find you don't even like yourself...but with work, eventually that'll change."

I know he's right. It certainly proved true for Nik. By God's grace, it's true for all of us.

Learn how to be alone.

TUESDAY: *Commitment*

"It was very early in the morning and still dark. Jesus got up and left the house. He went to a place where he could be alone. There he prayed." - Mark 1:35

"But the news about Jesus spread all the more, and great crowds came to hear Him and to be healed of their sicknesses. Yet frequently withdrew to the wilderness to pray." - Luke 5:15-16

Father, I need to spend more time with You. Specifically, I need to spend more time with You in silence. As this world seemingly moves faster and faster, You beckon me to slow down, get quiet, and listen for Your still small voice, to worship You, to elevate You to Your rightful place in my life, and by extension, revel and be renewed by what You say about me.

I repent today for not making time away with You my highest priority. The silence can be a scary place. Left alone to my thoughts can lead to a fertile atmosphere for the enemy to take ground in my life. Help me, Holy Spirit. Strengthen me in my weakness. Help me to resolve to spend more time in the quiet with You, ultimately to tune my spirit to hear from You.

Thank You, Jesus, for meeting me in this place.

Amen.

WEDNESDAY: *Assessment*

1. Is spending quiet time with God a regular practice in my life? If not, why not?
2. Is my prayer life "one-directional," meaning I talk a lot, pray a lot, and ask for a lot, and I don't spend nearly enough time listening (i.e., studying what Your Word says and meditating on its truths)?
3. Do I spend dedicated time with Jesus prior to making big decisions or taking major actions? If not, why not?
4. Do I spend dedicated time with the Spirit in times of gratitude or grieving?
5. Do I spend dedicated time with the Father to renew my soul, especially after long seasons of pouring out? Do I process my life happenings with Jesus?

THURSDAY: *Battle Plan*

1. What do I need to do to prioritize spending time alone with God?
2. What distractions in my life do I need to eliminate? How do I need to rework my schedule?
3. Who do I need to talk to help me better structure this time?
4. Where am I going to go to establish this practice regularly?
5. When am I going to do this (daily)?

FRIDAY: *Gut Check*

1. What will I do when my schedule, the enemy, or circumstances threaten me from keeping this practice?
2. What lies am I believing that I cannot go to God alone?
3. When I sin (which is inevitable), will I commit to going to Him in solitude, or will I stay away from Him in shame?

4. Even during those days and seasons when it feels like God is not meeting me in that space, am I committed to keeping it up? What will I do when I feel discouraged?
5. Do I genuinely believe God wants to spend time with me? If yes, why? If not, why not?

SATURDAY: Baby Steps

Sitting quietly for any length of time can almost feel impossible. In an age of instant information, instant grocery shopping, instant connection, and instant gratification, the arts of patience and solitude have fallen out of practice. Despite that, our souls need it! So like anything else, start small. Find a quiet space in your home. Go out on your back deck. Sit in your car. Walk in the woods. Stand on the shoreline. And be quiet for a moment. If you can be quiet a moment more, do it. Work up to 5 minutes, then to 10. Read a few passages from the Psalms or a parable Jesus gave His disciples. Think about it. Play the words back in your head. Ask God to illuminate His Word to you. Bring your troubles before Him. Bring your gratitude, too. Then just be silent.

Start today. Do it again tomorrow. Make it a habit. Grow it over time. Journal about what you meditated upon. Write down what He revealed to you. Grow a holy reverence for the fact that the God of heaven wants to spend time with you.

SUNDAY: Reflect and Rest

Father God, what did I learn this week about being in quiet, meditation, prayer, and sitting in solitude? How can I grow in this practice and incorporate this as a daily rhythm in my life?

Almighty Father, thank You for reminding me that You want to spend time with me. And not just when I am in crisis or need something. But because You desire to have a relationship with me through all of it – the highs and the lows, the surreal and the mundane. Remind me of the truth You taught me this week and the lies I need to release.

Lord, help me in building the practice of solitude into my life. In the midst of all the craziness and busyness of this life, please grow in my conviction to slow down, pause, pray, and ponder.

Thank You, Lord, in advance for all you will show me during these times together.

Amen.

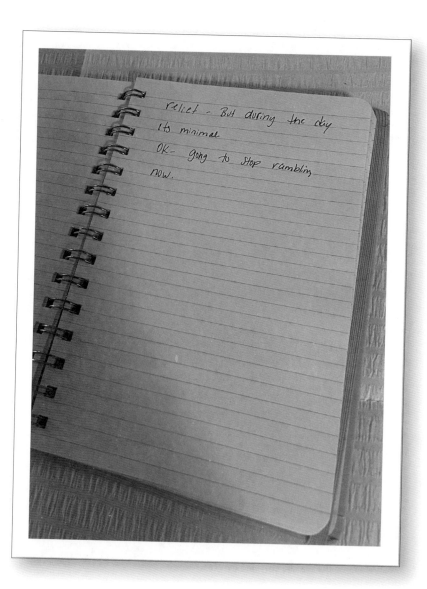

relief – But during the day
its minimal
OK – going to stop rambling
now.

ASSUME NOTHING

MONDAY: *What She Taught Me*

"Okay, Going to stop rambling now." - Nik's final journal entry from June 11, 2022

Thirty hours before she went to heaven, Nik was still meticulously reviewing tracking numbers. She wanted to make sure all the "T"s were crossed, and the "I"s were dotted.

She certainly wasn't going to leave that up to Amazon & Etsy.

Blankets for our dads and our kids. Necklaces for the moms. Earrings for her tribe of close friends. A watch for me. She wanted to be sure her people knew she was still thinking about them. Still loving them. Simple, small gifts – left behind in memory of her.

My wife loved me. But she still left me something that I can look at each day to be reminded of her love. A love that was selfless and pure. Kind and absolute. Faithful and vigilant.

My kids didn't need those blankets to know they were her whole world. There was no doubt of that. But she left them so they could curl up and be comforted in her words. To embrace them. Because she knew she wouldn't be able to embrace them down here anymore.

She loved us. But she was not going to assume that the memory of that love wouldn't fade. To assume we would always be able to recall what true love does and how true love operates. Assumption is dangerous.

Jesus NEVER operated under assumption.

You would have thought Jesus had done enough. Enough preaching. Enough teaching. Enough healing. Enough loving. Yet on the night He was betrayed. Once again He didn't assume His friends would grasp how much

He loved them (and us). So He showed them – with a basin of water to wash their feet. With broken bread and poured-out wine. A grand, profound practice to be observed often – left behind in memory of Him.

Assumption has no place in a genuine relationship.

So I've really tried to stop assuming when it comes to my people. I've resolved to slow down, spend the time, and love them as Nik loved me. Even if I think they already know. To take no relationship for granted. In memory of her and in reverence to Him. To be intentional.

To assume nothing.

TUESDAY: Commitment

"The evening meal was in progress…Jesus knew that the Father had put all things under his power, and that he had come from God and was returning to God; so he got up from the meal, took off his outer clothing, and wrapped a towel around his waist. After that, he poured water into a basin and began to wash his disciples' feet, drying them with the towel that was wrapped around him." - John 13:2-5

"…Jesus took bread, and when he had given thanks, he broke it and gave it to his disciples, saying, 'Take and eat; this is my body.' Then he took a cup, and when he had given thanks, he gave it to them, saying, 'Drink from it, all of you. This is my blood of the covenant, which is poured out for many for the forgiveness of sins'…" - Matthew 26:26-28

Lord, I operate under a lot of assumptions. I assume others know my heart. I assume others know my intentions. I assume others know how I feel about them and the situations we find ourselves in.

I can be self-consumed and distracted. I can be so preoccupied with the urgent that I neglect the important. Sometimes I do this unintentionally. Sometimes it's just an accident. But to be honest, other times, it's because I have not disciplined myself to be intentional in my relationships.

Jesus, You always prioritized people. People always knew where they stood with you. Whether You were encouraging someone or correcting them, it was always done out of love and intentionality to see them edified, valued, and cared for well. Those who knew You best would go on to model this to others.

Help me, Jesus, to become more like You in this regard. Help me stop assuming and to start being intentional in my relationships.

Amen.

WEDNESDAY: Assessment

1. In general, do those closest to me know how I feel about them? If not, why not?
2. Do I take intentional actions to express love, kindness, gentleness, etc.? What are those actions? How often do I do these things?
3. Do I assume others should intuitively understand my perspective, actions, and attitudes, or do I explain myself to those around me?
4. Am I so overly distracted, burdened, busy, or self-consumed that I miss opportunities to be present with those who rely upon me, look up to me, or could use my company, assistance, or counsel?
5. Do I have intentional goals for my dearest relationships? If so, what are they?

THURSDAY: Battle Plan

1. What actions and activities must I immediately put in place to be more intentional with those closest to me (spouse, children, parents, siblings, friends)?
2. Who do I need to seek forgiveness from because I have operated in a paradigm of assumption that has ultimately resulted in a rift or distance that really should be resolved?

3. Does my schedule allow me to be intentional in critical relationships (i.e., spending quality time)? If not, what needs to be, at a minimum, reprioritized or even canceled altogether to allow me to have the time necessary to sow into those relationships?

4. What do those closest to me require that they can only get from me? How can I ensure I am providing that which is required?

5. Operating in assumption tends to be a default mindset. What checks and balances can I implement to keep me from returning to this thinking?

FRIDAY: Gut Check

1. Am I honestly willing to be intentional? How?

2. What is the measurable fruit that I am not being a person who operates under assumption?

3. Who can hold me accountable in this area?

4. Am I willing to admit that I have failed here in some regard? Am I willing to seek forgiveness and work toward restoration?

5. Am I willing to put away distractions to work on important relationships? How so?

SATURDAY: Baby Steps

Being intentional doesn't just happen. Things don't naturally move into order and "as they should be." Because of sin, this broken world and the people in it (you and me) naturally allow things to move into disorder and chaos. Even the relationships that mean the most to us. If you are going to stop this cycle, you have to be intentional. To crawl and claw back that which has slipped away. It may take time, it may take a lifetime, but it will be so worth it. But if you are going to have any shot at it, you need to start. Resolve to start today.

Be intentional with your person, have a meaningful conversation, go out on the date, make the phone call, face the dilemma, take the step you know you need to take to show you care. And then resolve to keep after it. The first step forward may result in three steps backward. But over time, and by His grace, you may build a relationship that is better, stronger, and more God-honoring than it ever has been before. Besides, the results are only partially up to you. It takes two to tango. That said, your actions (or lack thereof) are your responsibility. Be sure you can give a good account. Take the step.

SUNDAY: Reflect and Rest

Lord Jesus, what did I learn this week about my assumptions and my intentionality? What is the key area in my life that I must be more intentional?

Jesus, thank You, Jesus, for meeting with me this week. For working on my heart and showing me the importance of intentionality. I know God that this lesson is not a "one and done" thing. This is a practice that I will need to work on daily. Please help me to do just that.

Help me, Lord, to remember to be intentional about my intentionality. For the good of not only myself but for the good of those around me. By doing this, I will become a better version of myself. I will become a better reflection of You in a world that so desperately needs You.

I ask all of this for Your glory and my good.

Amen.

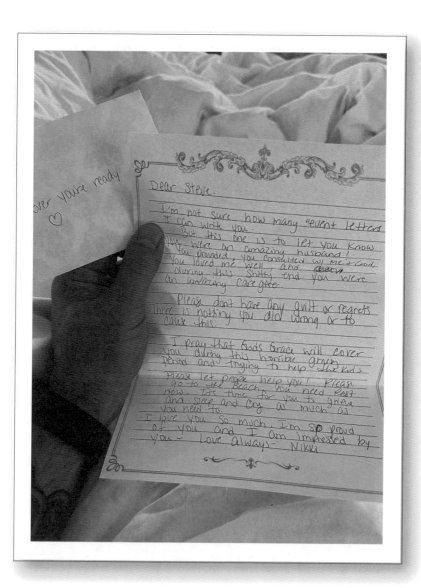

ver you're ready
♡

Dear Steve,

I'm not sure how many "event letters" I can write you. But this one is to let you know you were an amazing husband! You provided, you consulted w/ me & God, You loved me well, and always during this shitty end you were an amazing caregiver.

Please don't have any guilt or regrets. There is nothing you did wrong or to cause this.

I pray that God's Grace will cover you during this horrible grieving period and trying to help the kids. Please let people help you! Please go to the Beach. You need Rest now. It's time for you to grieve and sleep and cry as much as you need to.

I love you so much. I'm so proud of you and I am impressed by you. Love Always~ Nikki

BEACHES ARE INCREDIBLE

MONDAY: *What She Taught Me*

"Please go to the beach. You need rest now…" - Excerpt from Nik's "Goodbye Letter" to me in June 2022

For most of our life together…Nik could run laps around me. That chick had one gear, Fast. Furious. Forward. Seemingly every moment was spent being productive. Getting things done or achieving a task. She was vigilant not to fall into the trap of a little sleep, a little slumber, a little folding of the hands…

Yet once a year, she would plop down in a beach chair, get in a low gear, stare out at the breakers, and rest…in Him.

It reset her mechanism. It brought her peace. It gave her perspective. She felt at home. Enjoying her people in His creation. Enjoying Him.

Nik recognized her propensity to operate "heads down." Overwhelmed by the concerns of her own world. With all the tasks, traumas, tribulations, and triumphs of life clawing for her attention. To be so busy "doing" that she would lose sight of the Creator who holds all life together. The religion of running. The idol of self-dominion.

So she'd sit with Him. On a beach. For a long while. To remind herself how awesome He was and how reassuring it was to know her Father was in control.

In the beginning, was the Word, and the Word was with God, and the Word was God. (John 1:1) He said, "Let the water under the sky be gathered to one place, and dry ground appear." And He called the dry ground "land" and the gathered waters He called "seas." (Genesis 1:9-10a)

It brought her great peace and comfort to be in that place. On the very shoreline He fashioned. To be reminded of the stresses of this life. All the uncertainty we endure. Even the tragedies that take place. All of it fades against an Almighty God. The Creator who so loved her.

Perspective matters.

Yes, I am called to steward this life. To raise my children well. To honor God with the provision He has given me. Yet, at the same time, to remember all of this, all of it, is His. For the sea is His, for He made it, and His hands formed the dry land.

That was her comfort. As it is mine.

Beaches are incredible.

TUESDAY: Commitment

"In the beginning God created the heavens and the earth. Now the earth was formless and empty, darkness was over the surface of the deep, and the Spirit of God was hovering over the waters. And God said, "Let there be light," and there was light. God saw that the light was good, and he separated the light from the darkness. God called the light "day," and the darkness he called "night." And there was evening, and there was morning, the first day. And God said, "Let there be a vault between the waters to separate water from water." So God made the vault and separated the water under the vault from the water above it. And it was so. God called the vault "sky." And there was evening, and there was morning, the second day. And God said, "Let the water under the sky be gathered to one place, and let dry ground appear." And it was so. God called the dry ground "land," and the gathered waters he called "seas." And God saw that it was good." - Genesis 1:1-10

Come, let us sing for joy to the Lord; let us shout aloud to the Rock of our salvation. Let us come before him with thanksgiving and extol him with music and song. For the Lord is the great God, the great King above all gods. In his hand are the depths of the earth, and the mountain peaks belong to him. The sea is his, for he made it, and his hands formed the dry land. Come, let us bow down in worship, let us kneel before the Lord our Maker; for he is our Gog and we are the people of his pasture, the flock under his care. - Psalm 95:1-7

Lord, forgive me. Forgive me for growing callous to Your majesty. When I look at the stars in the sky, I should be in awe of You. When I look at the details of this world, I should esteem You. When I witness the intricacies of Your creation and its interplay with my life, I should be humbled and inspired that while this universe is so complex for me, it is not for You.

And while I could never grasp the magnitude of what You hold in order, You do, and yet Your thoughts about me remain innumerable. You are a great and awesome, powerful yet personal Creator. Thank you.

As I go into this week, let me be more mindful of Your grandeur. Not just to reveal what you have done but Who You are – my strong tower from where my help comes. Let my eyes rise from my circumstances. Let my grip loosen on that I feel I must cling to so tight. Let me find the rest You desire for me that can only be found in You.

Amen.

WEDNESDAY: Assessment

1. Who do I believe is in ultimate control in my life – God or me?
2. What is the line of demarcation between God's sovereignty and my responsibility? What areas in my life require my activity (i.e. greater effort) and what areas require dependence on God (i.e. less control)?
3. Am I a "control freak?" Would others agree with that assessment?
4. Do I spend time getting to know God, or is all my time spent interacting with aspects of His creation? Am I pursuing Him, or am I overwhelmed with everything that packs my schedule?
5. Does my life follow a healthy rhythm of work and rest? Do I seek refreshment in creation or spend time with my Creator?

THURSDAY: *Battle Plan*

1. What specific area(s) do I need to release control back to God? What does that look like?
2. How do I practically draw my strength from God's sovereignty rather than my ability?
3. What does stewarding my life well look like?
4. What does a daily, weekly, monthly, and annual plan look like to ensure I spend time revealing, thanking, and enjoying God's sovereignty in my life?
5. Who can I ask to hold me accountable for my plan?

FRIDAY: *Gut Check*

1. Do I really believe God's thoughts about me are countless? That He desires to reveal Himself to me and that He honestly wants the best for me?
2. Starting a new rhythm is one thing; holding to it is another. Will I commit to this new process?
3. Am I really going to relinquish control? If so, when?
4. What will be the measurable result of my trusting God's sovereignty and goodness?
5. If things turn out differently than I expect or want, am I still willing to follow God's leading in my life?

SATURDAY: *Baby Steps*

A healthy rhythm of life comes from understanding when to run and when to rest. The beautiful marriage of God's sovereignty interacting with our faithful activity has been the plan since before the Fall. He made it, and we are called to steward it. However, we cannot steward that with which He entrusted us if we don't spend time with the One who commissioned it. We must take time simply to bask in His glory.

Resolve today to spend time reveling in the majesty of God. Sit quietly and watch your children as they sleep. Rejoice not only for the creation but for the One who created it. Dare to have your mind's eye peer behind the curtain. Look back on the tapestry of your life and see His handiwork in it. Find solace in the great I AM. The One who was, is, and always will be. Blow Him up in your mind. Find comfort in His omniscience. His omnipotence. His omnipresence. In that newly found awe and respect...resolve to let go and trust Him. To find rest for your soul and relief from so much striving. He cares far more about spending time with you than the time you spend working for Him.

Sit with Jesus. Spend time with Him. And don't come with only grievances. Come in gratitude simply for who He is.

What did God reveal to you today?

SUNDAY: Reflect and Rest

Heavenly Father, what did I learn this week about striking a balance between my efforts and my dependence upon You? What areas of my life can I improve in this regard? What did I learn about trusting You?

Father God, I will never wrap my mind around who You are and all that You do. But I can stand on Your Word. And Your Word tells me that You draw close to those that draw unto You. Thank You for wooing me this week to come deeper with You.

Thank You, Lord, for illuminating the glory of Your creation. Help me to never grow callous to Your majesty. Help what I have learned this week to spur me to spend time learning more about You.

Lord, let my desire to worship Your glory never fade but only increase. Thank You, Lord, for all that You revealed this week.

Amen.

FAMILY SECOND

MONDAY: *What She Taught Me*

"I Love You Most...The End. I Win." - Inscription on gift from Nik on Father's Day 2021

We were her world. From the moment she said, "I do," until death made us part. We were right at the top of her list. Or at least right next to the top. There remains a great debate as to who was the favorite, we each have a theory. Bai's list has her trailing her siblings. Ri favors Everett as the winner. E would argue his sisters far surpassed his standing. By the way, they are all wrong. I was the favorite.

But honestly, it's a photo finish. We all could make a solid case for second best. That said, first place was assured.

Her God stood in that spot. Unrivaled.

In her suffering, she learned that most of the things we place on the thrones of our lives are ill-fit to provide the comfort required in our time of deepest need. Our career. Our reputation. Our finances. Even our family. Good gifts make poor gods. And when God-size grace is required, an idol makes for an unworthy substitute. It simply can't bear the weight.

Only One is worthy of that throne.

Understanding the importance of a properly ordered paradigm is the only way to endure. God first. Everything else must follow. For He is our Hope, and He is our Assurance. A surety that no matter how bad it gets down here, because of Jesus, all suffering will one day end.

But taking hold of that precious promise requires honoring the price paid for it.

The only way my wretchedness is reconciled is because Perfection was marred. The only way my filth is wiped clean is because the Spotless One was stained. He paid it all, taking my place.

The Great Exchange, His riches for my rags. His righteousness for my ruin.

Nik loved Him for that. She revered Him for it. I'm certain upon her passing, she walked right up to Him to thank Him face-to-face. He was her King, and she was His friend. He was her Lord, and she was His faithful servant. She honored Him as first and foremost in her life because of the price He paid for her eternal freedom. Yes, she loved us. But she loved Him more. Rightfully so. A proper paradigm: God first.

Family second.

TUESDAY: Commitment

You will have no other gods before Me. - Exodus 20:3

Anyone who loves their life will lose it, while anyone who hates their life in this world will keep it for eternal life. - John 12:25

Listen, I tell you a mystery: We will not all sleep, but we will all be changed, in a flash, in the twinkling of an eye, at the last trumpet. For the trumpet will sound, the dead will be raised imperishable, and we will be changed. For the perishable must clothe itself with the imperishable, and the mortal with immortality. When the perishable has been clothed with the imperishable, and the mortal with immortality, then the saying that is written will come true: "Death has been swallowed up in victory." "Where, O death, is your victory? Where, O death, is your sting?" - 1 Corinthians 15:51-55

Oh, how foolish I have been, Lord! I have taken You for granted! I have allowed that which I know to drown out the mystery of the Great Unknown. Forgive me, Father, for not ordering my worship correctly. For idolizing, pursuing, protecting, and honoring that which I love, be it the relationships I have, the material things I desire and possess, or even the persona I have attempted to create, above my relationship with You. I have lost my reverence. I have lost my awe. I have even taken my very salvation for granted. My thoughts and actions have found me out. I am so sorry, Lord.

Thank You once again for wooing me back into Your presence, beckoning me to sit and ponder Your majesty. To be reminded of all that You have done for me and all that You promise to do through me.

Thank You, Jesus!

Amen.

WEDNESDAY: Assessment

1. Is God first and foremost in my life? Do my thoughts, actions, and activities reflect a properly ordered paradigm?
2. What are the idols in my life? How did they become idols? Why do I worship them?
3. What is the sin that so easily besets me? What deep need am I attempting to satisfy that I feel God cannot? Why?
4. Do I honestly feel I control my idol, or does it control me?
5. Does anyone know about my idol? What wise counsel would they (or have they) give me about it?

THURSDAY: Battle Plan

1. What can I do daily that will keep the Great Exchange fresh before me?
2. How can I practically surrender lordship to God, especially concerning the area I struggle with the most?
3. What practical measures can I put in place to keep my idol(s) in their proper place or, if necessary, removed completely from my life?
4. As it pertains to idol(s), what lies must I stop believing?
5. Who can hold me accountable?

FRIDAY: Gut Check

1. Will I honestly commit to keeping God primary in my life? What does that look like practically?
2. What will I do when a situation tempts me to worship my idol, and I feel compelled to follow my desire rather than the guidance of the Spirit?
3. Am I ready to be done placing things on the throne of my life and start worshipping the only One worthy of it?
4. Have I grown callous to what was done on the cross? Do I need to repent?
5. Am I ready to make God not just my Savior, but my Lord?

SATURDAY: Baby Steps

We all have something in our lives with which we struggle. It could be an area of blatant sin or a good gift from above that we have elevated to the place of the highest (yet undeserved) regard in our lives. Regardless of what it is, sin or misappropriation, God is calling for us to lay those things aside (sin) or put them in their proper place (ordered good things correctly) to honor the only One worthy of our worship.

Today God is calling you to make a declaration and take the first step toward venerating Him. Go back to church. Read His Word. Admit the sin. Quit the habit. Start a Bible study. Make today the first day of cutting a new path that honors God and tell someone about it. Tell them to check in on you tomorrow to see if you are still at it. You won't always get it right. You might have a few good days than a couple of bad ones. You might string together a really good week, then have a really bad night. It likely won't be a path that is constantly trending upward. That said, don't use those bad days or experiences as an excuse to quit. Commit to keeping God first and foremost in your life. He loves you too much to leave you where He found You. So, honor Him by pursuing Him and, in so doing, becoming more like Him.

SUNDAY: *Reflect and Rest*

Lord Jesus, what did I learn this week as it pertains to the idols I have in my life? How can I practically pull them off the throne of my life? How will I elevate You to Your proper place?

Jesus, My King, thank You for being so patient and long-suffering with me. I am so grateful for this past week and what it revealed in terms of my priorities, my disordered paradigm of worship, the need to continually tear down idols in my life, and my propensity to be so caught up in creation that I forget to honor the One who created it. I know this will be an ongoing process in my life. I know that I will no sooner pull down an idol in my life, and another will fight to fill the vacancy, or I will simply return to the disordered paradigm out of my own selfish desire. Help me to keep things in their proper order and place. To enjoy the blessing of this life You have given me, but to never forget that all that I have now and all that I have for all eternity is from You.

Thank you for this week, Lord. Please never let me grow tired of You.
I love you.
Amen.

LIGHTEN UP

MONDAY: *What She Taught Me*

"Hehe…Gotcha!" - Every day of our marriage (or at least it felt like it - I only recently started walking upstairs again)

For the better part of two decades, any time I went up a staircase, I did so like I was being chased, for a good reason. For the entirety of our marriage, Nik found great joy in coming up the stairs behind me. Extending her pointer finger. And poking me right in the tailpipe. It didn't matter if I was walking up to our bedroom in pajamas or ascending the staircase of Congress in a suit. The poke was coming.

True story.

And she got me every time. My reaction was always the same. To spin around abruptly and slap haphazardly at a hand that had already been pulled back. Her reaction was always the same too. To look up at me and laugh so hard her nostrils would flare uncontrollably.

Life was way too serious to be taken so seriously all the time.

She hated it when I worried too much. She didn't like to see me downcast or heavy-hearted. When I took myself so seriously. Nik understood that we all make our plans, but ultimately He orders the steps. After years spent striving and straining our lives looked nothing like what we had set out to achieve as doe-eyed newlyweds. There was a lot more pain than we had planned. Nearly jumped the rails on more than one occasion. Yet we got through all of it. Because Jesus was always in our boat. Rain or shine. Clear sky or hurricane.

At the end of the day, there is enough stuff to get worked up about. There's enough cause for concern. I need not add any more severity to the situation. I want to be a person that conveys calm where unrest prevails. A certain levity where hope has evaporated. Because at the end of the day. He's got me. And He's got you too.

Lighten up.

TUESDAY: Commitment

"'Jesus was inside the boat, sleeping with his head on a pillow. The followers went and woke him. They said, 'Teacher, don't you care about us? We are going to drown!' Jesus stood up and gave a command to the wind and the water. He said, 'Quiet! Be still!' Then the wind stopped, and the lake became calm. He said to his followers, 'Why are you afraid? Do you still have no faith?'" - Mark 4:38-40

"We can make our plans, but the Lord determines our steps." - Proverbs 16:9

Lord, it is so good to know that, ultimately, You are in control, and I am not. When I look at the circumstances around me or what is happening in this world, I can feel myself becoming heavy. To become cynical. Critical. Angry and anxious.

God, I know You don't want that for me. You don't want me to be flighty or fickle, but you don't want me to be so serious and melancholy, either. You want me to be salt and light. You call me to be hopeful because You are Hope.

You call me to reach down and help pull up those who are downtrodden, depressed, and despondent. I can't do that if I don't operate in the confidence that You love me and will never forsake me. That You are for us and will never leave us.

Jesus, help me to lighten up. To relax a little bit. To operate in faith even when it all looks like it is all falling apart. I desire to be a beacon for You. Help me, Jesus, to step into this calling.

In Your precious name. Amen.

WEDNESDAY: *Assessment*

1. Am I easily rattled by the circumstances that surround me? Am I an anxious person? What is the source of my anxiety?
2. Am I able to laugh at myself? Am I able to be self-deprecating? Am I overly concerned about the opinions and beliefs of others – especially as it pertains to their view of me?
3. Where do I place my faith, especially in difficult times? Do others see me as a source of hope and encouragement?
4. Am I okay when things don't go as I planned? Am I flexible?
5. Am I sensitive to the Spirit's leading? Do I go before God in prayer before setting out in a direction? Am I okay with being somewhat uncertain?

THURSDAY: *Battle Plan*

1. What specific area, topic, or relationship do I need to work on lightening up (a bit or a lot)?
2. What does "lightening up" look like, practically speaking?
3. When I am anxious or melancholy for an extended period of time, what can I do to shake myself from the funk in a healthy way?
4. What can I specifically do to add more joy to my life in a healthy way?
5. How can I practically grow my faith in God and His sovereignty over my life?

FRIDAY: *Gut Check*

1. Am I willing to finally face my anxiety?
2. Will I admit that certain activities, thought processes, and possibly even relationships cause me unneeded mental, emotional, and even physical strain – and ascribe to do something about it?

3. Am I willing to admit that I am not God? That sometimes the world gets a vote on how things transpire? That I need to resign myself to the fact that sometimes things just aren't fair?
4. Am I willing to acknowledge that my response to difficulty is my responsibility while the outcome may be beyond my control? That I am called to be salt and light despite the circumstances?
5. Will I trust God despite what I see and experience? Will I resolve to remain faithful and hopeful for both myself and for those around me?

SATURDAY: *Baby Steps*

It can be a tall order to be a hopeful person in the current climate. There are many reasons to be cynical, critical, angry, and anxious. Financial strain. Relational drama. 24/7 newsfeeds. Constant connection on social media. It's too much. It robs us of our joy, and as a result, we are hopeless ourselves, let alone have enough hope to offer those around us. All we are is heavy and sad and tired and defeated.

But you are more than a conqueror in Christ. This world needs bright lights. A shining city on a hill that serves as a beacon of hope and dares to be a place of joy. You build a city one brick at a time. So today, lay your first stone. Do something that will bring someone joy. Buy your coworker a cup of coffee. Make your neighbor a meal. Extend the homeless guy a $20 and tell him Jesus loves him. Be salt and light. Listen to the prompting of the Spirit. He will tell you what to do. No one loves His creation more than Him. When He tells you, thank Him. Then go do it. Be sure to write it down to remember it. And look for another opportunity tomorrow. Hold your plans loose. Listen to Jesus. Love up on people.

Wash. Rinse. Repeat.

SUNDAY: Reflect and Rest

Jesus, what did I learn about myself this week? Am I overly critical, angry, or anxious? What am I going to do about it moving forward?

Lord Jesus, thank You for speaking to me this week. For helping me to get out of my own way. To look for opportunities to make other people smile, maybe even laugh. It felt good.

Thank You for the reminder that though in this world we will have trouble, You have overcome the world. It's not on me to fix everything. But it is on me to help build the faith of those around me by staying hopeful, despite the circumstances.

Help me in the coming days, weeks, months, and years to maintain a hopeful perspective. As this world grows darker, help me to be that city on a hill; always shining and pointing people to You, come what may.

Help me to be a person of joy for You.
Amen.

The next day when I was taking communion I told God, Lord it would be so easy for me to shut down right now, claim you don't exist, and that I've been trying to read the tea leaves believing that you will help me. But I can't do that I know too much and I have nowhere else to go. Where would I have any hope and what good would it do so here I am with a mustard seed of faith asking

NEVER STOP GROWING

MONDAY: *What She Taught Me*

"…I can't do that. I know too much, and I have nowhere else to go." - Note from Nik's phone from February 2022

Around the age of thirty, Nik and I got to see a well-known author give a talk. It was one of those events in your life where you learn something so profound, everything shifts. I wasn't expecting it. But it happened all the same.

Nik almost looked bewildered afterward. She had a thousand-yard stare. Her mind was moving a million miles an hour. After some time, she resolved something. And she stood a little taller. Back a little straighter. Eyes more fixed and focused.

She resolved that she couldn't go back now. She had to learn more. She had to grow. She knew it might be confusing at times. It was going to be a process. Maybe a little uncomfortable. Probably awkward too. But she couldn't stay ignorant any longer. She knew too much now. Seen too much. I mean, where else was she going to go?

It had to be very bewildering for those men when they met the Truth. One day you are fishing. Working at your tax booth. Then in a moment. Everything changes. And I mean EVERYTHING. What followed was a whole lot of awkward, embarrassing missteps. Misunderstood teachings. Stern rebukes. But there was a whole lot of awesome in there, too, miraculous spectacles. Undeniable marvels. Inconceivable wonders. They might not have understood it all. But they dared to keep growing despite themselves. They couldn't stay ignorant any longer. They knew too much now. Seen too much. As one of them remarked, where else were they going to go?

After her enlightenment, Nik made a commitment to grow. To grow in her understanding to become a more effective mom. To grow her capacity to become an exceptional wife. But more than anything, to grow in her knowledge of Him in hopes of becoming an extraordinary human being.

The result was a life well-lived. A life that brought Him glory and gave her great joy.

None of us will reach our full potential by accident. It takes the willingness to press through the awkward. But on the other side of awkward is the incredible and there is a lot of awesome along the way.

Never stop growing.

TUESDAY: *Commitment*

"As Jesus was walking beside the Sea of Galilee, he saw two brothers, Simon called Peter, and his brother Andrew. They were casting a net into the lake, for they were fishermen. 'Come, follow me,' Jesus said, 'and I will send you out to fish for people.' At once, they left their nets and followed him." - Matthew 4:18-20

"As Jesus went on from there, he saw a man named Matthew sitting at the tax collector's booth. 'Follow me,' he told him, and Matthew got up and followed him." - Matthew 9:9

"'...Yet there are some of you who do not believe.' For Jesus had known from the beginning which of them did not believe and who would betray him. He went on to say, 'This is why I told you that no one can come to me unless the Father has enabled them.'
From this time, many of his disciples turned back and no longer followed him.
'You do not want to leave, too, do you?' Jesus asked the Twelve.
Simon Peter answered him, 'Lord, to whom shall we go? You have the words of eternal life. We have come to believe and to know that you are the Holy One of God.'" - John 6:64-68

Honestly, God, it would be a whole lot easier for me to stay here. It's comfortable. I know this place. Honestly, even in my suffering. Even in my complaint. Even in my cynicism, it's comfortable here. Because I know this place. And it is easier to remain stagnant. Remain the victim. Remain content. Just to remain. But I know You want more for me. You didn't find me here to leave me here.

So give me the courage to grow. To maintain my gratitude for all You have done for me already while having a holy discontent with staying here. I fully recognize my growth will not be linear. It may be two steps forward and one step back most of the time.

So please guard my heart against discouragement. Help me lay down my pride. You used twelve unlearned men to turn the world on its head. I am ready for You to use me to do the same.

Help me, God, to grow.

Amen.

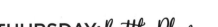

WEDNESDAY: Assessment

1. What area(s) of my life do I find myself stagnant?
2. Am I healthy in these areas: Spiritual, Mental, Emotional, Physical, Relational, and Financial? Why or why not?
3. Is there a dream or burden that God has placed on my heart that requires growth? What is it? Am I actively moving toward that goal? If not, why not?
4. Have I grown overly comfortable with my situation? Are there legit reasons why I am here? Am I using excuses to stay where I am at?
5. Am I scared of growing? If so, why?

THURSDAY: Battle Plan

1. What are some specific goals for each aspect of my life: Spiritual, Mental/Academic, Emotional, Physical, Relational, Financial?

2. What is a legitimate timeline to accomplish these goals? What are the checkpoints along the way to ensure I am on track to accomplish these milestones?
3. What are the resources and the relationships I will need to access and cultivate to help me achieve these aspirations?
4. Are any of the goals I have set unachievable at this time? Are there other, small goals, that I may accomplish that will set me up for achieving the larger goal in the future?
5. Who can I share this plan with? How can they help hold me accountable?

FRIDAY: Gut Check

1. If you are fearful of starting this process, are you willing to face the fear? What would God say to you about it?
2. If you have been making excuses, are you finally willing to admit it?
3. Do you think you are worthy of growth? If you don't, why not?
4. What are you going to do when this gets hard?
5. The goals you set will take a year to accomplish, are you going to put the work in every day to achieve them? How are you going to hold yourself accountable?

SATURDAY: Baby Steps

I get it. Sometimes staying in one place can be really appealing. Sometimes you are actually supposed to stay where you are. But let's be honest. Most of the time, you aren't called to stay there forever. God wants us to grow. God wants us to reach all the potential that is within us. But getting started can be so embarrassing. So humbling. Scary even. So it makes sense to stay. But at what cost? It might seem worth it now, but play it out in your head. If you stay here, how much opportunity will you squander 6 months from now? How about a year? If you stay here, will that relationship be viable in a few more months? Is your health going to hold out that much longer?

Real talk, it will probably get harder before it gets easier. The first day going to the gym is the worst. The first day without a cocktail might seem impossible. Committing to doing what's necessary to salvage the marriage may feel insurmountable after that first counseling session. But it will be worth it in the end. You don't have to do it all in a day. Probably can't, anyway. But you can start. Do the one thing you know you can do today to start the process. Cut up the credit card. Sign up for the gym membership. Use the membership you already have. Take a picture of the action. Capture the memory. Do something tomorrow that proves you took another step. Take a picture of that too. Place these photos in a folder on your phone. In one year, see how many photos you have taken. Look back at them and marvel at all that God has done. But for today...do something worthy of that first photo.

SUNDAY: Reflect and Rest

Holy Spirit, where are You calling me to grow? This past week, what wisdom, direction, and/or conviction did You lay upon me to grow? How can I see this done?

Holy Spirit, thank You for kicking me in the butt this week. Thank You for not letting me sit stagnant anymore. It is so encouraging to me to know that You loved me where you found me, but You love me too much to leave me there.

Thank You for reminding me that there is still work to be done.

Thank You for reminding me that You desire to use me to continue to move Your Kingdom forward. What a gift God!

Let me never take this for granted again. Let me remember all the work You did for me this week and praise You for it.

You are so good to me, God!

Amen.

Dec. 3, 2019

Today is a Thursday, after my 1st _____ ino infusion. A miracle has happened. Since Monday, I feel like I have woken up. My mind is clear, my energy is good, and I only have tummy pain. I have been so grateful for this gift. I have also had a few good poops — which was a major part of my stress last week. I've been able to walk to the bus stop, go to the store, pick up Rian from swim.

I don't know if this will last but like I said I'm thankful. The kids have been struggling a bit — we are going to put them in counseling and hopefully that will help.

_____

Praise is the most powerful weapon
Battle for healing is not yours to → send praise ahead.
Valley of Beracah. → Bless
Exchange your bitter for grateful

WORSHIP IS A WEAPON

MONDAY: What She Taught Me

"Praise is the most powerful weapon" - Excerpt from Nik's journal from November 7, 2019

I'm glad I signed up for Audible. It at least gave me something to listen to these last 3 years. Every time I'd go to listen to my Pandora account, I couldn't. Nik was always on it. I could have gotten another service. Spotify. Apple Music. Just never got around to it.

Didn't seem to be much of a priority.

On the other hand, ensuring Nik had access to those lyrics was a priority. It was how she fought. It was how she set her frame. It was how she lamented. It was how she praised. It was her rampart. It was her battle cry.

Worship was her weapon.

More than any other portion of Scripture, He quoted the Psalms. As one author put it, those verses are His songbook. And just like we can sing every word of a tune long since we last heard it, Jesus summoned those sweet stanzas everywhere He went. In teaching His disciples. In fulfilling the prophesies. In setting the religious and political regality in their place. Christ wielded His words of worship as a weapon. Sharper than any two-edged sword. Dividing soul and spirit. Joint and marrow. Discerning the very thoughts and intents of the heart (Keller, 2015).

Know this, you and I have an enemy sweet friend.

We do not battle flesh and blood. Though we may see the consequences of the fight play out down here. No, our true battle lies against the rulers of darkness. The wickedness is found in the heavenly places.

Choose your weapon wisely.

Bring your munitions of praise. Bring your armament of lament. Bring your ordnance of gratitude. Bring your arsenal of grief. Bring it all. Each battle will call for a different song.

In so doing we call down heaven upon the earth. We summon angels. We lay waste to demonic strongholds. We war with all the fury our grace-bought hearts can muster.

So fight until the very sky cracks open and the one called Faithful and True ends the war forever. And on that day, we will all be singing songs of His victory.

Worship is a weapon.

TUESDAY: *Commitment*

Blessed is the one who does not walk in step with the wicked or stand in the way that sinners take or sit in the company of mockers, but whose delight is in the law of the Lord, and who meditates on his law day and night. That person is like a tree planted by streams of water, which yields its fruit in season and whose leaf does not wither, whatever they do prospers. - Psalm 1:1-3

For the word of God is alive and active. Sharper than any double-edged sword, it penetrates even to dividing soul and spirit, joints and marrow; it judges the thoughts and attitudes of the heart. - Hebrews 4:12

Thank You Jesus for showing me the importance of worship. You teach me and show me that it is through lifting my eyes from my circumstances and raising my voice, be it in prayer, praise, lament, sorrow, or joy, that I connect with You in a deeper way. That in my worship the space between heaven and earth is narrowed. I am reminded that the Kingdom of God is here and still arriving. That, when I worship and confess with my tongue that You are Lord of Lords and King of Kings, Satan and his dominion lose ground in my life.

Spirit of the Living God, take me out to deeper waters with You this week through my worship. Let me connect with You in a richer way. Let the bond we share be forged even stronger. Whatever I am going through Lord, whether it be a season of rejoicing or suffering, I am reminded that I walk in favor because I can worship You through it all. You are the only One worthy of my worship. Let me bring myself fully to You.

In Your most precious name.

Amen.

WEDNESDAY: Assessment

1. Is worship a prominent part of my life?
2. Is my worship contingent upon my circumstances? If so, why?
3. Where is my focus when I worship? Is my worship done in a way that I magnify God and His glory?
4. Do I have a private worship life? Do I worship Jesus outside of the church house?
5. Are the songs I sing, the articles I read, and the things I give my attention to consistent with a heart bent toward honoring God in worship?

THURSDAY: Battle Plan

1. How can I make worship a consistently accessible weapon in my life?
2. What influences (music, TV shows, etc.) must I remove from my life that impede creating an atmosphere of holy worship in my life?
3. Practically, where can I incorporate worship into my day?
4. What circumstances am I currently enduring that I need to bring to Jesus through worship? What do I need to lament to Him about? What do I need to praise Him for?
5. What lie must I tear down that is keeping me from worshipping Jesus?

FRIDAY: *Gut Check*

1. Am I willing to get honest with God about what is hindering me from worshipping Him?
2. Will I commit to removing that which does not bring honor to God as it pertains to what I watch and/or what I listen to (music, television, movie preferences, etc.)?
3. Do I believe God is worthy of my worship? Do I have issues with God that are hindering me from worshipping Him? Have I brought those issues to Him? If not, why not?
4. Do I allow my feelings and/or my circumstances to dictate when/if I worship? What am I going to do about that?
5. Am I going to commit to worshipping God even when I am enduring difficulty?

SATURDAY: *Baby Steps*

We all were designed for worship. We all worship, in some form or fashion. Unfortunately, due to our sin nature, we have a propensity to worship the wrong thing. Only God is worthy of our worship. Only He is worthy of our praise. Only He can understand our suffering. He is the only one to whom we can lift our gaze and find genuine comfort.

Today is an opportunity to raise Him on high. Today is an opportunity to bow at His feet. Set aside some time to praise Him on your mountain. Take a few moments and cry to Him in your valley low. Sing a song of gratitude. Sing a song of sorrow. Sing of His greatness. Sing of His faithfulness. Stay in this moment until your spirit shifts and you no longer are enraptured by your circumstances, but rather, enveloped by His presence. Commit to come back to this place. Daily, if at all possible. Read one psalm a day, if nothing else. Make it a discipline. Watch it steady you. Watch it change you. Watch it make you more like Him. Only He is worthy of our worship.

SUNDAY: *Reflect and Rest*

My King, what did You reveal to me this week about worship? What am I worshipping currently? Do I worship You rightly? How can I continue to be mindful of this aspect of my life?

Father God, You alone deserve all my praise. You alone deserve all my worship. Father God, thank You for helping me to lift my gaze this week. To look up from that which is circumstantial and delight in the One that is sovereign.

As I reflect back on this week, I pray that the intimacy I experienced with You inspires me to draw closer to You in worship every day until I meet You face-to-face. You are so patient and longsuffering with me God.

Lord help me not to misappropriate Your patient love and excuse myself from what I was designed to do, to worship You all the moments of my life.

Thank You, God, for loving me so fully and completely. Help me to revel in You all the days of my life.

In Your name.

Amen.

PUT OTHERS FIRST

MONDAY: What She Taught Me

"It's Okay Nin…I'll see you real soon" - Nik's goodbye to her Grandmother via Phone on June 13, 2022

It probably was the most selfless thing I've ever seen.

By 9 p.m. on June 13, Nik knew she was about to take the trip home. She held out as long as she could for us. She wrote the letters. She made the lists. She ordered the gifts. She attended the graduation. It was time to go.

There was only one thing left to do: to say goodbye well.

Over the next 3 hours, she took the time she had left. The strength she had remaining, and spoke life over all of us. Encouraged us. Spoke to the gold she saw in our lives. Charged us not to waste the good stuff He put in us.

We sat around that bed. All of us. Our family. And listened intently to the words of a sage whose wisdom far surpassed any of our own. Her family and mine. My kids and me. She even took the time to call some friends. Leave some voice memos. And call her beloved grandparents: Pap and Nin.

She comforted us when it seemed like it should have been the other way around.

I cannot begin to imagine the agony of that moment. As Mary looked up and saw her promised Son. The Messiah. Broken beyond recognition. Bloodied beyond repair. Yet in that moment. The Christ was not concentrating on His suffering. He was not focused on His agony. Instead. He looked down at His mother. And the disciple whom He loved standing at her side.

In that moment, there was only one thing left to do, to say goodbye well.

In the time he had remaining. He gave Mary and John His charge. "Woman this is your son. Friend this is your mother." Forever cementing the relationship and bond between His beloved. A bond that would continue until they would be with Him again. In Glory.

He was still comforting His closest people when it seemed like it should have been the other way around.

The gifts we have from Him are not our own. We are called to take all the good stuff that He has put in us and pass it along to those who will succeed us. Our sons. Our daughters. Our friends. Our family. Those who know us the best. And those that will only hear our stories. Our gifts are not our own. Use them wisely.

Put others first.

TUESDAY: Commitment

"So the last will be first, and the first will be last." - Matthew 20:16

"Finally Pilate handed him over to them to be crucified. So the soldiers took charge of Jesus. Carrying his own cross, he went out to the place of the Skull (which in Aramaic is called Golgotha). There they crucified him, and with him two others, one on each side and Jesus in the middle. Pilate had a notice prepared and fastened to the cross. It read: "jesus of nazareth, the king of the jews." Many of the Jews read this sign, for the place where Jesus was crucified was near the city, and the sign was written in Aramaic, Latin and Greek. The chief priests of the Jews protested to Pilate, 'Do not write 'The King of the Jews,' but that this man claimed to be king of the Jews.' Pilate answered, 'What I have written, I have written.' When the soldiers crucified Jesus, they took his clothes, dividing them into four shares, one for each of them, with the undergarment remaining. This garment was seamless, woven in one piece from top to bottom. 'Let's not tear it,' they said to one another. 'Let's decide by lot who will get it.' This happened that the Scripture might be fulfilled that said, 'They divided my clothes among them and cast lots for my garment.'

So this is what the soldiers did. Near the cross of Jesus stood his mother, his mother's sister, Mary the wife of Clopas, and Mary Magdalene. When Jesus saw his mother there, and the disciple whom he loved standing nearby, he said to her, 'Woman, here is your son,' and to the disciple, 'Here is your mother.' From that time on, this disciple took her into his home." - John 19:16-27

Lord, it can be difficult at times to think to put others first. Sometimes I admit I can be selfish. Often I just become so self-absorbed in my circumstances that I lose sight of those around me. I live in a culture that celebrates the individual. That values an enlarged platform. That champions the self-made man. To do whatever is necessary to win, succeed, and gain that which my heart desires. It's a culture that does not honor our fellow man.

You desire a different culture for me: a Kingdom Culture. A culture that honors thy brother and thy sister as thyself. You desire for me to honor You by honoring Your most precious creation, mankind.

Help me, Jesus, become more selfless. To place the needs of others above my own. To serve my fellow man well. To put others first. To operate as You did. As a humble servant in service to the King and my fellow man.

In your name, I pray.
Amen.

WEDNESDAY: Assessment

1. Am I a selfish person? Would others consider me selfish?
2. Do I think of how my actions will affect others prior to taking those actions?
3. Do I honor my family? My friends? My coworkers? Strangers? Do I look to elevate the needs of others above my own?
4. Am I present with those I find myself around, or am I constantly distracted and/or self-absorbed in what I am doing?
5. Do I look for intentional opportunities to serve others? Do I go out of my way (even at personal cost) to seek to be a blessing to my fellow man?

THURSDAY: Battle Plan

1. Who have I taken for granted (i.e. a parent, a spouse, a friend, a coworker, etc.)? Specifically, how I have placed my needs and desires above their own, and how can I address this?
2. What is the first step I can take to become a more self-aware, less selfish, and more present person?
3. Who can speak into this area of my life and reveal any blind spots I may have?
4. Who do I need to prioritize right now? Who needs my help?
5. What practice can I adopt, alter, change, or give up that will help make me more sensitive to the needs of others?

FRIDAY: Gut Check

1. Am I going to apologize for being selfish? To who? When?
2. Am I going to place the needs of others above my own when it is inconvenient to do so? How so?
3. What is a measurable assessment of growth in this area? Who can hold me accountable for it?
4. Am I going to put the needs of others above my own, regardless of the reactions I receive or the lack of gratitude that I may experience?
5. Am I committing to this process primarily out of obedience (i.e. it's what I am supposed to do), or out of a heart of gratitude (i.e. it's what I get to do because God did it for me first)?

SATURDAY: Baby Steps

Look up. There is a whole world out there that needs you. Put the phone away. Turn the TV off. Stop scrolling. It's time to get present. It's time to observe. It probably won't take long. The inventory of people who could use your help right now is likely going to stack up pretty quickly. Your dad could use a phone call. Your wife would love to have a genuine conversation. Your kid needs your help. Ask Jesus, "Who can I serve right now?" It won't take long before someone comes to mind. Whoever it is. Whether you think they deserve it or not. Listen to the prompting and make the move.

Some of the most impactful moments of a person's life come when it is least expected. You may never know the depth of your impact. When you decide to buy the groceries for the single mom in line behind you. When you cut the grass of the elderly neighbor across the street. When you call your grandmother just to check in. When you thank a service member for standing in the gap for you. You might never know what it means to that individual, but they will. They will experience the love of Christ through you, and they will be changed. Your God will know it, too. And He will be so proud of You when He tells You about it when You see Him in heaven.

So do it. Do the thing that you were designed to do, Love God by loving His people.

Put someone else first.

>>>———

SUNDAY: Reflect and Rest

Father God, what did I learn this week? What did You reveal to me as it pertains to my interactions with other people? How can I better serve those around me?

Gracious and Heavenly Father, thank You for being so patient with me. I can be so selfish and so self-absorbed, even if I don't mean to be. Thank you this week for helping me see the hurt that is around me and empowering me to do something about it. Thank you for using me the way You did. Remind me of what You taught me this week about prioritizing others. Remind me of the specific people that I can come alongside and help. Help me find opportunities to serve others despite my circumstances. Help me to be salt and light. Thank You, Lord in advance for all that You are going to do through my life for the advancement of Your Kingdom.
Thank You, Lord.
Amen.

WASH YOUR FACE
AND MAKE THE BED

MONDAY: *What She Taught Me*

"This house is a hot mess…" - Nik commenting on her home on any given day.

It never was, really. She ran a tight ship. Always cleaning something. Making it more presentable. Even at the end. In our two decades together seldom did we have to scramble around to put things away due to an unexpected visit. Quite frankly, the house was always beautiful.

She always looked amazing too. Always had her makeup and hair done. Dangly earrings on. Even at the end. Honestly, I think it ticked off some of the women who knew that about her. She didn't care. She liked "looking pretty for me" (her words). Quite frankly, she was always beautiful.

She took great pride in having a presentable home. She took great strides to be sure to take care of herself. She stewarded well that which He had given her.

After it was all created. The sun and the moon. The land and the sea. The birds and the animals. He saved the best for last, us. He set our first parents in that place and He commissioned them with a task. To steward all that He had made. To keep it as it should be, always beautiful.

Work was not the curse. Labor existed before the Fall. From the beginning, our kind has been called to tend and watch over His precious creation. It just got a lot harder after the serpent's deception.

But that doesn't mean it isn't still our job.

There are a lot of reasons to not take care of ourselves or the tiny Kingdoms in our charge. There are a lot of factors that easily justify abdicating our responsibilities. Lots of excuses to show indifference to the everyday blessings of this life. Wasting the original commission of mankind.

But at the end of the day, none of those reasons matter. None of the explanations will hold up. We can have all the excuses in the world for our apathy, but that doesn't mean it isn't still our job.

And on that day in His presence, we will have to give an account for it. What we did. And what we didn't. So get up.

Wash your face and make the bed.

TUESDAY: Commitment

For you created my inmost being; you knit me together in my mother's womb. I praise you because I am fearfully and wonderfully made; your works are wonderful, I know that full well. My frame was not hidden from you when I was made in the secret place, when I was woven together in the depths of the earth. Your eyes saw my unformed body; all the days ordained for me were written in your book before one of them came to be. How precious to me are your thoughts, God! How vast is the sum of them! Were I to count them, they would outnumber the grains of sand, when I awake, I am still with you. - Psalm 139:13-18

So God created mankind in his own image, in the image of God he created them; male and female he created them. God blessed them and said to them, "Be fruitful and increase in number; fill the earth and subdue it. Rule over the fish in the sea and the birds in the sky and over every living creature that moves on the ground." Then God said, "I give you every seed-bearing plant on the face of the whole earth and every tree that has fruit with seed in it. They will be yours for food. And to all the beasts of the earth and all the birds in the sky and all the creatures that move along the ground, everything that has the breath of life in it, I give every green plant for food." And it was so. - Genesis 1:27-30

Father God, thank You for the commission over my life. You have created me so uniquely, so intricately, so beautifully that in Your perfect eyes, I am Your most precious creation. Yet, You do not place me in some glass jar to be kept preserved and safe. You place me into the very world You fashioned into being and call me to take dominion over it.

Lord, let my awe and appreciation of this task never grow callous or dim. Each day allow me to wake with joyful expectations of the work You have waiting for me. To honor You in both how I care for myself and that which You have placed in my charge.

Thank You, Jesus, for this most incredible assignment.

Amen.

WEDNESDAY: Assessment

1. Do I see myself as God's most precious creation? Do my actions reflect it?
2. Am I taking adequate care of myself?
3. Do I see "my dominion" (i.e. my home, my family, my finances, my possessions, etc.) as gifts to be valued and stewarded well? Do my actions reflect it?
4. Am I content with what I have been given/earned? If not, why not?
5. Would those closest to me consider me a good steward of both myself and that which God has given me? If so, why? If not, why not?

THURSDAY: Battle Plan

1. What is the area of my life right now that needs the most attention due to a lack of proper stewardship?
2. What is a measurable metric that I can use to determine if I am becoming a better steward in this area?
3. What does being a better steward look like in 30, 60, and 90 days from now? Six months? One year?

4. Who can hold me accountable for growing in this area?
5. What resources must I access to achieve this goal? Do I have them? If not, how can I get them?

FRIDAY: *Gut Check*

1. Stewardship requires accountability. Will I hold myself accountable? Will I enlist the support of others to be held accountable?
2. Do I trust God to grow me in this area even when this process becomes difficult?
3. What must I stop doing today to make this a priority?
4. What must I start doing today to make this a priority?
5. Am I willing to commit to doing the work, no matter what? What does that look like practically?

SATURDAY: *Baby Steps*

What an incredible assignment: to partner with the Creator of the universe and be on mission for and with Him. It can seem like a daunting task. It may feel overwhelming. It may even feel impossible. Perhaps you have never thought of your life's work in stewardship as important before. Perhaps you feel like you have been negligent in this area for so long that there is no way to recover from where you find yourself.

You'd be wrong.

If you aren't dead, God is not done with you. There is work yet to be done. Both on yourself and in your sphere. You likely already know what needs the most attention. Maybe it's time to finally go get that check-up with your doctor. Maybe it's time to stop paying the minimum balance on the credit card. Maybe it's time to stop spending hours on end in front of a screen. I'm certain it's time. So do something about it today. Call and make the appointment. Put down the phone and go for a walk. Cut up the credit card. Clean out the clutter. Throw away the trash. Get your finances in order.

Start to make your home and your life presentable again. It honors you. It honors creation. It honors God. Break the cycle of apathy and indifference. Begin a new cycle of respect and care. Start today.

SUNDAY: *Reflect and Rest*

Holy Spirit, what important aspects did I learn about my stewardship this week? Where am I stewarding my resources and relationships well? What areas need improvement?

Lord, how exciting! How exciting to have purpose! How exciting to have good work worth doing. Sometimes I feel adrift. Sometimes I feel like I lack purpose.

But this week You reminded me Lord that I am not here by accident. You reminded me that I am built on purpose for a purpose. You commissioned me at this specific time in this specific place with these specific resources and relationships to make an impact for You.

Thank You for reminding me of that fact. Thank You, Jesus, for reminding me this week that I am called to steward this incredible life you have given me. What a gift!

I love You, Lord.

Amen.

Isaiah 35: 3-4

Encourage the exhausted, and
make staggering knees firm. Say
to those with an (anxious and
panic-stricken heart,) "Be strong,
Fear not! Indeed, your God
will come with vengeance [for the
The retribution of God   ungodly]

DANCE TO "DOG DAYS"

MONDAY: What She Taught Me

"Encourage the exhausted, and make staggering knees firm. Say to those with an anxious and panic-stricken heart, 'Be Strong, Fear Not!...'"
- Isaiah 35:3-4a (AMP)

It did not matter what she was doing. It did not matter where she was. It did not matter who she was with. When the first staccato note of that Florence + the Machine classic hit, it was game on.

And participation was not optional. You were coming along for the ride. Pride. Ego. Love and longing. You had to leave it behind. She wanted to do what the moment called for, and she didn't want to do it alone.

Who gets a "plus twelve" invite to a wedding? I mean honestly. When you stop and think about it. Jesus had to be a really fun guy to be around. That Galilean jubilee leaves no question. Cana hadn't seen a celebration like that ever...or since. Because He did what the moment called for, an unexpected miracle that became an unforgettable memory.

But He didn't do it alone.

He sent others to fill the jars. Someone else did the pouring. Even the taste test was delegated.

It didn't matter what He was doing. It did not matter where He was. It didn't matter who He was with. When a person collided with Jesus, it was game on.

And participation was not optional. Others came along for the ride. Pride. Ego. Love and longing. They had to leave it behind. The moment called for movement.

There is something about being present. About being where my feet are planted. To seize the moment and go all-in on what Jesus wants me to do. It might seem silly. It might challenge my ego. It might require courage. It might require humility. But whatever it requires, I try to remind myself, Jesus will go before me and do all the heavy lifting. I just need to be obedient.

So be bold. Be brave. Be worthy of the moment.

Dance to "Dog Days Are Over."

TUESDAY: Commitment

On the third day a wedding took place at Cana in Galilee. Jesus' mother was there, and Jesus and his disciples had also been invited to the wedding. When the wine was gone, Jesus' mother said to him, 'They have no more wine.'

'Woman, why do you involve me' Jesus replied. 'My hour has not yet come.' His mother said to the servants, Do whatever he tells you.'

Nearby stood six stone water jars, the kind used by the Jews for ceremonial washing, each holding from twenty to thirty gallons. Jesus said to the servants, 'Fill the jars with water'; so they filled them to the brim. Then he told them, 'Now draw some out and take it to the master of the banquet.'

They did so, and the master of the banquet tasted the water that had been turned into wine. He did not realize where it had come from, though the servants who had drawn the water knew. Then he called the bridegroom aside and said, 'Everyone brings out the choice wine first and then the cheaper wine after the guests have had too much to drink; but you have saved the best till now.' - John 2:1-10

Jesus, You are the God of "right now." You are not distant. You are not far off. You are ever-present. Every moment of every day You desire to teach me, to use me, to grow me, and to empower me. To be Your representation here on earth until Your return. To not waste a moment of this gift You have given me, my uniquely designed and perfectly authored life. You want to see me use this gift for Your glory and Your renown. To use it and enjoy it. To be intentional with it and to not waste it. To spend it in a worthy cause for others to point them to who You are, The great I AM.

Jesus, help me be more present in the moment. Help see clearly what You would have me do in my daily comings and goings. To be silly when the moment calls for it. To be vulnerable when vulnerability is called for. To be helpful when I am surrounded by a person in need. To be so bold as to step outside of my comfort zone and do exactly what the moment calls for, to spend my days in a life well-lived, enjoyed, and rung out for Your purposes and plans.

Thank You, Jesus, for inviting me along this incredible ride called life. Amen.

WEDNESDAY: Assessment

1. Am I a "present" person? Do I live in the now? Do I relegate too much of my time thinking about the past or over-planning for the future? If so, why?
2. Am I a situationally aware person or am I too self-absorbed to notice potential opportunities to make an impact on the lives of others?
3. Does my ego, fear of failure, or potentially harmful impact on my reputation prevent me from being bold and taking risks even when I feel God directing me to step into that risk?
4. Do I see challenging situations as opportunities or obstacles? Do I see people in need as a chance to serve or a liability to be managed?
5. Do I enjoy life? Would others say I do?

THURSDAY: Battle Plan

1. What specific practices must I put in place to be more situationally aware and more present in the moment?
2. What specific practices do I need to eliminate to be more situationally aware and more present in the moment?

3. What specific area of my life do I need to lighten up and/or not take myself so seriously so I can enjoy the gift of this life in a deeper way?
4. What specific relationships/interactions do I need to be more intentional about so as to better serve those around me?
5. What fear must I face that is preventing me from stepping into what God has for me?

FRIDAY: Gut Check

1. Am I honestly willing to go all-in when the moment requires it, even if I am uncomfortable doing so?
2. What prideful part of my personality do I need to repent of in order to be more present and effective for the needs of others?
3. Do I trust God to go before me and do the heavy lifting in a situation that requires my activity? Do I find myself feeling ill-equipped or fearful often? If so, why?
4. Am I okay with knowing that the results of my actions towards others, though well-meaning and well-intentioned, may not always be received as such or may outright fail?
5. Am I willing to commit to growing in this area of intentional living for the long haul?

SATURDAY: Baby Steps

Intentional living does not come easily. Putting the needs of others in front of our own is not our default setting. Doing what the moment requires can be difficult, especially when it comes at the cost of our time, our resources, and even our reputation. But this life is not solely built for doing what we want for our benefit alone. This life was meant to be enjoyed by partaking in all of the opportunities that are set before us daily with and for others. Yes, some are fun. Some are enjoyable. But the truth is, many of those moments cost us something. Sometimes they cost us dearly. Yet, this life is meant to be poured out as a drink offering in service to others with a heart of gratitude toward the King who designed it.

So what does that look like for you today? Where is the place that God is calling you into intentional activity? If you aren't sure yet, ask Him. He'll tell you. But don't feel like you have to look around too hard or do some grandiose thing. Dance with your wife in the kitchen. Play "Go Fish" with your grandson. Call that friend that God laid on your heart. Do something today that takes intentionality that ministers to the soul of another while bringing honor to the One who created them. Oh…and as always…do it again tomorrow and the day after that, and the day after that…

SUNDAY: Reflect and Rest

Wonderful Counselor, what did I learn this week about being present? What distractions do I need to remove from my life that is robbing me of what lies before me in the moment?

Holy Spirit, thank You for helping me see the forest for the trees. Truth be told, I can get so busy grinding it out, so wrapped up in my own world, I can stop living intentionally, neglecting to be on mission to represent You in this world. To drink in all that You have for me, to do down here and to do so being "others focused."

I don't want to miss it, Lord. I don't want to look back on my life and see all the squandered opportunities in which I did not live to the full, not just for my own gain, but for the joy and edification of others. I want to live a grand life that points people to You.

Thank You for walking so closely with me this week, for giving me eyes to see, and ears to hear. You are so good to me.

Amen.

Nikki Healy
May 24, 2019 · 👥

In September when I signed up for my first substitute job I was beyond terrified!
Today I finished my 12 week journey as an 8th grade long term language arts substitute. I never thought 14 year olds would be "my people ".. but they are! Steve says it's because we share the same humor:)
I was honored to be a part of room 117 and I will miss them so much🖤

#longtermsubstitute #iteachmiddleschool
#substituteteacher
#pasadena
#8thgrade
#jokesfordays

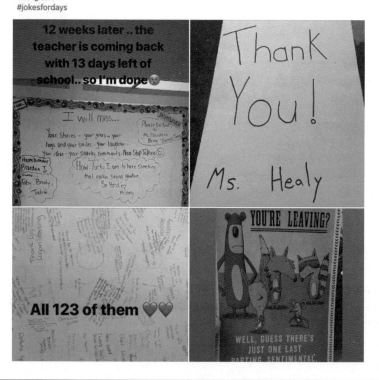

RAISE ADULTS

MONDAY: *What She Taught Me*

"Prepare the child for the path not the path for the child" - Nikki's parenting ethos

There are few things on the planet more foreboding than a classroom full of middle-schoolers. They can be critical. Overly sensitive. Indifferent. Cynical. And sometimes downright mean. As such, they can be quick to dismiss. Disregard. Diminish.

But Nik loved 'em.

She tried her hand at many a craft over the years. Lots of odd jobs. Lots of part-time gigs. Some were wildly successful. Some a wildly wasteful use of her time. But when she started substituting at the local middle school, she found the kind of joy that can only come from doing that for which you were designed.

She sought to extract the treasures in them the way a diver seeks out a pearl in an oyster. The way a miner chases the gold hidden by the mountain. It was in there. You just had to go find it.

More than interpreting lines on a graph or understanding sentence structures. She sought to engage with the next generation. To help them realize that despite our desire to the contrary, you can't stay a kid forever. We all grow up. Ready or not.

It seemed like a nuisance to the adults nearby. A distraction at best. Not to Jesus. He knew that these little hearts and minds would not stay little forever. These little people would someday become the ones in charge. So He placed the very Kingdom of Heaven within their grasp. A childlike faith to serve as their lifetime guide. A gift so precious that the enemy would attempt to steal it daily and replace it with a spirit of cynicism and indifference. Oversensitivity and a bent to be just downright mean. Bit by bit. Day by day. Year over year.

I can get so caught up in my adulting. Meanwhile, the whole time, I have three mini-me's in tow that need my experience and counsel. To be made aware of my successes and my failures. What I've built and what I've ruined. What part of His gift I have held fast and what I have squandered? What matters and what is chasing after the wind?

Because He has placed the same treasures in them, too. I just need to help them find them. Because they're up next. Ready or not.

Raise adults.

TUESDAY: *Commitment*

People were bringing little children to Jesus for him to place his hands on them, but the disciples rebuked them. When Jesus saw this, he was indignant. He said to them, "Let the little children come to me, and do not hinder them, for the Kingdom of God belongs to such as these. Truly I tell you, anyone who will not receive the Kingdom of God like a little child will never enter it." And he took the children in his arms, placed his hands on them and blessed them. - Mark 10:13-16

Start children off on the way they should go, and even when they are old they will not turn from it. - Proverbs 22:6

Jesus, I am but one link in the chain. Truth be told, in a few short years after my passing, few will remember what material things I left behind. The money I will have amassed will be disbursed. The possessions that I have collected will be scattered. All that will remain will be what I have cultivated in the hearts of those who have succeeded me. How to live. How to love. How to hold their head up in defeat and how to walk humbly in victory.

This is the greatest gift I can give them, my life experiences. The lessons I have learned. The measures You have taught me. The perspective I have gained in the years spent walking with You. In so doing, I will protect the greatest gift You have given them outside of Yourself, the childlike faith You have placed in all of our hearts upon our entry into this world. In sharing Your faithfulness despite my frivolity and faltering. In witnessing to Your steadfastness whether I won or I lost, I pass along the great lesson of this life, that despite what we see or experience, You are always there, You can always be trusted, and You are always good.

Help me, God, become more intentional in showing this to those who will follow me. To my children. To my nieces and my nephews. To the snot-nosed neighbor kid down the street. To the foul-mouthed teenager that frequents my path. You've placed the Kingdom of Heaven in them, Lord. It is my job to help them find it. It is my job to help them protect it. It is my job to leave a legacy worthy of those who have done so for me.

In Your most precious name.

Amen.

WEDNESDAY: Assessment

1. In general, how do I feel and, by extension act towards the generation that is coming up behind me?
2. Where do I derive the information I have about the next generation?
3. Do I interact with the next generation in an intentional way? If not, why not?
4. How does the younger generation perceive my generation? How do they perceive me specifically? Why? Are their comments or critiques valid?
5. Do I see my role in raising the next generation as significant? Do my actions support that belief?

THURSDAY: Battle Plan

1. Who are the specific individuals in the next generation that are in my sphere of influence either relationally or simply through proximity?
2. With whom do I need to focus on simply building a relationship, rather than looking for opportunities to train and teach?
3. What are some general things I think would be worth understanding regarding the life that lies ahead of them?
4. What are some of the specific things that I want to impart based on my experience at their ages?

5. Where and when are the intentional places and times I could look for the opportunity to engage them?

FRIDAY: Gut Check

1. Am I afraid of engaging individuals from the next generation? Why?
2. Am I willing to prioritize the necessary relational work over my desire to teach and train those in my stead?
3. Am I willing to listen more and talk less?
4. Will I commit to approaching younger people with their best interest at heart rather than a disdain for what I consider to simply be immaturity or lack of understanding?
5. Am I willing to admit that I may learn as much from them as they learn from me? Will I count upon the Holy Spirit's leading in the process? How?

SATURDAY: Baby Steps

The greater the generational gap, the more likely the larger the separation for relatability. In a world where everything is changing so fast, older people can quickly fall behind or simply be ignorant of the latest trends and passion points of those who are coming behind them. This can cause older folks to either feel insecure or antiquated when engaging with the youth. If not insecure or antiquated, then maybe just annoyed or perturbed by the perceived lack of respect, authority, and/or experience. If left unchecked, the gulf between the current group of adults and the ones up next in the queue can remain unresolved and unabridged.

But that isn't the charge. We are instructed for the older to train up the younger. To come alongside and help them. Prepare them. Train them. Teach them. Show them. This is all theirs someday soon. The ability to steward it well depends upon our assisting them to do so.

So you have to take this seriously. You can't relegate your perception and interaction with the next generation to be surmised with the statement,

"These kids today" (insert dismissive eye roll). Who is it today that you can start to shift the narrative? Who is it, that because of the actions you start today, will look back twenty years from now and can barely speak your name without getting misty-eyed because of the intentional way you sought to grow them up? Picture them in that moment.

Now, picture them if don't step up and do what you know God would have you do. Not as they are now, the dewy-eyed youth with the whole wide world spread out before them, but the thirty-three-year-old mom of three trying to figure out how to raise her kids amidst the tyranny of urgent chaos that relentlessly besets her home. The forty-two-year-old executive whose once black hair has now gone grey worries about all the time he spends at the office and all the time he doesn't spend with his son.

This goes one of two ways: they will either be prepared for the path before them or they won't. You are part of the process.

Today...do the one thing you know you need to do to start preparing them for the life they will lead. 'Cause it's comin'...ready or not.

>>>——

SUNDAY: Reflect and Rest

Father God, how has my paradigm shifted this week as to how I view the next generation? What are my roles and responsibilities for those that are coming behind me? How can I help them, encourage them, protect them, and guide them?

Lord God, Thank You for awakening me to the magnitude of the task set before me. You love the little children, yet You have placed upon me the trust to train them up in the way that they shall go, in the hope that, when they grow older, they will not depart from it. What a humbling task, Lord. Its size and scope are equally ominous as it is magnificent. In no way could I do it alone. Which is why I am beyond grateful that You go before me to see it through. Help me find the courage to minister to these young hearts and minds. Help me to find the words to guide and encourage them. Help me to help them. Help me to love them well.

Thank You for going before me, Lord.

Amen.

MAKE YOUR PLANS, BUT NEVER SAY "NEVER"

MONDAY: What She Taught Me

"I ain't never saying 'never' again."- Nikki's Facebook post comically recounting all the "Never Will I Ever" that happened in her life, circa 2014

Nik laughed at the notion of a five-year plan. Don't get me wrong, she appreciated the sentiment. She was an ardent planner. Old school. Paper calendars only.

She was just wise enough to know that, despite solid planning, the world gets a vote. And sometimes our best-laid plans don't survive first contact with the enemy. And sometimes God just seems fit to send us another way.

Even the best strategy is often just a plan from which to deviate.

At 19 she was certain she was going to be an FBI agent with no relational obligations save a dog. Certainly had no plans for marriage. But God saw otherwise. By 28 she was staunch in her belief that her life as a military wife was as certain as the sunrise. No other path for her family was conceivable. But God saw otherwise. By 30 she was convinced that she would never leave sunny SoCal. The most preferred of places.

But God saw otherwise. He often does. Jesus tells us so. As he did when speaking about the young prodigal.

I'm sure that young boy never saw himself eating with the pigs. I'm sure he never intended to squander the inheritance. I'm sure he never thought it would turn out the way it had. But the world got a vote. And his best-laid plans didn't survive first contact with the enemy.

So with a convicted heart, he sheepishly headed back home. He was convinced he would need to explain himself. To try and somehow make amends, but he never expected what happened instead. His Father ran towards him. Not to berate the boy. Rather, to embrace him.

He couldn't have seen it. But God saw otherwise.

I make my plans. But often without seeking His wisdom before setting out on my course. Yet in His grace, His divine love situates me in circumstances that far surpass my wildest expectations.

And in those times when the world's will wins out or I succumb to the schemes of the enemy. When I wise up and return home. He graciously embraces me before sending me on my way again. The right way this time.

So I'm learning to hold my plans loosely. And to listen to Him more intently. After all, His plan is far better than my own.

Make your plans but never say never.

TUESDAY: Commitment

"In their hearts humans plan their course, but the Lord establishes their steps." - Proverbs 16:9

"Jesus continued: 'There was a man who had two sons. The younger one said to his father, 'Father, give me my share of the estate.' So he divided his property between them.

Not long after that, the younger son got together all he had, set off for a distant country and there squandered his wealth in wild living. After he had spent everything, there was a severe famine in that whole country, and he began to be in need. So he went and hired himself out to a citizen of that country, who sent him to his fields to feed pigs. He longed to fill his stomach with the pods that the pigs were eating, but no one gave him anything.

When he came to his senses, he said, 'How many of my father's hired servants have food to spare, and here I am starving to death! I will set out and go back to my father and say to him: Father, I have sinned against heaven and against you. I am no longer worthy to be called your son; make me like one of your hired servants.' So he got up and went to his father.

But while he was still a long way off, his father saw him and was filled with compassion for him; he ran to his son, threw his arms around him and kissed him.

The son said to him, 'Father, I have sinned against heaven and against you. I am no longer worthy to be called your son.'

But the father said to his servants, 'Quick! Bring the best robe and put it on him. Put a ring on his finger and sandals on his feet. Bring the fattened calf and kill it. Let's have a feast and celebrate. For this son of mine was dead

and is alive again; he was lost and is found.' So they began to celebrate."
- Luke 15:11:24

Father, there is a time and a place for good solid planning. You told us that a man does not build a tower without counting the cost. Taking the time to plan is good, noble, and is required if I am to be a good steward of that which You have entrusted to me.

That said, it is fraught with peril and the potential for dangerous missteps if I am not careful. I can and have failed to bring You into my planning process. To spend the time necessary seeking Your face and asking for Your wisdom. When necessary to seek out wise counsel from Godly men and women that You have placed in my life to help me along the way.

Then there is the manner in which I tend to hold my plans. So tightly. So, so rigid. So protective. My way or the highway. So when things don't go as planned or in those times when I face stiff resistance, I can become frustrated, confused, annoyed, angry, or despondent.

Lord, remind me that You are constantly working all things together for the good of those who love You. Remind me that, even if the path seems uncertain. Even when my plan falls apart. You are with me. Help me to plan, Lord. But remind me to not put my faith in the plan but in You.

Amen.

WEDNESDAY: Assessment

1. What is my perspective on planning? Is it a healthy one? Should I spend more time planning, or do I "over-plan"?
2. Do I prioritize seeking Jesus while making my plans? Are His potential plans or considerations part of my planning process? If not, why?
3. Do I ask Godly men and women to speak into my planning process when it would be prudent to do so? Do I have trusted voices in my life that can help me think through difficult circumstances or seasons?
4. How do I react when things do not go as planned? Am I a "why me?" person?
5. Do I get angry with God when things go awry or seem uncertain? What do I do with those emotions?

THURSDAY: Battle Plan

1. What areas in my life do I need to be more regimented as it pertains to making and executing a plan (i.e. Spiritual Formation, Relationship Development, Physical Health, Financial Planning, etc.)?
2. As it pertains to this area, what would Jesus have me do? Who can help me develop a healthy plan and hold me accountable to it?
3. What is an area of my life that I am over-planning and/or not giving to God for development? Do I need to repent? Do I need to seek forgiveness from another whom I should have involved in this process (i.e. spouse, child, friend, etc.)?
4. What does a Godly planning process look like for me moving forward?
5. What specific incidence or circumstance in my life resulted in my and/ or others' pain or hurt as it pertains to a "failed plan?" How can I process this in a healthy way with Jesus?

FRIDAY: Gut Check

1. How do I really feel about this new perspective on planning? Am I okay with it? Does it make me uneasy? How can I grow in my comfort with it?
2. What accountability measures can I put in place to ensure my God-honoring plans are set up for success?
3. What distractions must I remove from my life to stay on track when I encounter the inevitable resistance I will face in attempting to carry them out?
4. Am I really going to get honest with God about my hurt, disappointment, sorrow, and/or confusion regarding plans of mine that have failed? Especially those that I believed were commissioned by Him.
5. Despite where I may end up, whether on a mountain high or in a valley low, do I still trust that God is working all things for my good?

SATURDAY: Baby Steps

It is a lot like holding a handful of sand. If you attempt to hold it without any form, fingers spread apart, palm flat, the sand will fall away at the slightest of jostling. Yet, if you squeeze it too tight, fist clenched closed, the sand will rapidly eject from your grasp as there is no room for it. The best way to hold a handful of sand is to scoop it tenderly, palm cupped gently, in the tension between intently and loosely.

This is how God tells us to make our plans. To seek His face, His leading, His direction, and then to set out on that path while all the while knowing the adventure will likely look far different than we could have ever imagined. This is why He is a light unto our feet and a lamp unto our path. If He were not to reveal the next step, surely we would stumble. But if He were to illuminate all that lay in front of us, we likely would be frozen in fear or disbelief.

It takes great confidence and trust in Him to plan rightly. To recognize the importance of our will while finding peace in His sovereignty. So before setting out to start your plans, spend some time with Him. Clear the air if you need to. Thank Him for the provision and protection He has given you thus far if you haven't ever done so. Give to Him your uncertainties and your hurts. Give Him your hopes and your dreams. A good plan starts by spending time with the One that architected it all. Before you act, plan. And before you plan, spend time with Jesus.

SUNDAY: Reflect and Rest

Lord Jesus, what did I learn this week in regards to being diligent in my planning while still being sensitive to Your leading and activity in my life? Where do I need to plan better? Where do I need to be less regimented?

My King Jesus, the One who designed it all. From the cosmos to the very cells that comprise my being. Lord, thank You for the reminder this week that ultimately You hold all of this together. Ultimately, it will be Your plans that will be done. Ultimately, it will be Your will that be completed.

Yet You have graciously invited me into that process. You call me to partner with You in the redemptive work You are doing. Moving forward, help me, Jesus, view my plans rightly, that I am commissioned by You to make my plans, but to trust that You will ultimately order my steps.

Amen.

APRIL SHOWERS
BRING MAY FLOWERS

MONDAY: What She Taught Me

"Jesus specializes in new beginnings. Stop looking back – New view ahead." - Excerpt from Nik's journal from July 2019

It wasn't always sorrowful in our house. We had years full of joy too. We experienced both ends of the spectrum. Happiness and heartache. Constantly ebbing and flowing between those poles as time marched on. Feasting and fighting. Laughing and crying. Running and resting. Ours was a life that ran the gamut.

In retrospect. What our final years together taught me is that everything is fleeting. Everything shifts. Everything changes. Often without warning. Often on random and otherwise nondescript days. Days that previously had no anticipated meaning at all. And yet – in an instant – becoming unrivaled in their significance.

The day she said, "I'm pregnant." The day the doctor said, "It's cancer." The day we met. The day she left. The first "I love you." The last "I'll see you real soon."

History counts him as the wisest man who ever lived. Solomon – the son of the great king David. His acumen brought him power and platform. Peace and prosperity. No one was considered more discerning or perceptive. As such. His contemplations on life's circumstances are worth considering.

"To everything there is a season. And a time for every purpose under the heavens. A time to be born. A time to die. A time to plant. A time to reap. A time to kill. A time to heal. A time to break down. And a time to build up. A time to weep. A time to laugh. A time to mourn. And a time to dance."

Solomon's counsel to us – Eventually. This too shall pass. The good will give way to the bad. Then sorrow gives way to joy. The fullness of delight will give way to the emptiness of lament. Only to have the moments spent in the deep valley then eclipsed by the glory of a summit experience.

Each giving way to its reciprocal. And vice versa. Over and over. Until we walk into glorious rest. In Him. Then and only then. Will our joy be complete and everlasting.

So for now. Remember. In every season. Eventually. This too shall pass.

He is making everything beautiful in its time.

April showers bring May flowers.

TUESDAY: *Commitment*

"There is a time for everything, and a season for every activity under the heavens: a time to be born and a time to die, a time to plant and a time to uproot, a time to kill and a time to heal, a time to tear down and a time to build, a time to weep and a time to laugh, a time to mourn and a time to dance, a time to scatter stones and a time to gather them, a time to embrace and a time to refrain from embracing, a time to search and a time to give up, a time to keep and a time to throw away, a time to tear and a time to mend, a time to be silent and a time to speak, a time to love and a time to hate, a time for war and a time for peace.

What do workers gain from their toil? I have seen the burden God has laid on the human race. He has made everything beautiful in its time. He has also set eternity in the human heart; yet no one can fathom what God has done from beginning to end. I know that there is nothing better for people than to be happy and to do good while they live. That each of them may eat and drink, and find satisfaction in all their toil, this is the gift of God." -
Ecclesiastes 3:1-13

"Now listen, you who say, 'Today or tomorrow we will go to this or that city, spend a year there, carry on business and make money.' Why, you do not even know what will happen tomorrow. What is your life? You are a mist that appears for a little while and then vanishes. Instead, you ought to say, 'If it is the Lord's will, we will live and do this or that.' As it is, you boast in your arrogant schemes. All such boasting is evil. If anyone, then, knows the good they ought to do and doesn't do it, it is sin for them - James 4:13-17

Father God – Every aspect of my life is subject to change. Nothing stays as it is for long. My city. My station. The relationships I value. Even my own physical condition. All will change. All will transform. And all will eventually fade away. Nothing is constant. Nothing except You.

You are eternal and everlasting. You are unchanging and unmoving. Let me forever anchor my hope in that fact. So often Lord, I am moved by my circumstances. My perspective and countenance are set by the fleeting conditions I am experiencing in the moment.

Father give me both the wisdom to experience those moments to the full – to laugh and to cry. To shout and to weep – while never letting go of the foundational truth that You are present and always with me. That I am an eternal spiritual being having a temporal human experience. Let me never forget that the joy I receive here is but a shadowy glimpse of the glory of heaven. Let me never forget that all the pain I endure in this life will pass away when I enter Your celestial city. Let me be anchored and balanced by the truth that all of this will one day pass and my best is yet to come.

Amen.

WEDNESDAY: Assessment

1. Do I genuinely enjoy the good seasons of life? Do I find contentment in them? Do I recognize them when I am experiencing them or do I only notice them after they have passed?

2. How well do I endure the hard seasons of life? Do I look for growth opportunities in them or simply find myself complaining?

3. Am I eternally or temporally minded? Do I care more for the things of this life or am I investing in the one that will follow? What do my actions say about this?

4. How do I approach my future? Do I fear it? Am I cynical about how things will shake out? Or am I pragmatic in my approach to planning? Or am I optimistic about the unforeseeable? What experiences shaped my viewpoint on this?

5. Do my past mistakes and/or misfortunes rob me of my present? Do my concerns for my future steal the moments of my "here and now?"

THURSDAY: Battle Plan

1. In this season of life, what should I be focusing on? What requires my attention?

2. In this season of life, what distractions do I need to remove? What is keeping me from doing that which needs my attention?
3. In this season of life, what are the relationships that I should be investing in right now? What does that investment look like practically speaking?
4. In this season of life, whom should I be seeking counsel and guidance to navigate these times in the best manner possible?
5. What God-given lessons from my past can best help me navigate these times? If I find myself in uncharted territory, how do I better seek God's face to obtain the wisdom necessary to navigate these times in the best manner possible?

FRIDAY: *Gut Check*

1. Looking back, do I see God's faithfulness in every season of life? If not, have I brought that to Him? Will I talk to someone about those confusing times when I felt abandoned?
2. Have I thanked God for all the seasons of undeserved blessing? Where do I need to better express my gratitude?
3. Have I thanked God for all the seasons of difficulty that have ultimately made me stronger and more resilient? If not, why have I not? Am I better for it or am I just bitter?
4. In retrospect, have I missed opportunities for growth or forging deeper relationships because I was focused on that which was less important during certain seasons of life? Do I need to repent? Who do I need to ask for forgiveness for my neglect?
5. Do I trust God with my future? If not, why?

SATURDAY: *Baby Steps*

It comes as no surprise to us each year when the spring rain gives way to the summer's heat. Only to have the blistering temperatures to be cooled by the autumn wind. For colorful fall foliage to drop and eventually be covered by the snow of the winter. Then for spring to return again. Perpetually repeating the cycle again and again. Over and over. Year over year.

Yet in our own lives. We can be so surprised by the sudden change in the seasons. To be dismayed, downcast, and utterly destroyed by the dark days spent in the valley. Losing all hope for reprieve. Conversely, we can miss the potential memories that could be made while we remain, albeit for a moment, upon the mountaintop. So preoccupied with our business we miss the golden opportunities that lie at our feet, an unplanned romantic getaway, a chance to play catch with our child while they still desire our company, a quiet evening spent on the porch, staring up, and getting lost in the glory of creation.

This life is fleeting. Which is what makes it so precious. The moment you are experiencing right now you will never have again. And God has something for you in it. Even those things that are most difficult to endure, if only to experience them here as they will not be a part of life that is to come.

So what season do you find yourself in today? Is God calling you to revel in gratitude for all the blessings you are experiencing? Is He asking you to bring your lament to Him so that you can be comforted despite being in the dark?

Whatever it is. Don't miss the opportunity friend. It likely won't come back round again.

This life is a gift. Don't miss it.

>>>———

SUNDAY: Reflect and Rest

Everlasting Father, what key things did I learn about myself this week? How do I process the seasons of my life, but when I am experiencing them and remembering them? What season am I in right now? What are You calling me to do in this time?

Father God, often I am lost in the tyranny of the urgent. I miss the forest through the trees. I become so engrossed in what I am doing in the moment, I lose sight of the greater narrative that is being written. I take the good seasons for granted. I complain when I experience a long stretch of pain. Father in every season You have something for me. An opportunity for impact and a chance to grow closer to You. Help me Lord to learn to appreciate all the seasons of life. For the gifts that are found in them and the lessons learned because of them. Thank You, Lord, for the gift of life. It is precious. Let me squeeze everything out of it that You have for me. Day by day and from season to season. Thank You, Lord. Amen.

BE HONEST

MONDAY: *What She Taught Me*

"We need to talk" - Spring of 2011

A few years into our marriage, Nik sat me down. Her eyes were full of tears and her voice trembled as she spoke. It came out of nowhere for me. But not for her. It was time. And with all the resolve she could muster. She laid it all out.

Amidst that conversation, Nik owned a lot. Lots of mistakes. Lots of missteps. She knew she was forgiven. But coming to me was part of her restoration. Couldn't move forward without dealing with the past. She was scared but she was certain. She was broken but she was choosing to be brave.

I was humbled by her brutal honesty. Trusting me in her vulnerability. Trusting Him in her obedience.

In the end. It became a beautiful new beginning, for both of us.

It certainly was not the dinner party Simon had envisioned. Yet Jesus remained unfazed. He didn't restrain the woman from what she set out to do, washing His feet with her tears. Her voice likely trembling as she dried them with her hair.

It came out of nowhere for Simon. But not for her. It was time. And with all the resolve she could muster. She laid it all out. Couldn't move forward without dealing with the past. She was scared but she was certain. She was broken but she was choosing to be brave.

A beautiful blueprint recorded in His Word. One Nik revered and in turn modeled for me.

I have so many reasons not to be honest with Jesus and those that I've hurt. To hide my sin and my shame. To protect my ego and my reputation. For fear of what will come to pass or what may be ruined as a result.

But there is no freedom in that place. There is no hope for redemption in the hiding.

We all make mistakes. We all fall short. But that doesn't have to be the end of the story. It's okay to be scared, still being certain of our need to be unburdened. We can be broken while still choosing to be brave.

This is where the narrative is re-written. By Him.

Be honest.

TUESDAY: *Commitment*

"Have mercy on me, O God, according to your unfailing love; according to your great compassion blot out my transgressions. Wash away all my iniquity and cleanse me from my sin…

Create in me a pure heart, O God, and renew a steadfast spirit within me. Do not cast me from your presence or take your Holy Spirit from me. Restore to me the joy of your salvation and grant me a willing spirit, to sustain me." - Psalm 51:1-2, 10-12

"When one of the Pharisees invited Jesus to have dinner with him, he went to the Pharisee's house and reclined at the table. A woman in that town who lived a sinful life learned that Jesus was eating at the Pharisee's house, so she came there with an alabaster jar of perfume. As she stood behind him at his feet weeping, she began to wet his feet with her tears. Then she wiped them with her hair, kissed them and poured perfume on them.

When the Pharisee who had invited him saw this, he said to himself, "If this man were a prophet, he would know who is touching him and what kind of woman she is, that she is a sinner."

Jesus answered him, 'Simon, I have something to tell you.'

'Tell me, teacher,' he said.

'Two people owed money to a certain moneylender. One owed him five hundred denarii, and the other fifty. Neither of them had the money to pay him back, so he forgave the debts of both. Now which of them will love him more?'

Simon replied, 'I suppose the one who had the bigger debt forgiven.'

'You have judged correctly,' Jesus said.

Then he turned toward the woman and said to Simon, 'Do you see this woman? I came into your house. You did not give me any water for my feet, but she wet my feet with her tears and wiped them with her hair. You did not give me a kiss, but this woman, from the time I entered, has not stopped kissing my feet. You did not put oil on my head, but she has poured perfume on my feet. Therefore, I tell you, her many sins have been forgiven, as her great love has shown. But whoever has been forgiven little loves little.'

Then Jesus said to her, 'Your sins are forgiven.'

The other guests began to say among themselves, 'Who is this who even forgives sins?'

Jesus said to the woman, 'Your faith has saved you; go in peace.'" - Luke 7:36-50

Jesus, it just seems safer to hide. It seems so much more appealing to keep it hidden away. I know it was wrong. I know I messed up. I know I've hurt others and myself in my words, thoughts, and deeds. It seems so much easier to just keep carrying it alone, but it just isn't. I am so heavy-laden. I am so full of guilt and shame. I can't escape it. It will not leave me alone. So, Lord, I know it is time to face it. It is time for me to own it and the consequences that come with it.

So, Lord, I am starting now. I am scared but I am certain You want me to bear this no longer. So, Lord, I confess. I have sinned against You. I have done that which You would not have me do. Please forgive me. Forgive me for my transgressions and let me stand on Your Word that says that there is no condemnation for those that claim Your name as Lord and King.

This is the first step, Lord. There will likely be others. I will need to change my ways. I may need to make amends with others. But this is the first step.

Thank You for giving me the courage to take it. Thank you for loving me so much that You refuse to leave me in this place of suffering. Thank You for restoring me to life again.

Amen.

WEDNESDAY: Assessment

1. Is there an area of sin, misunderstanding, mistake, or hurt (either inflicted or endured) that remains unresolved in my life? What is it?
2. How has this area affected my relationship with God?
3. How has this area affected my relationship with others?
4. How has this area affected the view I have of myself? My self-worth?

5. What other results/symptoms are present in my life as a result of maintaining this area of unhealth and/or unconfessed sin?

THURSDAY: *Battle Plan*

1. What is it that God is specifically laying on my heart that I need to repent? If not repent, what is it that I specifically need to go to Him and be honest about?
2. Who do I need to seek forgiveness from? What does that look like?
3. If I have been hurt, who is it that I need to go to and let them know of my wounding/offense? What does that look like?
4. How do I need to specifically prepare myself for these conversations – with God and with others? What attitudes and feelings do I need to get in check?
5. What does real health and/or restoration in these areas/relationships look like after these matters are addressed?

FRIDAY: *Gut Check*

1. What excuse do I need to remove that is preventing me from moving forward and handling this situation rightly?
2. Am I scared? If so, why?
3. Even if these conversation(s) go poorly in my eyes, do I believe God will still work this situation for the good of all those who love Him, including myself and those involved?
4. When am I going to do that which I know God would have me do? Be specific.
5. Can I resolve to be honest without being rude, defensive, mean, or argumentative?

SATURDAY: *Baby Steps*

Being honest can be scary. Being real and authentic can be difficult. It can be even more so when we are offended, or we have caused an offense. Something in our brokenness goes into self-preservation mode. It's a lot easier to be guarded than to be vulnerable. It seems a lot safer to stay hidden than to be transparent. It seems that way, but it's not. The longer we hold onto our hurts, sins, hang-ups, and offenses, the more they wear us down into bitter, despondent, and hopeless people.

God doesn't want this for us. God doesn't want this for you.

So stop doing the same thing and expecting a different result. Stop cuddling the sin that is killing you, if not the relationships dearest to you. Stop avoiding facing the wounding that has shaped you and the jaded way in which you view others and the environment you operate. If you want a different result, you are going to have to take a different approach.

And since this is a new one, it might be a little difficult to cut down the new path at first. It isn't the well-worn highway of shame or avoidance you have been traversing for such a long time. But this path leads to life and life to the full. So sit down. Gather your thoughts. Pray for wisdom. Pray for an opportunity to address the matter. Pray for your heart and your words. Pray for the recipient's response. Ask Him to go before you and make the seemingly bleak if not impossible be restored and bright.

And then go have the conversation…it will take 15 seconds of courage, but once you start, the rest will come more naturally. The hard part is just starting. You can do it. He wouldn't be commissioning you to do it if you couldn't.

SUNDAY: Reflect and Rest

Holy Spirit, what were my key takeaways from this past week? What ground did I take back in choosing to be honest? What victories did I experience because of Your movement in my life?

Holy Spirit, thank You! It feels so good to put that burden down. It feels so good to place that at the foot of the cross and know You paid for it all. Please give me both the courage to keep moving forward while at the same time, the strength to not go back and pick it back up. I continue to pray for all others that were involved. Healing takes time. Rebuilding trust takes time. Yet I know that you specialize in making broken things new. Please continue to minister to our hearts collectively as we continue in the restorative process. In Your most precious name. Amen.

Liked by **maryychurch** and **239 others**

nikkihealy5 Today I tried to start decorating my house with Christmas decorations...Music going, boxes out, Steve on the roof..

Normally it's my most favorite time of the year...I've been taking about it for weeks, planning it out, buying new stuff..

Yet as I was pulling decorations out I couldn't shake a deep OFF feeling...

Pull up Nikki, What's wrong with you Nikki, This is your FAVORITE Nikki, Everyone is here and helping, You live in an awesome house Nikki, You have awesome decorations Nikki..

Then it starts.. Man I'm slow today, I feel really fatigued, Your leg was more swollen this morning, That spot is still really hurting, The cancer has probably spread already, Remember the Dr. said he felt more lymph nodes, Nothing your doing is working, The cancer is probably everywhere, The chemo Isn't going to work, Don't tell Steve, You don't want to worry him..

What if this is your last Christmas..

STOP.. I will not die but live to tell what the Lord has done Psalm 118:17

Wow Nikki you are so mental, Your CEA was so low last week, Your live and lungs are stable, You have a plan, You read the scriptures, You take communion daily, God has told many people he will heal you..

Wendy would have been so happy to just watch.. here you are moving around and sad about it.. Nikki you have made it 3 Christmas's with cancer..that's huge..

Tears start to fall, pour out.. all while the girls are wrapping ribbons around the tree...

Next thing I know I'm sobbing, the girls stop and we discuss how Christmas decorationing has now become the memory associated with cancer..

Year 1 .. October..you have cancer let's decorate..

Year 2.. October.. you are now stage 4 let's decorate..

Year 3.. October.. after all you did you still have cancer..

Yet I AM still here, I am moving around, I am hugging my kids, shopping, and decorating..

This is the fine line I walk...Gratefulness and Grief..

It is ok to walk this line, as much as try we cannot escape our humaness..

Until then.. I will be here setting up lights, while wiping tears, while laughing, while being grateful to see another year, while being sad for my friends that aren't, while hopeful next year has a different association..

View all 69 comments

jessica.booker Most amazing person!! We will always be praying for you 💜 💜 💜

ellebellecreative Love you sweet friend. 💜

November 6, 2021

 **nikkihealy5**   •••
Envita Medical Centers

REAL IS RELATABLE

MONDAY: What She Taught Me

"...I will be here setting up lights, while wiping away tears, while laughing while being grateful to see another year, while being sad for my friends that aren't, while hopeful next year has a different association.." - Nik's Instagram post from November 2021

We did it the way she liked this year. Despite the circumstances. Even without her. Way too early for most folks. But Nik always wanted the house decorated as soon as possible. She loved it. The soft glow at night. The peace it seemed to bring into our home.

But that year was different.

On November 6th, 2021. Nik wrote about it. While the rest of us were still forcing our cheer. Nik was being Nik. Being honest with her questions. Being honest with her state of mind. Amidst the twinkling lights. There were tears. Amidst the carols. There was a lot of confusion. And she wasn't hiding it. She was being real. Inadvertently giving us permission to do the same.

It was a long evening after that Passover supper. Tarrying in the garden deep into the night. Some in His company were putting on the façade of bravery. But Jesus was busy being Jesus. Being honest about His state of mind. Turning to His Father in His agony. Processing through prayer. Sweating drops of blood in sorrow. Amidst the backdrop of the stars He hung was His sadness. Amidst the cosmos He created was His concern. And He wasn't hiding it. Even in His resolve to submit to the plan. And let Thy will be done.

There is real pressure to have it all together these days. To grin and bear it. To put on the appearance of resilience despite a lack of understanding.

But often I'm just not okay. And faking that I am serves me little, and it serves those I lead less.

Nik taught me that it's okay to not be okay. She showed me you can be sad while still trusting the certainty of His love. To be scared yet still resolve to submit to Him. Thy will be done.

She reminded me that even my God had His night in Gethsemane. And in letting others see my struggle. Implicitly it gives them permission to do the same. To start being honest with themselves. And to start being honest with Him too.

Real is relatable.

TUESDAY: Commitment

"Then Jesus went with his disciples to a place called Gethsemane, and he said to them, 'Sit here while I go over there and pray.' He took Peter and the two sons of Zebedee along with him, and he began to be sorrowful and troubled. Then he said to them, 'My soul is overwhelmed with sorrow to the point of death. Stay here and keep watch with me.'

Going a little farther, he fell with his face to the ground and prayed, 'My Father, if it is possible, may this cup be taken from me. Yet not as I will, but as you will.'

Then he returned to his disciples and found them sleeping. 'Couldn't you men keep watch with me for one hour?' he asked Peter. 'Watch and pray so that you will not fall into temptation. The spirit is willing, but the flesh is weak.'

He went away a second time and prayed, 'My Father, if it is not possible for this cup to be taken away unless I drink it, may your will be done.'

When he came back, he again found them sleeping, because their eyes were heavy. So he left them and went away once more and prayed the third time, saying the same thing." - Matthew 26:36-44

"My God, my God, why have you forsaken me? Why are you so far from saving me, so far from my cries of anguish? My God, I cry out by day, but you do not answer, by night, but I find no rest." - Psalm 22:1-2

Lord, I'm tired. I'm worn down. I'm weary. I soothe myself with distractions. I try and keep busy. But in the quiet. I am anxious and concerned. I feel so lonely. I am tired of faking it. I am tired of grinning and bearing it. I've carried this weight so long that I don't remember what it feels like to be unburdened.

In faith, I am coming to You. In faith, I am choosing to stop trying to do this on my own. I am expecting that You will meet me in this place. I am expecting that You will place divine appointments in my life that will result in healing, freedom, and restoration. I understand that this may be a process. That joy may not come tomorrow morning...but it will come.

Give me the strength and tenacity to be honest and authentic. Both with You and those that You place in my life to help me. It's hard right now, Lord. But I am still believing the best is yet to come.

Amen.

WEDNESDAY: Assessment

1. What is/are the thing(s) in my life that I am reticent to be transparent about? Both with God and "my people?"
2. Why am I reticent to do so?
3. What am I afraid of when it comes to sharing honestly?
4. Do I trust God with my healing in this place? If not, why not?
5. Do those closest to me know how I am really doing?

THURSDAY: Battle Plan

1. What does health/restoration in these areas look like?
2. What are the practical authentic steps I can walk out in my healing?
3. Who can I bring along with me? Who can help me?
4. Who do I need to share my journey with? How will it help them?
5. How do I communicate my process in a healthy way? Who needs to know and who does not?

FRIDAY: *Gut Check*

1. Will I face the fear of this level of vulnerability? How and when?
2. What will I do if my transparency results in difficult conversations with others?
3. What does accountability look like in choosing to be real with God and others?
4. How will I act if my reputation is affected by my choosing to be authentic?
5. What lie of the enemy do I need to tear down right now in this area so as to pursue my health?

SATURDAY: *Baby Steps*

Being real can be a tricky thing. Some of us find comfort in keeping our true selves hidden away. Some of us tend to overshare due to our insecurity. Finding a way to be brutally honest while still maintaining our dignity can seem almost impossible.

Yet, there is a way.

It starts with coming clean with Jesus. Laying it all out there. Our hurts. Our worries. Our fears. Our embarrassments. Our mistakes. Our shame. Our anger. And our questions. He isn't scared of any of that. He knew you when He formed you in your mother's womb. Nothing you say to Him will surprise Him or cause Him to pause over loving You. So talk to Him.

Tell Him all of it. All the raw and all the real. Lament. Cry. Scream if you have to. He can take it. Then ask Him what You should do about it. Ask Him who you should talk to about it. Ask Him not only what you should do but how you should do it. How should you model your authenticity for your spouse, for your coworkers, for your friends, for your children?

He will show you the narrow path. It all starts by seeking His wisdom.

SUNDAY: Reflect and Rest

Heavenly Father, in what way did You call me to be more vulnerable this week? What relationships were affected by my choosing to be honest? How were they affected? What are You calling for me to do next?

Father God, it was so good to finally get honest with You and allow me to be authentic and honest with those to whom I am the closest. To stop striving. To stop acting like I have it all together when I don't. To give myself the liberty to say, "I'm not okay."

It's in that honesty that I can have real, meaningful conversations with You and with others. It's in that vulnerability that real relationships are formed. Thank You, Father, for giving me the courage to be transparent. For my health and for the health of those around me.

I love You, Lord.

Amen.

EAT GOOD FOOD
AND DRINK FINE WINE

MONDAY: *What She Taught Me*

"#butiwillwin" - Nik's Instagram post from November 2019

Not her preferred holiday for sure. But I think it grew on her over the years. It grew because of what it started. Her favorite season of the year. It grew because of what it came to represent. An opportunity to slow down. And be thankful. Regardless of the circumstances.

It really hit home in 2019. A little over 6 weeks after her original diagnosis. At Friendsgiving, already the effects of the chemo were setting in. Cold hands. Neuropathy. The first signs of the increased discomfort that would come.

Nothing makes you more grateful for your blessings than when they are gone.

Good health. Good friends. Good times. Good food. And good wine.

I wish that weren't the case.

But sometimes He needs to make me lie down. Often He needs to lead me to the still waters. I wish I had gone willingly. But often. I don't. I need to be forced. To slow down. To pause. To rest and reflect.

It's in that place I can gather at a table that He has prepared before me despite the presence of my enemies – the circumstances I am enduring. The losses I have taken, and still revel in all that He has done. For me and mine.

Surrounded by dear friends and family. In that place. We can gather and be grateful. For the relationships we have forged. The provision that He has given. And the promise that no matter how things turn out. The best is yet to come.

Nik got really good at that. Being grateful. For big things and small. For lifelong friends. For moments of laughter. For a steak properly prepared. For an embrace that brought comfort. And a glass of really good wine.

Nik was so grateful. And goodness and love followed her all the days of her life.

And now she dwells in the house of the Lord. Forever.

Yes sir. Nik did win. And as a result. She is feasting better than any of us that remain "down here." As we await "up there." But one day. Because of Christ. We will all join her. And the host of those that have gone before us with the hope of heaven.

But until then. We are commended to enjoy the blessings of this life. And we should. Especially when it comes to the wine.

TUESDAY: Commitment

The Lord is my shepherd, I lack nothing. He makes me lie down in green pastures, he leads me beside quiet waters, he refreshes my soul.
He guides me along the right paths for his name's sake.
Even though I walk through the darkest valley, I will fear no evil, for you are with me; your rod and your staff, they comfort me.
You prepare a table before me in the presence of my enemies.
You anoint my head with oil; my cup overflows.
Surely your goodness and love will follow me all the days of my life, and I will dwell in the house of the Lord forever. - Psalm 23, NIV

Holy Spirit, I have so much for which I should be grateful. The relationships that are dear to me. The undeserved blessings that have provided and protected me. Even the very breath I breathe. And all of it. ALL of it. Comes from You.

I admit I get wrapped in my circumstances. I get busy in my comings and goings. I seldom pause to rejoice in all that You have done in my life.

Awaken my spirit within me! Open my eyes to see my blessings anew! I don't want to take this life for granted anymore God! I want to see and sing about all that You have done for me.

Spirit, create in me a heart of gratitude. So I can delight in all that You have done. That I might worship You more fully and freely.

Thank You, Lord.

Amen.

WEDNESDAY: Assessment

1. Would I consider myself to be a grateful person? If so, how so? If not, why not?
2. Would those closest to me consider me grateful?
3. Do I have a critical or ungrateful spirit as it pertains to certain areas in my life? If so, why?
4. Am I content despite my circumstances? Do bad experiences, situations, or circumstances easily steal my joy?
5. When was the last time I specifically sat down and thanked God for specific blessings in my life beyond that of a quick, "thank you?"

THURSDAY: Battle Plan

1. What is one area in my life that I could be more grateful?
2. How can I specifically cultivate a spirit of gratefulness?
3. What is one (or more) area(s) that I need to ask God's forgiveness for my lack of gratitude?
4. Who are the individuals that I need to go seek forgiveness from due to my lack of gratitude?
5. What specific language, paradigm, or attitude must I tear down that, if left unchecked, breeds a critical spirit within me?

FRIDAY: *Gut Check*

1.   What excuse must I remove as it pertains to my lack of gratitude?
2.   What unmet expectation (valid or otherwise) must I confront and/or address in order to remove bitterness from my life?
3.   What hurt or wounding must I confront and/or address in order to remove bitterness from my life?
4.   What fear must I face as it pertains to seeking forgiveness, both from God and others, for my lack of gratitude?
5.   Am I willing to do the work necessary to foster a heart of gratefulness? Do I trust God in this process?

SATURDAY: *Baby Steps*

Complaining is easy. Wallowing is easy. Sometimes it's even valid. Losing a job is a hard thing. Losing a loved one to cancer is horrible. Divorce sucks. All of that is true. All of that needs to be felt, processed, and worked through. But becoming a person who always complains is not okay. Getting stuck in depression is not okay. God desires more for us.

Then there is the stuff that isn't really worth complaining about. Getting cut off in traffic. The grocery store being out of something you need. Yet these things grind on us all day every day and we find ourselves being cantankerous about the very things God has blessed us with.

The cycle has to be broken.

And it can be. It starts with listing all the blessings in our lives. From the most basic to the most dear. The commonality of a sun that rises each day. To the wife or husband that you get to hold when times get tough. We all have blessings. But few of us have taken the time to reflect upon them and compile them.

Do that today. Go somewhere quiet with a few blank sheets of paper and a good pen. List out the blessings in your life. Try to write out as many as you can. Then thank God for them. As you come to the names on your list, set it in your mind to call them and tell them how grateful you are for them and more importantly why. You don't have to do it all at once. Perhaps just one person a day. See how they react. See how much it feeds their soul.

Love God. And love people.

It starts simply by saying, "thank you."

SUNDAY: Reflect and Rest

Holy Spirit, remind me what You taught me this week about how I view my blessings. Reveal to me again the areas You have highlighted in my life for which I need to be more grateful.

Thank You so much for meeting with me this week, God. Thank You for opening my eyes and my heart to that which I have been neglecting.

I ask, God, that this spirit of gratitude and gratefulness would continue to grow in me. I don't want to be a critical or cynical person. I don't want to be a spoiled petulant child.

I want You to know how much I honor and appreciate all that You have done for me. I want others to know how much I appreciate them. I want to cultivate a life of gratitude, and that requires a regenerated heart.

I thank You for starting that work in me. I am confident You will see it completed.

Thank You, God.

Amen.

PRAY A LOT

MONDAY: What She Taught Me

"Jesus – My feelings this morning:" - Nikki's journal from April 2022

For hours on end. She would talk to Him. Singing praises of gratitude. Crying out in tears of lament. Meditating on His promises. Sitting in solitude. Sometimes praying for herself. More often advocating on behalf of others. All the way to the end. Nik prayed. A lot.

She'd pray over us. And she asked to be prayed over. She would praise Him despite her pain. She would journal her desires in the midst of her doubts. She would write Him letters of thanksgiving on her darkest days of tribulation. She would share her worries for those she loved and her concerns for those she barely knew. In all things. Nik prayed.

She left those reverent moments more at peace than when she entered them. Not because of an answer received or a download given. Rather a transcendent tranquility found simply in spending time intentionally in His presence.

Jesus made it a practice to pray often. Sometimes praying for Himself. More often advocating on the behalf of others. Prayers for protection. Prayers for strength. Prayers of praise. Prayers of lament. All the way to the end. Jesus prayed.

If God needed to pray. I need to pray. A lot.

People often ask me. "What can I do for you besides pray?" I appreciate the sentiment. They seek to provide a practical alleviation to the burden I am carrying. I get it. I appreciate it. And often it's needed.

But not more than prayer.

Nik showed me the power that comes from being a person of prayer. The supernatural way we can be strengthened amidst our suffering. Choosing gratefulness despite our grief. To live in the tension between sorrow and joy. Experiencing both simultaneously.

The source of our solace is found not in our activity. It is found in grateful supplication to our King.

So, if you wonder how you can help others or wonder where to find your own peace when it seems fleeting, in every situation, it's with prayers rooted in gratitude. Petition your Father. And be expectant of a holy calm that isn't predicated upon the circumstances at hand.

Pray A LOT.

TUESDAY: Commitment

"After Jesus said this, he looked toward heaven and prayed: 'Father, the hour has come. Glorify your Son, that your Son may glorify you. For you granted him authority over all people that he might give eternal life to all those you have given him. Now this is eternal life: that they know you, the only true God, and Jesus Christ, whom you have sent. I have brought you glory on earth by finishing the work you gave me to do. And now, Father, glorify me in your presence with the glory I had with you before the world began.

I have revealed you to those whom you gave me out of the world. They were yours; you gave them to me and they have obeyed your word. Now they know that everything you have given me comes from you. For I gave them the words you gave me and they accepted them. They knew with certainty that I came from you, and they believed that you sent me. I pray for them. I am not praying for the world, but for those you have given me, for they are yours. All I have is yours, and all you have is mine. And glory has come to me through them. I will remain in the world no longer, but they are still in the world, and I am coming to you. Holy Father, protect them by the power of your name, the name you gave me, so that they may be one as we are one. While I was with them, I protected them and kept them safe by that name you gave me. None has been lost except the one doomed to destruction so that Scripture would be fulfilled.

I am coming to you now, but I say these things while I am still in the world, so that they may have the full measure of my joy within them. I have given them your word and the world has hated them, for they are not of the world any more than I am of the world. My prayer is not that you take them out of the world but that you protect them from the evil one. They are not of the world, even as I am not of it. Sanctify them by the truth; your word is truth. As you sent me into the world, I have sent them into the world. For them I sanctify myself, that they too may be truly sanctified.

My prayer is not for them alone. I pray also for those who will believe in me through their message, that all of them may be one, Father, just as you are in me and I am in you. May they also be in us so that the world may believe that you have sent me. I have given them the glory that you gave me, that they may be one as we are one , I in them and you in me, so that they may be brought to complete unity. Then the world will know that you sent me and have loved them even as you have loved me.

Father, I want those you have given me to be with me where I am, and to see my glory, the glory you have given me because you loved me before the creation of the world.

Righteous Father, though the world does not know you, I know you, and they know that you have sent me. I have made you known to them, and will continue to make you known in order that the love you have for me may be in them and that I myself may be in them."' - John 17:1-26, NIV

Gracious and Heavenly Father, I long for peace. A peace that is not predicated upon my circumstances. A peace that is not tossed about like waves on a sea. A kind of peace that is truly divine. That can only come from You. I long for understanding and to be understood. I desire to be seen and heard. I desire to praise in thanksgiving and, when necessary, wallow in lament. That honest exchange and the fulfillment that comes from it can only be found in a relationship with the One who created me and the One who understands my very being. So, Lord, let me become a person of prayer. Let me resolve not to turn to you as a last resort but rather the first option I pursue. All I want and desire is found in You. So let me begin that conversation today. And resolve never to end it.

Until the day I meet You face-to-face.

Amen.

>>> ————

WEDNESDAY: Assessment

1. How do I view the practice of prayer? Am I a prayerful person?
2. What does my prayer life look like? How often do I pray? Do I have set times of prayer (daily, weekly, etc.)?

3. Do I make it a habit to "talk to God" only as a last resort? Only when I need something or desire some outcome?
4. Who taught me how to pray? Am I comfortable praying, either independently or with others?
5. Do I make it a practice to pray for others, or are all my prayers predicated on my own state, desires, and needs?

THURSDAY: Battle Plan

1. What potential lies or misconceptions about prayer do I need to explore?
2. Who is a trusted agent I can ask about prayer? What questions do I seek to resolve concerning prayer?
3. What potential wounding, hurts, or disappointments do I need to address and face that are precluding me from having an honest conversation with God?
4. Practically, how can I cultivate a life of prayer – both scheduled and spontaneous?
5. Who in my life needs prayer right now? How can I pray for them?

FRIDAY: Gut Check

1. Do I believe prayer works? If not, why not?
2. Do I pray for what I want or for a desire to come into God's will?
3. Am I selfish in my prayer life? Do I seek to elevate my desires above the needs of others?
4. Do I have a healthy relationship with God? Do I even want to talk to Him on a regular basis?
5. What excuse, lie, convenience, or preference is keeping me from praying? Am I willing to remove it? If so, how? If not, why not?

SATURDAY: Baby Steps

Prayer can easily be mystified. Prayer can be made very complicated. We can think that if we are to pray, we should do so only in the King's

English, littering our sentences with "thees," "thous," and "beseeches." So, we feel inadequate. So, we don't.

Prayer can be made to feel hollow. Prayer can be made to feel inept. We can think of the times we have prayed. We have sought God. We have asked for His favor. And yet the answer was, "No," or worse yet, we feel like we were ignored. So we feel abandoned or neglected. So we don't pray.

Whether due to lack of understanding, our past experience, or a million other reasons that seem so valid to us at the time, we refrain from conversing with the One being who holds it all together. Space. Time. Thought. All of it. The all-knowing, all-present, all-powerful Creator of all things. We forfeit our blood-bought right to ascend our words, our desires, our tears, our anxieties, our petitions, and our praises. To the One who so fervently desires for us to hold court with Him.

...and at the end of the day...all prayer is, at its heart, an honest conversation between a Father and His child.

So, start today. He wants to talk to you. And if you don't know how to start...start here. And see where the conversation goes from there.

"Our Father in heaven, hallowed be your name, your Kingdom come, your will be done, on earth as it is in heaven. Give us today our daily bread. And forgive us our debts, as we also have forgiven our debtors. And lead us not into temptation, but deliver us from the evil one." - Matthew 6:9-13

SUNDAY: Reflect and Rest

Father God, what did I learn about prayer this week? What did I learn about my own prayer life? Where did I see You move? Allow me to reflect now and be humbled by the fact that You, the Creator of All Things, desire to have a relationship with me through prayer.

Thank You, God. Thank You. Thank You. Thank You. Because of the accomplished work of Your Son, Jesus Christ, I can boldly come into the very throne room of heaven and make my request known to You through prayer. In my joy and in my sorrow. In my gratitude and in my grief. You desire all of it. And in my turning to You, You graciously bring me into Your perfect and pleasing will. I am so grateful to have such a gracious and awesome God.

I love You, Lord.

BE SPECIFIC

MONDAY: What She Taught Me

"I love you Steve ♥"- Nik's journal entry to me from May 2022

Goodness gracious did we ever fight like cats and dogs when we were first married. The 7-week engagement didn't help. Not a whole lot of time to learn how to fight fair. To learn how to fight for each other, not against one another.

We would toss out words like "always" and "never" a lot.

"You'll never do that." Or "You always do this."

Verbal haymakers that were intended to create hurt rather than give credence to a perspective.

Only after years of frivolous fighting. Too many nights with the sun going down upon our wrath. We finally admitted we had been doing it wrong the whole time. To each other. And to Him.

We finally started getting specific. Finally started caring less about winning the argument and more about mending the wound. She learned. I learned. We learned together – you can make a point or you can make a difference. Seldom can you make both.

How easy would it have been for Him to condemn that woman? Naked and adulterous. Laying humiliated in the street. But Jesus didn't take the bait. He didn't buy what the accusers were selling. He surveyed what was happening and got specific with all involved.

To them – "He who is without sin can cast the first stone."

To her – "They do not condemn you. Nor do I. Go and sin no more."

Grace and Truth. In perfect accord.

Jesus never shrunk back from a difficult discussion. He never sidestepped a sticky scenario. He stepped into it. He spoke to it. He got specific. To bring clarity and restoration. Not shame or retribution.

Conflict is inevitable. Disappointment and offense are part and parcel of the human experience. But it's what I do with that hurt that determines if we still honor God despite our pain, or choose to elevate our cause above His commands.

We honor God when we put our egos in check. We honor God when we seek earnest resolution with those with whom we have strife. The goal should always be restitution. Not the elevation of our "righteousness." The battle may be noble, but so must be the way we fight it. The conversation may be necessary, but the way we approach it is important. How we struggle together matters.

Be specific.

TUESDAY: Commitment

"Jesus returned to the Mount of Olives, but early the next morning he was back again at the Temple. A crowd soon gathered, and he sat down and taught them. As he was speaking, the teachers of religious law and the Pharisees brought a woman who had been caught in the act of adultery. They put her in front of the crowd.

'Teacher,' they said to Jesus, 'this woman was caught in the act of adultery. The law of Moses says to stone her. What do you say?'

They were trying to trap him into saying something they could use against him, but Jesus stooped down and wrote in the dust with his finger. They kept demanding an answer, so he stood up again and said, 'All right, but let the one who has never sinned throw the first stone!' Then he stooped down again and wrote in the dust.

When the accusers heard this, they slipped away one by one, beginning with the oldest, until only Jesus was left in the middle of the crowd with the woman. Then Jesus stood up again and said to the woman, 'Where are your accusers? Didn't even one of them condemn you?'

'No, Lord,' she said. And Jesus said, 'Neither do I. Go and sin no more.'"
- John 8:1-11, NLT

"The Lord is compassionate and gracious, slow to anger, abounding in love." - Psalm 103:8

My King Jesus, you are the Great Peacemaker. Amidst the struggle and the strife. Amidst the pain and the hurt. You always stepped into the fray. Speaking in Truth. Operating in Grace.

You did not strain to hold onto a peace that was false. Nor did You lash out in rage and anger. You always struck the balance. You always kept the main thing the main thing. You always brought clarity in your correction. You always brought the opportunity for restoration in Your rebuke.

Jesus, would You help me to become a peacemaker for Your Kingdom? To be one that looks to set the wrong things right. To bind up the broken-hearted. To see Your redemptive work done.

This will require putting my agenda down and picking Yours up. Laying down my ego and walking humbly before You. But I know by Your strength and with Your wisdom, it can be done. And my relationships and this world will become a better place.

Thank You, Lord.

Amen.

WEDNESDAY: Assessment

1. Would I be considered a passive person? Do I elevate "keeping the peace" above all else? Do I avoid confrontation even when doing so creates an environment of unhealth?

2. Would I be considered a prideful person? Do I elevate my "need to be right" above all else? Do I consider winning the argument more important than seeing a difficult situation resolved in a Godly manner?

3. How do I fight? Do I speak in generalities, using words like "always" and "never?" Do I look to inflict pain, shame, or hurt on those whom I come into conflict with?

4. Do I take my arguments/opinions before the Lord prior to discussing them with those with whom I have an offense? Do I seek wise counsel before engaging in a difficult conversation?

5. Do I fight for people or do I fight against them?

THURSDAY: Battle Plan

1. What are the unhealthy relationships in my life that need to be addressed, either due to systemic unhealthy communication practices, past hurts or wounds that have affected the relationship, or actions/activities that I have avoided discussing out of an unhealthy desire to avoid rocking the boat?
2. Of these relationships, after prayerful consideration, which do I feel that God would have me address?
3. How should I go about addressing these matters? Where should it take place? When should it take place?
4. Are there people I trust in my life who could give me wise counsel and perspective prior to engaging with those with whom I have relational strife?
5. What is the goal of these conversations? What needs to be said that would be helpful? What needs to be avoided?

FRIDAY: Gut Check

1. Do I believe a healthy resolution is possible? If not, why not?
2. Am I willing to be wrong and admit fault when it is necessary? What does that look like?
3. Once a resolution is found, am I committed to not using past hurts as a weapon against those who have offended or hurt me?
4. Will I elevate God's purposes over my plans, ego, desires, or opinions? What does that look like?
5. Do I trust God in this process? If not, why not?

SATURDAY: Baby Steps

Conflict is hard, but it's inevitable. Having healthy conflict is even harder, and can be oh so elusive. Yet, we are not called to be peacekeepers. We are called to be peacemakers. We are not called to use might to make it right. We are called to be humble and seek healing. We are called to fight for one another. Not against.

There are so many barriers to healthy conflict. Some are understandable, hurts endured, wounds inflicted. Others are sinful, pride, shame, ego. But at the end of the day, if we can lay those all down, fix our eyes on Jesus and His redemptive tactics, and enter into the space with those we have disagreements, God-honoring redemption is possible.

The devil hates resolution. The devil hates healing. The devil wants you to be "right at all costs." The devil wants you to never say, "I'm sorry." The devil wants you wallowing in pain, shame, and guilt.

But Jesus doesn't. He wants better for you and He wants better for those with whom you interact. Because He loves them, too.

So right now, go to Him. Go to Him in prayer. Get real honest about your concerns when it comes to this conflict, both those that are long-standing and those that are still pending. Take to Him your thoughts and concerns. Your agenda or lack of one. Ask Him to speak into the situation. What is He telling you? What is it that you are to do right now?

Once you know what it is you are to do, resolve to do it. Write it down and put a date and time on it. Call the person and ask to set aside some time to talk. And before you enter into conversation, be sure to be prayed up. Ask God to show up and show off. To make peace where there was none before. It takes two to tango. But a strand of three cords is not easily broken (Ephesians 4:12). With Jesus, all things are possible.

>>> ———— •

SUNDAY: Reflect and Rest

Jesus, what did I learn about myself this week as it pertains to my approach to conflict? What did you reveal to me? What areas do I need to be mindful of moving forward? Where must I repent to You and seek the forgiveness of others? Where must I be bold and have the hard conversation even if I am scared to do so? Enlighten me on what You have revealed to me this week.

Thank You, Jesus. Thank You for showing me that healthy conflict resolution is indeed possible. Thank You for the relationships that will become healthier because of these practices. Thank You for the courage to mend that which was broken. Thank You in advance for the grace that is needed when the other party refuses to walk out a healthy resolution with me. I am so grateful that You are a God who wants to see his children be healthy. I am so grateful that You love me.

Thank You, Lord. Amen.

DO NOT SETTLE

MONDAY: *What She Taught Me*

"I called...and demanded the scan."- Excerpt from Nik's journal from October 2020

She had been convinced something had been wrong for a long time. But no one listened. No one who could do anything about it anyway.

It's probably stress. Could be hormones. Perhaps a pregnancy. Maybe your diet. You're too young. You're too healthy. You look great.

Even after diagnosis. After a year of treatment. After she was told there was no way it could have come back that fast. She had to convince them to look again. She had to demand it.

She was done settling for less. Taking the path of least resistance. She decided enough was enough. She decided to press in.

12 years is a long time. A long time to be in pain. A long time to be uncertain. Expending all she had looking for relief. Being dismissed. Being discounted.

So when she heard about Him being in town. She decided to push through the crowd. She fought through the doubt. The looks and the judgment. Probably past a few people who thought they knew better. She was going to get to the hem of His garment. No matter what.

Over the last 20 months of my wife's life. I watched in awe as she took back control. Asserting dominion over personal territory that had become overrun and borderless. Marred by overreaching opinions and expectations. God-given areas were once abdicated for fear of upsetting the apple cart.

She set boundaries. She stood up for herself. She found her voice.

And while her physical health weakened. Her spirit grew in strength.

And by the time of her passing. She had grown more secure and confident than ever before. Because she knew she mattered. And so did what she had to say.

Experts are there to guide us. Authorities are there to inform us. Our closest friends and family are there to help us along the way. But we should not confuse being protected with attempted possession. Substitute helpful counsel with unhealthy influence. We are to be respected and valued. We are to be considered and honored. But if we expect others to treat us properly. We must first start by standing up for ourselves. No matter what.

Do not settle.

TUESDAY: Commitment

"And a woman was there who had been subject to bleeding for twelve years. She had suffered a great deal under the care of many doctors and had spent all she had, yet instead of getting better she grew worse. When she heard about Jesus, she came up behind him in the crowd and touched his cloak, because she thought, 'If I just touch his clothes, I will be healed.' Immediately her bleeding stopped and she felt in her body that she was freed from her suffering.

At once Jesus realized that power had gone out from him. He turned around in the crowd and asked, 'Who touched my clothes?'

'You see the people crowding against you,' his disciples answered, 'and yet you can ask, 'Who touched me?''

But Jesus kept looking around to see who had done it. Then the woman, knowing what had happened to her, came and fell at his feet and, trembling with fear, told him the whole truth. He said to her, 'Daughter, your faith has healed you. Go in peace and be freed from your suffering.'" - Mark 5:25-34

Holy Spirit, I want to see myself as You see me. I want to break the lies that I have believed when it comes to my feelings, opinions, desires, and needs. The big lies that assert my thoughts do not warrant merit or discussion. The subtle lies that tell me it's just easier to "go along and get along." To relegate that which matters to me to inconsequential, silly, or irrelevant. God, if it matters to me, it matters to You. I know that I won't always be right, but I do need to be heard. I know that others may indeed have the answers, but I do need to be seen. You love me so much that You sacrificed it all for me. You love me. You respect me. You see me. You hear me. Help me, God, to value myself better. To stand up for myself when necessary. To speak up when it is warranted. I matter, Lord, because You say I do. Help me remember that and operate in that confidence. Thank You, Lord. Amen.

WEDNESDAY: Assessment

1. How does God see me? Do I view myself in the same way? If not, why not?
2. Do I value my opinion? Do I expect others to do the same?
3. Do my actions and activities reflect my self-worth?
4. Do I foster feelings of contempt or anger because I choose to keep my thoughts, feelings, and opinions subservient or unspoken when I feel they are warranted?
5. When something matters to me, do I speak up about it? Do I hold my ground when challenged? If not, why not?

THURSDAY: Battle Plan

1. What are the relationships that I need to establish or re-establish healthy boundaries? What do those boundaries look like?
2. Who do I need to communicate these boundaries to? How will I explain these expectations?
3. What actions or activities toward me that are disrespectful, unkind, or dismissive do I need to eliminate from my life? How will I do that?
4. What actions or activities must I hold to, however difficult, when I am being disrespected, treated unkindly, or dismissively?
5. How can I practically remove the lies I have believed about myself with the truth of God's Word and promises over me?

FRIDAY: *Gut Check*

1. What is the biggest barrier that I face in regards to growing and operating in a self-respecting manner? Am I willing to face it?
2. Do I truly believe I am worthy of respect?
3. Who do I need to forgive and release right now that has impeded my ability to operate confidently? Parent? Spouse? Friend? Myself?
4. Am I willing to honestly pursue the freedom that comes from operating according to my worth, to demand to be seen and be heard, even if it creates friction by upsetting established relational dynamics?
5. Am I willing to walk away from the strange comfort that comes with allowing others to have unhealthy influence or control of areas of my life that they should not? How will I hold myself accountable?

SATURDAY: *Baby Steps*

There are so many reasons to think less of ourselves. To shrink back even when we feel convicted to speak up. To hold ground. To offer our thoughts, opinions, or insights. Even when we feel dismissed. Even when we feel disrespected. Even when we are hurt.

It can be due to the reason we were brought up. A mistake we made in the past. A misperception we've believed. Or, even unhealthy relational dynamics that we have partnered with, willingly or otherwise.

But it's time to break the cycle. It's time to speak truth over the lie. The time to expect to be respected. The time to walk in the boldness and the confidence to which you are called. Not born out of selfish pride. Not seeking to set a self-serving agenda as supreme despite the consideration of others. No – this is not an adjustment to raise yourself up by pulling others down. This is a recalibration to ascend to a plain that stipulates you are worthy of respect because Jesus says so, and that fact is not contingent upon whether or not others hold to that truth.

You are probably going to rub some people the wrong way. That's okay as long as you respect them in the process. You might even step into a few awkward situations. That's fine as long as you keep your words and actions above reproach. But at the end of the day, you are worthy of respect. Do not settle for less. Take this mantra with you moving forward. Dare to hold ground you once were quick to concede. Push back in the discussion if you are unsatisfied with how you are being treated.

Today take back a small piece of territory that God has ordained for you. Reset the boundary. Hold others accountable. Respect all those with whom you interact. But remember to respect yourself, too.

>>>———-—

SUNDAY: Reflect and Rest

Holy Spirit, what was my biggest takeaway of this week? What relationship must I revisit and establish healthy boundaries? What areas have I conceded that You have called me to steward? What lies have I believed about my self-worth that I need to tear down? Remind me again what You have taught me in our time together.

"In the same way, You descended upon Jesus and the Father spoke, 'This is My Son. In Whom I am well pleased,' because of Jesus, You speak the same words over me.

Thank you for showing me that I am worthy of being respected. Thank You for reminding me that as a son or daughter of the King I should never settle for less than that of a King's kid.

You are so good to me, God. Please continue to convict me that I should be good to myself.

I love You, Lord.

Amen.

EXPRESS LOVE SO LOVE IS FELT

MONDAY: What She Taught Me

"Hey Sara…I love you. You have been the most wonderful best friend…"- Voice Memo to her best friend at 1:13PM on June 13, 2022

Nik and I spent nearly 20 years together. And I never felt more loved by another person than the way she loved me. She made sure that the way she loved was received as love. Not necessarily how she would prefer to give it. But how I needed it.

She had a knack for it. Making people feel loved. Making people feel known. Making people feel seen and valued. So much so that upon her passing. Countless people claimed her as their "best of friends." According to the accounts given. She had more best friends than I have friends in total.

It's because she made it a practice to always show up for others. To give them what they needed. A loving embrace. A kind word. An hour spent together. A thoughtful gift. A needed task accomplished. Their desire. Not her preference. From the day I met her. Until the day she went home. She loved well. Just like her King.

Jesus never seemed to do the same thing twice. His interactions were so specific and so intentional. Asking one, "Do you want to be well?" (John 5:6) Commending another, "Never have I seen such faith." (Matthew 8:10) Pleading for the crowd, "Forgive them Father they know not what they do." (Luke 23:34) Turning water into wine. Stooping down to wash feet. Crying with a friend. What was needed most. What showed real love. From the day He arrived. Until the day He went back home. He loved well.

Often I operate in a sort of default mode. I do the cursory thing. Expressing my love in a manner that serves my convenience and choosing. I am learning it is better to slow down. To be intentional and express love and gratitude toward others in a manner where it is received as such. Not notching a belt. Not doing the obligatory thing. But taking the time to make sure those I care about feel seen and heard. Honored and known.

Of all that we are commissioned to do. God would have us love. So let us be sure to do it rightly. Do it in a manner that pleases Him. Do it in a manner that esteems them.

Express love so love is felt.

TUESDAY: Commitment

"If I speak in the tongues of men or of angels, but do not have love, I am only a resounding gong or a clanging cymbal. If I have the gift of prophecy and can fathom all mysteries and all knowledge, and if I have a faith that can move mountains, but do not have love, I am nothing. If I give all I possess to the poor and give over my body to hardship that I may boast, but do not have love, I gain nothing.

Love is patient, love is kind. It does not envy, it does not boast, it is not proud. It does not dishonor others, it is not self-seeking, it is not easily angered, it keeps no record of wrongs. Love does not delight in evil but rejoices with the truth. It always protects, always trusts, always hopes, always perseveres.

Love never fails. But where there are prophecies, they will cease; where there are tongues, they will be stilled; where there is knowledge, it will pass away. For we know in part and we prophesy in part, but when completeness comes, what is in part disappears. When I was a child, I talked like a child, I thought like a child, I reasoned like a child. When I became a man, I put the ways of childhood behind me. For now we see only a reflection as in a mirror; then we shall see face to face. Now I know in part; then I shall know fully, even as I am fully known.

And now these three remain: faith, hope and love. But the greatest of these is love." - Corinthians 13:1-13

Father God, You are love. In its perfect form. Its essence and its being. All love comes from You and flows back to You. As Your crowning achievement.

It is Your greatest desire for us to reflect that love. To be that love. To show that love. First to You. And then to those around us. To do that it is paramount that we understand how those around us feel loved and desire to be loved.

We are each unique. Formed and fashioned specifically by You in our mother's womb. How we feel loved is as unique as the texture of our hair. The fleck of color in our eyes. The sound of our laugh.

Therefore, I should not relegate the expression of my love to that which I desire. Those things that inherently make sense to me. The way I feel loved. Rather, I should pay attention and apply the particular words, actions, or activities that make the other feel uniquely known, loved, and cherished.

Help me see them as You see them, Lord. Use me so they can experience the love of God in a very unique and personal way.

In Your most precious name.

Amen.

WEDNESDAY: Assessment

1. What is my love language (Physical Touch, Acts of Service, Words of Affirmation, Quality Time, Gifts)? Do I tend to express my love in the same way/terms I feel most loved?
2. Am I thoughtful in how I express my love?
3. Would those who know me best say that I express love in a healthy life-giving way?
4. Do I look for opportunities to show intentional love toward others? If so, how? If not, why not?
5. Do I tend to be self-absorbed? Do I miss opportunities to love others well because I am overly concerned with my current circumstances?

THURSDAY: *Battle Plan*

1. How do I become more practically aware of the needs of others as it pertains to loving them well?
2. Who specifically must I work harder at loving in a more effective way? What does that look like?
3. Who do I need to apologize to for expressing love in a way that is cursory, obligatory, or disingenuous?
4. Who is the most difficult person in my life to whom I know I am called to love well? How do I love them well despite how I may feel about it?
5. Which relationships have I taken for granted and, therefore, not prioritized love? How can I change that?

FRIDAY: *Gut Check*

1. Am I willing to lay down my preferences and prefer the desires/needs of others in order to love them well?
2. Will I commit to being more in tune with the needs of others? What does that look like?
3. When will I seek the forgiveness of the individual I have failed to love well?
4. Will I repent for showing love in a cursory, obligatory, or disingenuous way?
5. Do I believe God will grow me in my capacity to love better? If not, why?

SATURDAY: *Baby Steps*

It probably wouldn't take too much time. Who do you know right now that could really use a hug? How about a phone call just to check in? Who do you know that could really use encouragement right now? Can you think of any act of service you could do for that person who seems so taxed and stressed out? In all of our daily comings and goings, it's easy to lose the forest through the trees. It's so easy to become so inundated with our own worlds, that we stop to look up at those that intersect our path and consider their current plight.

Today, take a moment to show someone you love them. Someone that really needs to feel that love. And don't do it in some quick and cheap way. Do it in a way that is genuine and real. Do it in a way that will make them feel honored, valued, and known. You have no idea what that single interaction may do. Both for them and for you. Don't despise small beginnings. Love someone well today.

SUNDAY: *Reflect and Rest*

Father God, remind me of all that You taught me this week. Bring to mind again all those that You have called me to love better. How can I ensure that I make the practice of loving well part of my daily rhythm?

Thank You, Father God. I am so grateful that You have placed so many people in my life to love well. So many opportunities to shift and shape the direction of someone's day for their benefit and joy. Let me see them as such. Let me see them all as a people to be loved well and in so doing bring Your Kingdom to earth.

We love You, God, because You first loved us. Never let me forget that. You loved me when I was unlovable. You loved me when I was far from You. You loved me despite myself. And You loved me so personally and intimately. You brought me carefully and tenderly back into Your loving arms.

In no small part, You did that through the people with whom You surrounded me. Let me do that now for someone else.

Thank You, Lord. I love You.

Amen.

Nov. 10

What we thought was an ending
may very well be a beginning...

Today is Sunday before treatm
#2. I have to say my attitude
 nday and this week has been
 atchiness. I've felt fabulous th
 k (Besides pain) and feel like
 d self. I had tues-s
 - clear headed

WATCH YOUR FOCUS

MONDAY: *What She Taught Me*

"What you thought was an ending may very well be a beginning..."- Excerpt from Nik's journal from November 2019

Early on. She was very results-driven. We all were. Focused on the timeline. The number of chemos remaining. How many rounds of radiation were left. Days until the first surgery. Weeks until the next. How long. How much. How often. Counting the cost to endure.

Then October 2020 happened. She was supposed to be done. It was supposed to be over. But it wasn't. The race was reset. The hill to climb was that much steeper. The pain more intense. And she resolved very quickly this was all beyond her capability now. Not sure that it ever hadn't been in the first place. If she was going to endure this. However it was going to turn out. She was going to have to raise her gaze from her circumstances. And fix her eyes on Him.

It had to be very strange for David when he was forced to hide in that cave. Retreating from the very king he served. The man for whom he had slayed the giant. It all had to be so unsettling and confusing for that young, bright, ruddy man of God. But in his uncertainty. While his heart grew faint. He chose to be led to the Rock that was higher than he. To his strong tower from where his help would come. He chose to take refuge in the shelter of His wings. David did not allow his circumstances to dictate his decisions. The outcome was God's business. His part was simply to fix his eyes on Him. And walk in obedience.

In light of my experience, I've determined that I'm not going to figure it out. I likely will not have that lightbulb moment when all the shattered shards of my experiences are woven together in a clearly defined tapestry of purpose. At least not on this side of heaven. All that is God's business.

Some promising beginnings reach unexpected ends. Yet some endings lead to unexpectedly curious new beginnings. And through all of it, the good and the bad, He is working. So let's be less concerned about the circumstances. Whether we understand them or not. Our focus must be on Him and Him alone. He remains the only constant. And therefore. The One whom we can fully trust.

Watch your focus.

TUESDAY: *Commitment*

Hear my cry, O God; listen to my prayer. From the ends of the earth I call to you, I call as my heart grows faint; lead me to the rock that is higher than I. For you have been my refuge, a strong tower against the foe. I long to dwell in your tent forever and take refuge in the shelter of your wings. For you, God, have heard my vows; you have given me the heritage of those who fear your name. - Psalm 61:1-5

Yours, Lord, is the greatness and the power and the glory and the majesty and the splendor, for everything in heaven and earth is yours. Yours, Lord, is the Kingdom; you are exalted as head over all. - 1 Chronicles 29:11

Jesus, there is NONE like You, Lord! There is NONE that rivals You! There is NONE that could ascend Your throne. You set the very foundations of time. You spoke the cosmos into existence. The very air in my lungs is born of You. The beat of my heart is kept in rhythm because You have deemed it so.

So why then, Lord, do I grow so despondent in my circumstances? Why do I become so overwhelmed due to my current experience? Have I thought that You have forgotten me? Have I bought the lie that what I am enduring is beyond Your care or command?

What a fool I am. Forgive me, my King. I'm running to You now. Envelop me in the shelter of Your Wing. The storm may rage on. But it shall pass. And You will forever remain. No matter what is happening, please, Jesus, help me to keep my eyes firmly fixed on You. Amen.

WEDNESDAY: Assessment

1. Am I a person who is easily shaken by the circumstance in which I am enduring? If so, why?
2. Do I regulate my "intake?" Do I concern myself with the amount of news, social media, podcasts and gossip I listen to or partake? Do I balance that with the amount of time I spend in worship, solitude, prayer, and reading God's Word?
3. When I receive a negative report, what is my immediate reaction? Do I think down/negatively? Do I seek Jesus and His wisdom?
4. Where do I derive my comfort in difficult times? Do I self-medicate or self-soothe? If so, how and why?
5. Do I struggle to see God's plan outworking in my life? Do I spend a lot of time trying to "figure out what He's doing?"

THURSDAY: Battle Plan

1. What is the area in my life that I have the most difficulty trusting in God and submitting to His authority? What would it look like to turn that over to Him?
2. What practice or habit do I need to abstain from in order to avoid self-soothing or self-medicating? How can I replace that habit with a healthy alternative?
3. How can I better regulate the negative intake in my life that causes me fear, anxiety, FOMO, etc. (news, social media, etc.)?
4. Who can hold me accountable for developing and keeping these new practices? What does accountability look like, practically speaking?
5. Anxiety and worry are emotions that are inevitably felt at one point or another. Therefore, how and who can I process these emotions with in a biblically healthy way when they are heavy?

FRIDAY: Gut Check

1. Am I willing to trust that God is working all things together for my good, even when it doesn't seem like it? If not, why not?
2. Do I think my plans and desires are more important than God's? Do my actions support my answer?
3. Why don't I trust God when things are difficult? When I'm disappointed? When I get hurt?
4. Jesus suffered greatly for me. Why do I struggle with suffering greatly for Him?
5. Am I willing to stand firm in my faith even if I do not see goodness in the land of the living? Even if all my questions and confusion remain on this side of glory?

SATURDAY: Baby Steps

Things sure are a lot less stressful when we already know the ending. The second time we watch the suspenseful movie we love or read through our favorite spy thriller, there is a lot less anxiety associated with it. A lot less concern. A lot less "is this going to work out?!?" When we already know how the plot is going to turn out, we have a lot more peace. A lot calmer. Honestly, a lot more joy.

Can I tell you something?

As a believer in Christ, you already know how this is all going to turn out. That while we live in a broken wretched world, full of sickness, pain, turmoil, hate, and death – one day, one glorious day – Jesus will bring that all to an end. Some will see His triumphal entry. Others are already seated in heaven waiting in anticipation as He prepares to bring the rest of their brothers and sisters home.

Never forget, sweet friend – because of Jesus – the game is over. You have already won.

No matter what you may endure down here. One day it will all be over.

So go out there and live your life! Stop worrying about so many trivial and inconsequential things.

And for those legitimate things. Those things that God, under His sovereign purview, has given you to steward. For those things, when they cause you the greatest concern. It's time to give them back to Him. In the same way, a child brings a broken plaything to his father, there are times when it is necessary to bring your broken health, finances, relationships, and situations back to Him.

And watch the Master Artisan work.

What is it, today, that God wants you to bring back to Him in prayer?

SUNDAY: Reflect and Rest

My King Jesus, thank You for all you taught me this week. Remind me of the perspective I had going into the week and how You have reshaped it over the course of the past few days. What is my big takeaway as it pertains to my focus moving forward?

Thank You, Lord. Thank You this week for reminding me yet again that You are God and I am not. And that, while I am called to steward my life obediently, You hold all matters under Your ultimate care and sovereignty. My business is to do that which You have instructed me. The results are Your business.

Thank You for the reminder that things seldom will work out in the manner in which I anticipate. In fact, they might not work out at all. Unfortunately, because of sin, pain and suffering are part of the package deal of humanity.

However, despite all of that, I can remain hopeful. Because my hope is not in this world. It is solely in You.

Thank You Jesus. I love You.

Amen.

SUCK IT UP

MONDAY: What She Taught Me

"The greater the assignment…the greater the resistance"- Excerpt from Nik's journal from August 2019

She hated it. Everything about it. She didn't want the platform. She didn't want influence. She didn't want any of it. And she certainly didn't want the reason for it.

Had it been her way, it would have been a quiet life: Small-town living. No pomp. No circumstance. Just a husband. 3 kids. A dog. And a beach vacation once a year.

But that wasn't her assignment.

She had cancer. And people were watching. They wanted to know. Was her faith all show and no go? Or did she really believe He was always working for her good, despite the outcome? They wanted to know if she really believed Jesus was King.

So she showed them. Everyday. She got up. And continued her work.

I've taken a few hits in my day. Been to the hospital once or twice. But I have never been mistaken for dead. I wonder how bad the Apostle Paul must have looked. Stoned. Bloody. Marred. Dragged outside the city walls. After preaching the Good News of the Kingdom. The crowd had had enough. So they tried to kill him. Stone and rock. Gravel and dirt. Hurling it at him with all the insult and vitriol they could muster. And when they were finished with him. Paul lay in a broken heap on the ground. His friends thought him dead. No one could have survived that.

But then a curious thing happened…he got back up. And went back into the very city that attempted to murder him. And continued his work.

That was his assignment.

Nothing worth having ever comes easy. Nothing worth protecting ever comes without a fight. Nothing that is good, pure, and noble is obtained without great cost. So why do I complain when it's hard? Why do I despair when met with defiance? Why do I look to retreat when the resistance inevitably comes?

If God wanted another to take up the task. He wouldn't have given the assignment. The load to carry. The cross to bear. So instead of complaining about it. Maybe we should embrace it. Maybe instead of running from it. We should run toward it. Because people are watching. And they want to know if we really believe Jesus is King, despite the outcome.

Suck it up.

TUESDAY: Commitment

"In Lystra there sat a man who was lame. He had been that way from birth and had never walked. He listened to Paul as he was speaking. Paul looked directly at him, saw that he had faith to be healed and called out, 'Stand up on your feet!' At that, the man jumped up and began to walk.

When the crowd saw what Paul had done, they shouted in the Lycaonian language, "The gods have come down to us in human form!" Barnabas they called Zeus, and Paul they called Hermes because he was the chief speaker. The priest of Zeus, whose temple was just outside the city, brought bulls and wreaths to the city gates because he and the crowd wanted to offer sacrifices to them.

But when the apostles Barnabas and Paul heard of this, they tore their clothes and rushed out into the crowd, shouting: "Friends, why are you doing this? We too are only human, like you. We are bringing you good news, telling you to turn from these worthless things to the living God, who made the heavens and the earth and the sea and everything in them. In the past, he let all nations go their own way. Yet he has not left himself without testimony: He has shown kindness by giving you rain from heaven and crops in their seasons; he provides you with plenty of food and fills your hearts with joy.' Even with these words, they had difficulty keeping the crowd from sacrificing to them.

Then some Jews came from Antioch and Iconium and won the crowd over. They stoned Paul and dragged him outside the city, thinking he was dead. But after the disciples had gathered around him, he got up and went back into the city…" - Acts 14:8-20a

Holy Spirit, I admit that I want an easy life. A life free of pain and suffering. A life filled with pleasure and fulfilled desires. I spend much of my life in pursuit of it. I labor hard for it. I work to protect it. But that is not what You have called me to. That is not where You would have me expend my efforts. There is nothing wrong with wanting to see goodness in the land of the living. But I should have a healthy expectation that the life I lead should be one that is poured out like a drink offering in pursuit of the task You have assigned me.

So Spirit, lead me. Convict me. Move me. Give me the courage necessary to press into the hard, dark places that You have placed me so I can be salt and light. Allow me to count the cost of being Your disciple and still move in the boldness and confidence to call heaven down upon the earth. It will certainly cost me. It may result in a great loss.

Still, Lord, I desire to be used by You in a mighty way. But to be used mightily by God, I recognize that I must be willing to be mightily broken, God. Have Your way, Lord. And grant me the endurance to run this race with all the fervor I can muster.

By Your leading.
Amen.

WEDNESDAY: Assessment

1. What is my perspective on pain and suffering? Do I believe it to be a necessary part of the Christian life? Why or why not?
2. Am I risk or pain averse? Do I avoid discomfort at a great cost? Am I willing to forgo spiritual maturing or delaying gratification in order to avoid suffering?
3. Do I blame God when I suffer? Do I hold it against Him or our relationship? If so, how?
4. What is my reaction when those I love are suffering? How do I pray in these times?
5. What is the experience that has caused me the greatest suffering? What do I think about it? Have I processed it? Do I believe God used it for good?

THURSDAY: Battle Plan

1. In what area of my life right now am I called to suffer well for the Kingdom?
2. Practically speaking, what does suffering well entail? What habits would I need to adopt, change, or stop?
3. What difficulty, tragedy, or hurt do I need to stop complaining about and rather embrace as an opportunity to see God's Kingdom work done?
4. What specific event or circumstance of pain do I need to process in a healthy way rather than just wallow in pain?
5. Who can I invite into this process to encourage me and keep me accountable?

FRIDAY: Gut Check

1. Am I honestly willing to suffer?
2. Am I ready to talk to God about my pain and hurt?
3. Will I stay the course even if it does not go according to plan? Even if the result leaves me with more questions than answers?
4. Am I willing to put the needs of others – even those that oppose me and maybe even wish me harm – above my own so as to display Christ to them?
5. When am I going to honestly start this process?

SATURDAY: Baby Steps

Once you are in the fray. Instinct will take over. That's why training is so important. You will naturally react as you in the way in which you have been preparing. The way you have been training your mind. Kind of the way a runner responds when the gun goes off. The way a boxer bobs and weaves as he squares with his opponent. When the time comes. If you have trained properly. You'll know what to do.

That being said, you still will need to choose to enter the fight in the first place. It is quite tempting to stay on the sidelines. To keep your distance in the grandstands of life. But that is not the place you have been called. You are not a spectator. You are a participant. The only way to run your race well is to come down out of the cheap seats and set your feet on the uncertain and dangerous track.

So, resolve this in your mind, you are already dead.

Maybe not today. Maybe not tomorrow. Maybe not for another 60 years or so. But at some point (unless Jesus comes back). You will die someday. So you need to decide the kind of life you are going to live. One spent cowering. Spent on the frivolous pleasure that will have no eternal reward. Food. Drink. And philandering. That will all too soon turn to ash and soot in your mouth and hands.

Or you can choose to live a life rung out for Him. It may cost you everything down here. But it will gain you great reward up there.

It will require sacrifice. You will need to put down your complaint. You will have to forgo understanding much of it. But today you can begin to suffer well for your Savior.

He did it for you…so as much as is in you…resolve to jump in the fight. And when the stone lands true. And you find yourself on bended knee. Marred from its blow. Find your footing. Get up. And walk back into that city.

Embrace your assignment…and it's time.

SUNDAY: Reflect and Rest

Holy Spirit, in what way did You convict me this week? How do I now view suffering in light of how I viewed it prior to our discussions together? What deep truth did I gain that I will need to remember and hold dear moving forward?

Thank You, Spirit. Thank You for the convicting truths You laid before me this week. I realize now more than ever that the Christian life is a life poured out for Your glory. This life is a gift. But it is to be spent on the tasks You have chosen in advance for me to complete. So, let me not grow weary in the well-doing. And when I do, draw me back to You so as to be refreshed again. Embolden me to continue the assignment that You, in Your sovereign majesty, have given me. I recognize, Lord, that this will not be easy. But I know I can do all things through Christ Jesus. And You are always with me.

Thank You, Spirit. Amen.

SLOW DOWN

MONDAY: What She Taught Me

"A quiet soul needs quiet time." - Excerpt from Nikki's journal, in August 2020

What if? That was said a lot around our house. Before she was diagnosed. During her treatment. Candidly, I still said it a lot in the days and months that followed the end. I've learned that an untethered mind is a precarious place when considering the "What ifs."

A few days after Christmas. On what would have been our 19th anniversary. I went away to read through how Nik processed all of her "What ifs". I read through every journal dating back to a few months before her diagnosis. I read every word. Her last entry was just 3 days before she went home. When I was done. I read the letters she left me. Her final instructions on how to move forward without her.

I don't think they have need of one. But if there is a planning committee in heaven. She's on it.

It was in that place. In the quiet of that hotel room. In reading through the experiences of my late wife. The Words of Jesus came alive to me. Why do you worry about your life, Steve? Look at the birds of the air. Does your heavenly Father not feed them? Can your worry add a single hour to your life? So rather than worry. Seek Me first and My righteousness. And with faith watch what I add to your life.

Nik could not have anticipated all that she would endure. But Jesus did. And He carried her through all of it. I know because she told me by her own hand. And in reading her words. I found a strange comfort that while I am assured that this life will likely look nothing like what I anticipate – I will encounter nothing that will surprise the One who is leading me on.

The "What if" game is risky. Often threatening me with a foreboding future that may never come to fruition. Leaving me riddled with anxiety, stress, and fear.

I believe the game God would rather have me play is "What was." Not wasting my concerns on a largely unpredictable future. Instead reveling in His faithfulness throughout my past. Mountain high. Valley low. He's carried me through all of it. I just need to create the space to remember it. In so doing. I draw the confidence needed to continue.

Slow down.

TUESDAY: Commitment

"Therefore I tell you, do not worry about your life, what you will eat or drink; or about your body, what you will wear. Is not life more than food, and the body more than clothes? Look at the birds of the air; they do not sow or reap or store away in barns, and yet your heavenly Father feeds them. Are you not much more valuable than they? Can any one of you by worrying add a single hour to your life?

"And why do you worry about clothes? See how the flowers of the field grow. They do not labor or spin. Yet I tell you that not even Solomon in all his splendor was dressed like one of these. If that is how God clothes the grass of the field, which is here today and tomorrow is thrown into the fire, will he not much more clothe you, you of little faith? So do not worry, saying, 'What shall we eat?' or 'What shall we drink?' or 'What shall we wear?' For the pagans run after all these things, and your heavenly Father knows that you need them. But seek first his Kingdom and his righteousness, and all these things will be given to you as well. Therefore do not worry about tomorrow, for tomorrow will worry about itself. Each day has enough trouble of its own." - Matthew 6:25-34

King Jesus, I have such a tendency to worry about what the future holds. I wonder how it is all going to pan out. I'm concerned that my past missteps, mistakes, and mishandling will rob me, and others, of the preferred future I believe You have for me. I think what I have done is unredeemable. I believe the circumstances are too insurmountable. The experiences are too inescapable. I have allowed the devil to condemn me of my past and cause concern for my future which in turn has resulted in me being robbed of my present. I know You don't want that for me, Lord. You have claimed me as redeemed. You see me as righteous. That does not mean I will not experience turmoil and strife moving forward, but it does mean that You will carry me through all of it. You always have, Lord.

Even on my darkest day, in my worst season. You were there beckoning me to call out to You: to be ministered by You; to be comforted by You; to be led by You. Help me, Jesus, see all of the incredible means by which You have manifested Your wonderful ways in my life. Let me see You in every blessing. Let me be reminded of Your presence deep in the valley. You have always been there, Lord. Let me find rest and peace in Your constant and consistent presence. Reveal to me the ways You have worked in my life so that I can honor You as You are due. Help me, Jesus, not to be a person of worry. Help me, Jesus, to be a person that fully trusts in the plan You have for my life – come what may. Thank You, Jesus. I love You. Amen.

WEDNESDAY: Assessment

1. Am I a person that worries a lot? Do I tend to concern myself with matters that are beyond my control? Do I naturally tend to think of the worst-case scenario panning out? If so, why?
2. Do I think my past actions, missteps, experiences, or mistakes will condemn my future? Do I believe that I will never overcome my past? If so, why?
3. Do my concerns for the future or the regrets of my past rob me of being present? If so, how?
4. Do I think God is ultimately in control of my life? That while I have choices, He is available to guide me and lead me through every season?
5. Has a past disappointment resulted in me losing trust in God and His plan for my life? If so, what happened and when? How did it make me feel? How has it affected my relationship with Him?

THURSDAY: Battle Plan

1. What is the primary area of my life that I trust God the least and therefore worry the most about regarding its effect on my future?
2. What past sin, action, mistake, or experience do I need to bring to Jesus because it affects my self-image, my relationship with God, and my hope for the future?
3. Who do I need to invite into this process to give wise counsel, perspective, and a potential route to healing?

4. Who do I need to confront either to ask for forgiveness or inform how their past actions and/or words have affected not only my present but how I approach and see the future?

5. When can I schedule some quality quiet time with God to work through some of these matters? What do I need to rearrange in my schedule in order to prioritize this?

FRIDAY: Gut Check

1. Am I ready to get honest with myself about how my worry and concerns for the future are affecting me?

2. Am I willing to get honest with God about my disappointments and concerns – not only about my past but how those experiences have affected my perspective on future matters?

3. Am I willing to seek forgiveness for the things I have done in the past that are affecting my present and, therefore, the trajectory of my future? If so, how? If not, why not?

4. Am I ready to confront the one that harmed me in the past; therefore, impacting my present and trajectory of my future? If so, how? If not, why not?

5. Am I going to commit to slowing down and spending quality time with God in order to grow my relationship with Him and see His sovereign work in my life? If so, when and where? If not, why not?

SATURDAY: Baby Steps

Can I be honest with you? Worrying is really easy. I mean, we don't even need to work at it. It comes naturally. Something happens around the age of 2 or so, and suddenly, worrying becomes our default mode. But do you know what is crazy? It wasn't part of the original design.

In the cool of the garden, before the fall, Adam and Eve walked in perfect harmony with God, facilitating the work He laid before them – with zero worries, despite being in charge of His perfect garden; despite being in direct contact with the great I AM. Adam and Eve actually found joy in their present and hope in their tomorrow. But then things got messed up. They chose temptation over temperance. They bought the lie that brought the whole thing down. And as a result, God opened their eyes. For the first time, they saw all they were now responsible for and all the inadequacy they brought to the table – and they worried. It has been like that ever since.

So here you sit – millennia removed from that decision – yet still part of that original bloodline. And now you worry. But what if you decided to try and change all of that?

Instead of carrying the weight of the world and attempting to control so many variables that will either reject or be unaffected by your influence, what if you surrendered your concerns back to the Creator? The One that holds it all together. Because you never had full control anyway. And you never could. But He can. And He does.

Easier said than done. I get it. But there is a path that gets you there. The best way to trust God with your future is to look back and remember His faithfulness in your past. So start there. Do it today. Remember the season of great victory, when God moved mountains on your behalf and made the seemingly improbable (if not impossible) happen. Remember the season of sorrow, in your lamenting and woe, how God, either through divine instruction or a caring person, ministered to your soul in the most personal of ways.

Sometimes it can be hard to see. Sometimes it takes time to see His artisan hand at work. But if you slow down long enough, and meditate upon it, He will reveal Himself to you. And in that revelation, you will grow your trust in Him and, by extension, your hope for your future.

So, slow down today…meditate on God's work in your life. And be sure to thank Him for it.

SUNDAY: *Reflect and Rest*

Lord, what do You want me to remember about this week? What do I need to come back to so as not to forget the wisdom You gave me? How has my perspective on worry and my future shifted?

Thank You, Jesus, for all You showed me this week. Lord, I do not want to be a person consumed by worry. Neither do You want that for me. I know that there will be seasons and circumstances in my life when it will be hard not to become overly concerned. When not to be stressed or anxious. But in those days, let me be reminded of Your sovereignty and control in my life; that You have counted the number of hairs upon my head and form fit and fashioned me in my mother's womb for Your purposes. And nothing – not death nor life, neither angels nor demons, not fears for today nor my worries about tomorrow, not even the powers of hell can separate me from Your love. I've got this, Lord, because You've got me. I love You. Amen.

STAND STRAIGHT. SHOULDERS BACK. LOOK THEM IN THE EYE. AND SMILE.

MONDAY: What She Taught Me

"She said to me always, 'Stand up straight and smile.' A phrase that has more meaning than face value." Our oldest child's, Bailey, comments at Nik's funeral on June 21, 2022

She wasn't always so resolute. She was quite reserved in her early years. Because of her beauty. People often mistook her as being stuck up. Perhaps rude. Holier than thou. But nothing could have been further from the truth. Actually. She was often intimidated. Often scared into submission. But that all changed over time.

Nik learned the hard way. Manipulators will always manipulate those who allow it. Bullies will always bully those who acquiesce. And sometimes, strength only respects strength. So choosing to be strong matters. Because the truth is the truth. Even if no one believes it. And a lie is a lie even if everyone has bought it.

But resolve will always be tested.

It had to blow the evil king's mind. Here was an entire nation of exiles bowed down before him. A conquered populace groveling at the statue made in his honor. Everyone. Everyone that is except three young Hebrew men. Refusing to bend their knee. Refusing to honor him as God. Even after his threats. Even after his assurance that they would be burned alive. These three men stood. Determined to hold fast to their faith.

But resolve will always be tested. So into the furnace they went.

Yet they remained unscathed. Not even the smell of smoke clung to them. And curiously enough, three were not seen in that oven, but rather four. The forth had the appearance of the Son of God.

Nik taught her children the hard-fought lesson she learned: what we hold dear will always be challenged. And the only way to hold on to what you know to be true is to choose to stand for it. Win or lose. The temporal result does not matter. After all. The truth is the truth. Even if no one believes it. And a lie is a lie if everyone has bought it.

She taught us that the strength to stay standing is not dependent upon us. That's on Him. It's the choice to be brave and choose to stand in the first place. That initial move remains ours and ours alone.

Stand straight. Shoulders back. Look them in the eye. And smile.

TUESDAY: Commitment

At this time some astrologers came forward and denounced the Jews. They said to King Nebuchadnezzar, "May the king live forever! Your Majesty has issued a decree that everyone who hears the sound of the horn, flute, zither, lyre, harp, pipe and all kinds of music must fall down and worship the image of gold, and that whoever does not fall down and worship will be thrown into a blazing furnace. But there are some Jews whom you have set over the affairs of the province of Babylon, Shadrach, Meshach and Abednego, who pay no attention to you, Your Majesty. They neither serve your gods nor worship the image of gold you have set up."

Furious with rage, Nebuchadnezzar summoned Shadrach, Meshach and Abednego. So these men were brought before the king, and Nebuchadnezzar said to them, "Is it true, Shadrach, Meshach and Abednego, that you do not serve my gods or worship the image of gold I have set up? Now when you hear the sound of the horn, flute, zither, lyre, harp, pipe and all kinds of music, if you are ready to fall down and worship the image I made, very good. But if you do not worship it, you will be thrown immediately into a blazing furnace. Then what god will be able to rescue you from my hand?"

Shadrach, Meshach and Abednego replied to him, "King Nebuchadnezzar, we do not need to defend ourselves before you in this matter. If we are thrown into the blazing furnace, the God we serve is able to deliver us from it, and he will deliver us from Your Majesty's hand. But even if he does not, we want you to know, Your Majesty, that we will not serve your gods or worship the image of gold you have set up."

Then Nebuchadnezzar was furious with Shadrach, Meshach and Abednego, and his attitude toward them changed. He ordered the furnace heated seven times hotter than usual and commanded some of the strongest soldiers in his army to tie up Shadrach, Meshach and Abednego and throw them into the blazing furnace. So these men, wearing their robes, trousers, turbans and other clothes, were bound and thrown into the blazing furnace. The king's command was so urgent and the furnace so hot that the flames of the fire killed the soldiers who took up Shadrach, Meshach and Abednego, and these three men, firmly tied, fell into the blazing furnace.

Then King Nebuchadnezzar leaped to his feet in amazement and asked his advisers, "Weren't there three men that we tied up and threw into the fire?"

They replied, "Certainly, Your Majesty."

He said, "Look! I see four men walking around in the fire, unbound and unharmed, and the fourth looks like a son of the gods."

Nebuchadnezzar then approached the opening of the blazing furnace and shouted, "Shadrach, Meshach, and Abednego, servants of the Most High God, come out! Come here!"

So Shadrach, Meshach and Abednego came out of the fire, and the satraps, prefects, governors and royal advisers crowded around them. They saw that the fire had not harmed their bodies, nor was a hair of their heads singed; their robes were not scorched, and there was no smell of fire on them.

Then Nebuchadnezzar said, "Praise be to the God of Shadrach, Meshach and Abednego, who has sent his angel and rescued his servants! They trusted in him and defied the king's command and were willing to give up their lives rather than serve or worship any god except their own God..."
- Daniel 3:8-28

But when they arrest you, do not worry about what to say or how to say it. At that time you will be given what to say... - Matthew 10:19

Holy Spirit, I recognize that I am prone to keep my head down. I feel safer staying seated, quiet, and reserved; to not cause a stir; to not stand up for that which I believe. I admit at times, I am intimidated by the opposition. That I don't feel equipped to defend what I know to be true. I am frightened by what will happen to me. Frightened as to being made to look like a fool. But Lord, I know that You have not given me a spirit of fear, but rather a spirit of power, love, and a sound mind. When the time comes, You will quicken the spirit within me to know what to say if I seek Your wisdom and guidance first. You promise to be with me when I know I am called to stand firm. So, God, let me be a person of boldness and courage. Give me the bravery necessary to muster the 15 seconds of courage it will take to choose to stand up for that which is right, noble, and good. Regardless of how it turns out, Lord. I know You are calling me to stand, Lord. And I trust You will give me the strength for whatever comes next. Amen.

WEDNESDAY: Assessment

1. Am I a courageous person? Do I look people in the eye when I speak? Does my body language convey confidence? If not, why not?
2. Do others view me as confident? Do I find myself in situations where others try to manipulate me often? Have I been a target for bullying? If so, why?
3. What is my response to confrontation? What do I do when my beliefs are challenged, or I witness something that is wrong, predatory, or mean?
4. Do I defend those I love at a personal cost to myself? Do I defend those that I don't know at personal cost to myself? If so, how? If not, why not?
5. Do I believe I must be fully equipped and ready prior to entering a difficult situation or confrontation? Do I rely on the Spirit of God to guide me in those circumstances?

THURSDAY: Battle Plan

1. Where is God calling me to be bolder for standing up for what I know to be right?
2. What does "standing up" look like practically?
3. Whom do I need to face that is challenging my beliefs? Why do they intimidate me, and how can I deconstruct that fear?
4. How can I prepare adequately for this situation? What specific requests must I bring before God regarding this situation? Who do I need to recruit as an advocate, counselor, or encourager in this situation?
5. How do I sustain the strength to operate as a person of courage and a champion of truth?

FRIDAY: Gut Check

1. What is my greatest fear in choosing to be courageous?
2. Do I feel inadequate about the task before me? If so, why?
3. What lies am I believing as it pertains to standing up for what I know to be true?
4. Do I trust God's promises over me? That He will never leave me nor forsake me – no matter how this turns out?
5. Do I care more about my temporal comfort than the championing of eternal truths? Do my actions reflect this belief?

SATURDAY: Baby Steps

Choosing to push past fear, intimidation, and potential harm in order to do the right thing is a lot easier to desire than to put into action. It's just easier to stay seated. It's easier to hide and lob lofty opinions and self-righteous drivel from behind a keyboard like some social media troll. Choosing to genuinely stand up for your faith; choosing to stand in the gap for a person in need (especially when that person may be an outcast themselves); choosing to do the right thing and being a person who talks the talk and genuinely walks the walk can be scary.

But that's our job as followers of Christ.

To do the hard thing. To be the shining beacon on a hill that can't be put out. Where we can get it twisted is when we think we are responsible for keeping the beacon burning. That was never our job. Our job is to choose to be the beacon; to stand for righteousness when all those around us are acquiescing under the influence of peer pressure and secularly driven culture. No more!

No one says you are called to rail against those outside of our camp. No one says you are called to take up arms against those who disagree. There is no win in exchanging vitriol for vitriol.

But what you are called to be is a person of integrity. To be a person whose actions mirror their belief systems.

So where are you being duplicitous? What is the area, relationship, or activity in your life that does not match up with the heart of God for you? Where are you being called to stand up? Put your shoulders back. Look the giant in the eye. And smile?

Come on…you know what it is. And I bet you know what it is you are supposed to do next. Time to come down out of the grandstands, hotshot. Time to strap up and get in the game. You will definitely take some hits while you are out there…might even cost you everything. But know this… if you stand for truth, you are assured that no matter how it turns out down here, you will hear "Well Done," up there.

Choose to start being courageous…today.

SUNDAY: Reflect and Rest

Holy Spirit, what is the big takeaway for me this week? How can I operate in the boldness of the saints that have gone before me? Where are You specifically calling me to be bolder moving forward?

Thank You, Holy Spirit, for convicting me this week, for showing me so blatantly where You are calling me to be more confident and bolder.

Lord, moving forward, please continue to give me hyper self-awareness in this area. Not only when I am directly challenged but even in the small manners of how I carry myself daily: to walk tall, to pull my shoulders back, to look people in the eye, and ultimately smile and be kind.

You have already given me all the courage I need, I just need to operate with the gift that is at my disposal.

Thank You, Lord, in advance for using me in such a mighty way.

For Your glory, and my joy.

Amen.

of ~~God~~ no matter what is
happening around us.
Not spared — But god
will be with them

* You can be both in the center
of God's will, and still stuck
in what appears to be a
hopeless situation.
+ God has a purpose for
the storms he allows

And of His fulness have all we received, and grace for grace.
~ John 1:16

DON'T INTERRUPT

MONDAY: What She Taught Me

"You can be both in the center of God's will and still stuck in what appears to be a hopeless situation…" - Excerpt from Nikki's journal from July 2020

I was so angry.

When we learned that the cancer had exploded. I told a friend, "I was done." When he inquired as to what that meant. All I could say in reply was, "With this. All of it."

Without further explanation. He knew what I meant.

Done with the faith-filled proclamations. Done with all the well-intentioned prophetic encouragements. Done with the constant disappointment. Done with all of it.

We had spent three years fighting with everything we had. Countless tears expended. Endless miles traversed. Innumerable hours spent in fervent prayer. All of it, seemingly for naught. It didn't make sense. And I was over it.

In my lack of understanding and fatigue. I thought God was done. So, I was too.

Poor Peter, man. Brother went from hero to zero in a second. One minute being praised by the King. The next being reprimanded by the One who had just esteemed him above all others. But Pete had gotten it twisted. When he remarked that Jesus was the promised Messiah. He was fully aligned with God's perfect perspective. But when he disagreed with the way God sought to enact His plan – the elevation of his desires over those of the Savior resulted in his rebuke.

After 3 years. A lot of fatigue. And a lack of understanding. Peter unknowingly sought to shipwreck the whole thing. Graciously – he'd learn later – it never was about Pete's plan. It was always about God's sovereign will.

For my part, I didn't come around quickly. It took months. And countless stories. Tales about how Nik's fight and faith had resulted in others finding hope. Not hope in temporal relief. Not even hope in an earthly cure. Rather the Everlasting Hope that, despite the cost, despite the lack of understanding, hope can only be found in meeting and submitting to Jesus.

This story was never about me. Nor was it about Nik. There is but one story. And it is His. And in it. What God is doing through those that choose to follow Him.

And that story is still being written. For His glory. And our eternal joy.

Don't interrupt.

TUESDAY: *Commitment*

When Jesus came to the region of Caesarea Philippi, he asked his disciples, "Who do people say the Son of Man is?"

They replied, "Some say John the Baptist; others say Elijah; and still others, Jeremiah or one of the prophets."

"But what about you?" he asked. "Who do you say I am?"

Simon Peter answered, "You are the Messiah, the Son of the living God."

Jesus replied, "Blessed are you, Simon son of Jonah, for this was not revealed to you by flesh and blood, but by my Father in heaven. And I tell you that you are Peter, and on this rock I will build my church, and the gates of Hades will not overcome it. I will give you the keys of the Kingdom of heaven; whatever you bind on earth will be bound in heaven, and whatever you loose on earth will be loosed in heaven." Then he ordered his disciples not to tell anyone that he was the Messiah.

From that time on Jesus began to explain to his disciples that he must go to Jerusalem and suffer many things at the hands of the elders, the chief priests and the teachers of the law, and that he must be killed and on the third day be raised to life.

Peter took him aside and began to rebuke him. "Never, Lord!" he said. "This shall never happen to you!"

Jesus turned and said to Peter, "Get behind me, Satan! You are a stumbling block to me; you do not have in mind the concerns of God, but merely human concerns."

Then Jesus said to his disciples, "Whoever wants to be my disciple must deny themselves and take up their cross and follow me. For whoever wants to save their life will lose it, but whoever loses their life for me will find it…"
- Matthew 16:13-25

"'For my thoughts are not your thoughts, neither are your ways my ways,' declares the Lord. 'As the heavens are higher than the earth, so are my ways higher than your ways and my thoughts than your thoughts.'" - Isaiah 55:8-9

Jesus, I am so grateful that you are the Savior of my life. You are the only One who could have salvaged my wretched soul. No other could have brought me back into communion with my heavenly Father. I am so thankful for the ultimate sacrifice You made on my behalf. Yet, while I am grateful to have You as my Savior, I admit that often, both knowingly and unknowingly, I do not hold You in Your rightful place in my life as my Lord. I am thankful for the undeserved gift of salvation, but I am quick to dismiss the respect for Your sovereignty that should rightfully follow accepting such a gift. You are in control, Lord. You always have been. Yet I try to rule my little Kingdom and those that traverse it as if I were the ultimate authority. Help me, Jesus, to recognize when I value my desires over Yours. Help me to willfully submit to Your purposes. Even when I am confused, scared, and hurt – help me find my footing. Rest in Your perpetual faithfulness, and find peace and comfort in Your leading. Amen.

WEDNESDAY: Assessment

1. How do I react when situations go poorly or not to plan?
2. Do I feel God has an obligation to answer some prayers? If so, why? If not, why not?
3. Is there any area or incident in my life that I feel God has abandoned me? That He has failed to answer my heart's cry for reasons I cannot understand?
4. What has been the effect on my relationship with God regarding my unanswered prayers, things not going according to plan, etc.?
5. Do I tend to elevate my desires and plans above all else (God's desires, or others' considerations)?

THURSDAY: Battle Plan

1. What is the past situation where I feel God "failed me" that He and I need to talk about/revisit because it has negatively affected our relationship?

2. What are the current circumstances I am enduring that I feel God is failing to move on my behalf that I need to discuss with Him because it is negatively affecting our relationship?

3. How can I restore my faith and trust in God's plans and purposes for my life?

4. Who can speak into my life as it pertains to growing my trust in God?

5. What desires, actions, and/or mindset must I submit to God? What is He asking me to trust Him with in my life (despite my lack of understanding) right now?

FRIDAY: Gut Check

1. Despite my hurt and anger, am I willing to move forward with restoring my relationship with God over past disappointments? If so, how? If not, why not?

2. Will I commit to submitting to God's will, desires, and commands over my own desires and wants? If so, how?

3. Do I truly believe that God is faithful and that He is working ALL things together for the good of those who love Him and are called according to His purposes? If not, why not?

4. Am I now willing to make Jesus not only the Savior but the Lord of my life? What does that look like?

5. Am I willing to repent for trying to manipulate, control, or manage areas of my life that I know are out of order according to God's economy?

SATURDAY: Baby Steps

It's good to be king. It feels good to be in control. It feels good to get what you want when you want it. And sometimes being in control isn't a bad thing. Getting what you desire isn't necessarily wrong. However, demanding to be in control is wrong. And severing our relationship with our Creator when things don't go our way is exactly what the enemy of our soul desires. But I get it. It makes so much sense. From our seat and from our perspective, when things don't go the way we want or even the way we feel is righteous – the child gets sick, the spouse is discovered to be having an affair, the loved one dies – it seems that the only right response is to shake our fists at heaven and demand justice. It may even seem right to walk away from Him altogether.

But as attractive as that course of action may appear…sweet friend, that is not the path that leads to life. In fact, it will only lead to bitterness, depression, anger, and potentially your own death.

There is a better way.

But you likely won't want to take it at first. There is too much confusion, too much hurt, too much pain. But it's the only way to walk out of hell. I know you don't want to stay here. And whether you believe it or not, God doesn't want you to either.

So take the first step today. Start the conversation with Him. Tell Him how angry you are. Tell Him how much His allowing that to happen hurt you. Be brutally honest. He's a big God. He can take it.

And if you aren't ready to talk to Him about it yet. Talk to someone. Someone you trust that has a relationship with Him. Tell them how you feel about the disappointment. Tell them how you feel like He isn't showing up for you.

Start the process and commit to keeping at it until you start gaining ground back. It might take a minute. But if you don't stop, you'll get there.

The first step will likely be the hardest. But you can do it.

Start today.

SUNDAY: Reflect and Rest

Jesus, what did You reveal to me about control this week? What did I learn about how my past disappointments have affected our relationship? Where do I need to continue to do work to align my priorities with Your own?

Thank You, Jesus, for all that You revealed to me this week. Lord, I know that in growing in my understanding of You, my faith and trust in You will grow. I must rely on that trust when things go wrong – as they invariably do living in a broken world. I need to stand on that faith when things do not go according to my plan. So, Jesus, help me commit to learning more about You, Your sovereign nature, Your eternal promises over me, and Your loving guidance in my life. I know You want what is best for me. Even when I don't see or understand what You are doing, even in the disappointments of my past, You waste nothing, Lord. You are still writing Your story. And in Your grace, You have invited me into that process. Help me, Jesus, to continue to hold my plans loosely and to listen for Your still small voice. Your way is always the best way, God. I know that. Help me never to forget it. Amen.

① I have a gift only I can give

② Someone has a need only I can meet

③ Joy is in the journey where the gift and need collide.

Gods path for your life is a collision course

④ The journey to give your gift will break you - But also make you

Be easy on pp. - Luke 6

Give your all - Mark 12

Be a cheerful giver - 2 Cor 9

BE PATIENT AND TRUST THE PROCESS

MONDAY: What She Taught Me

"The journey to give you your gift will break you, but it will also make you." - Excerpt from Nik's Journal from July 2019

One day. Out of nowhere. The girls got into a super-heated argument. Curious. Because, despite the fact they couldn't be more different, our daughters, Bailey and Rian, were usually thick as thieves. But on this particular morning in sunny San Diego, the two of them couldn't have been any more frosty towards one other.

And Nik wasn't having it.

Quickly she gathered them up. Stooped down to their level and laid it out: long after we were gone, they would have each other. Love it or leave it. This relationship was likely going to be the longest of their lives. So, it is worth cherishing. Worth growing and building over time. She told them that someday. They would need it. They would need each other.

Despite not fully understanding it. They, along with their brother, Everett, have worked diligently to build those sacred bonds. Through thick and thin. Good days and bad. They've worked at it. Because years ago. Their mom told them to, and it turns out she was right.

Through all of this. They needed each other.

According to the account. Ananias couldn't believe it. I mean. You gotta be pretty confused to ask God to repeat Himself. But he hadn't misheard Him. Turned out God really did want to enlist the very man who, until very recently, was arresting and even killing those who believed as he did. A man who had built a platform on the premise that Jesus was a fake. Now here was Ananias. Being commanded to go and commission that same man for God's purpose. A man who, until very recently, was known as Saul of Tarsus.

Go figure. Turned out God was right. Turned out. Ananias and the rest of the early Church would need the Apostle Paul. And so would we.

Sometimes things don't make sense. Sometimes we don't have full scope. Sometimes His divine direction only reveals the depth of its wisdom long after dispensing it.

But you don't have to fully understand the counsel if you fully trust the source. You don't need to entirely grasp the guidance to walk in humble obedience.

Be patient and trust the process.

TUESDAY: Commitment

In Damascus there was a disciple named Ananias. The Lord called to him in a vision, "Ananias!"

"Yes, Lord," he answered.

The Lord told him, "Go to the house of Judas on Straight Street and ask for a man from Tarsus named Saul, for he is praying. In a vision he has seen a man named Ananias come and place his hands on him to restore his sight."

"Lord," Ananias answered, "I have heard many reports about this man and all the harm he has done to your holy people in Jerusalem. And he has come here with authority from the chief priests to arrest all who call on your name."

But the Lord said to Ananias, "Go! This man is my chosen instrument to proclaim my name to the Gentiles and their kings and to the people of Israel. I will show him how much he must suffer for my name."

Then Ananias went to the house and entered it. Placing his hands on Saul, he said, "Brother Saul, the Lord, Jesus, who appeared to you on the road as you were coming here, has sent me so that you may see again and be filled with the Holy Spirit." Immediately, something like scales fell from Saul's eyes, and he could see again. He got up and was baptized, and after taking some food, he regained his strength. - Acts 9:10-19

For we know in part and we prophesy in part, but when completeness comes, what is in part disappears. When I was a child, I talked like a child, I thought like a child, I reasoned like a child. When I became a man, I put the ways of childhood behind me. For now we see only a reflection as in a mirror; then we shall see face to face. Now I know in part; then I shall know fully, even as I am fully known. - 1Corinthians 13:9-12

Father, I readily admit that I think I understand more than I do. I often believe my vision is clearer than it is. But in so doing, I can be myopic. I can be dismissive. I can be self-righteous and sanctimonious. I can be so assured that I know the way that the narrative should play out. So much so, that when it does not go how I think it should, I can become callous, bitter, and cold. In my disbelief and hurt, I can demonize others – blaming them for thwarting my "best-laid plans." I can even walk away from my relationship with You because I feel You didn't do what You were supposed to. Lord, You don't want that for me. You don't want broken promises, disappointments, and shattered relationships to be the entirety of my story. Each of these experiences are exactly that, experiences. Nothing more and nothing less. They are only part of the narrative. The meta-narrative of what You are doing through all of this is to bring Your creation back into order. And You have invited me into that story. Help me hold to the long game Father. Help me, come what may, to believe You are working all things for good. Amen.

WEDNESDAY: Assessment

1. Am I a driven person? Do I work hard at "getting my way?"
2. How do I react when things don't "go according to the plan?"
3. Do I consider others and their perspectives as I pursue my desires?
4. Are my emotions even keeled or volatile as it pertains to my reaction to unexpected/undesirable circumstances? What would those closest to me say about my temperament when I deal with the unforeseen or unpleasant?
5. Has dealing with unplanned or unexpected circumstances affected my relationship with God and/or others? If so, how?

THURSDAY: Battle Plan

1. In what area of my life do I feel God is calling me to be more patient and trust the process?
2. What failed plans or life's disappointment do I need to resolve with God? Who can help me with this?
3. Have I negatively altered or ruined a relationship due to my reaction to the unforeseen or unexpected? If so, how would God have me restore that relationship?

4. To whom do I need to go back and extend grace because I have wrongfully levied judgment on their well-intentioned, though perhaps ill-informed, actions?
5. How can I better be someone that holds their plans loosely while firmly chasing after all that Jesus has for me?

FRIDAY: *Gut Check*

1. What matters to me more, seeing my desires fulfilled or being a willing vessel in seeing God's purpose accomplished through my life?
2. Do I believe God has been faithful in my life – whether I have gotten what I have desired or not?
3. Do I believe that God is working all things for the good of those that love Him and are called according to His purpose? If not, why not?
4. Do I trust God with my future and the future of those I care about? Do my actions and reactions reflect this belief?
5. If I don't see God fulfilling my heart's desire on this side of glory, do I still believe He is good and has what is best for me?

SATURDAY: *Baby Steps*

Sometimes I think life would be so much easier if we just knew how it was all going to roll out. How it all was going to go. The victories we would achieve. The tragedies we would endure. Even if they were unavoidable. At least we could brace for impact. At least we could be better prepared.

I once heard a preacher say, "Many of us desire to know what the future holds in store for us. But I submit to you that if the Good Lord revealed to us what we would endure over the past six months, two years, etc., many of us would have run the other way as fast as our legs would carry us. Yet we find ourselves here this morning, in church, and in His presence. And with confidence, I can say He has never left or forsaken one of us."

Choosing to trust God is no small thing, especially with that which we hold the most dear. In our insecurity, we feel we can better steward our relationships and circumstances than anyone else, including the King of the Universe. But that is simply not the case.

God is sovereign. His will shall be done. But God is a good and loving Father who looks to comfort and console us through that process. So where is it that you need to better trust Him? What relationship do you need to give over to His leading? What past hurt do you need to take to Him for mending?

It starts with a conversation, one that may take time and a lot of commitment on your part. But an important one, nonetheless. God is calling you to trust Him with what matters to you the most. It'll both grow your relationship with Him and your belief in what is possible.

It likely will end up looking different from what you had set out to accomplish. Nothing like you had foreseen. You might not even understand it until you step into heaven. But one day, it will be sure to blow your mind when His ultimate craftsmanship in your life is revealed.

Where is God calling you to trust the process? Are you willing to step into that process today?

>>>————➤

SUNDAY: Reflect and Rest

Father, what did you teach me this week about trusting You? In what ways did You remind me of Your faithfulness throughout my life? What past hurts, wounds, or disappointments do I still need to take time to process and work through as it pertains to things not going "according to plan"?

Thank You, Father, for being so patient with me. Not just this week. But throughout my life. The number of times I have felt more competent and capable of understanding what way is best are too innumerable to count. Truth be told, You no doubt have saved me from untold amounts of pain should I have gotten what I had desired or set out to achieve. In the same way, the reasons for the hurt and suffering I have endured have and will continue to have farther-reaching purposes than could ever be conceived by my constrained human mind. The simple fact remains, You are God, and I am not. You see it all, and I do not. All of this, including my very being, is Yours. That being the case. I am standing on Your Word. I am choosing to believe in Your promises. I have resolved that You are good and that You love me. Therefore, I will trust this process even when I do not understand it. I will choose to be patient when my comprehension is stretched thin. Because I know You are for me. And You are using me to tell Your redemptive story. All of it is worth it.

Because You are worthy, Lord. I love You.

Amen

MAKING OTHERS FEEL AWKWARD IS FUNNY (AND SO IS THE MIDDLE FINGER)

MONDAY: What She Taught Me

"Nik was loyal, caring, tender, humble, selfless, and keenly self-aware. She loved her family, her friends, the beach, Christmas, summer, eating crabs, drinking good wine, celebrating her children, and making others feel awkward with her affinity to flip the bird to anyone that tried to take her picture." - Portion of Nikki's eulogy as read at her funeral on June 21, 2022

Not everything Nik did was edifying. She wasn't the prototypical pastor's wife. For sure. Chick was snarky. Irreverently funny. And downright inappropriate, often, I might add.

As such. This week is a departure from what you've grown accustomed to. A deviation from the norm. I hope you give me grace. So she can be remembered rightly. Not just in the saintly ways. But the unrefined ones too. After all. We all remain works in progress. Nik was no different. Though I don't think she had much interest in changing this part. But that's between her and Jesus.

Next week we will return to our regularly scheduled broadcast. Promise.

She loved to scare our kids for a laugh. She'd secretly set my lock screen with silly selfies. She'd say the most inappropriate things at the most inopportune times. And she'd fly her middle finger anytime a camera became present. I have the proof.

She just thought people took themselves way too seriously. And everyone seemed so angry all the time. On the news. In media. On Insta/face/snap/chat-a-gram. Everywhere. Opinions are paraded as facts. Preferences postured as sacrosanct.

Everyone just needed to lighten up.

She didn't take herself seriously so she wasn't taking you seriously either. At the same time. She wasn't going to hold you to a standard she hadn't kept herself. All fall short of the glory of God. And she always kept that in mind, to love others as Christ had so undeservingly loved her.

Solid strategy when you consider the source.

The truth is. We all mess up. We all have a past. So extending grace isn't a bad play in dealing with our fellow man…but that doesn't mean you can't have a little fun at their expense along the way.

Making others feel awkward is funny (and so is the middle finger).

TUESDAY: Commitment

As it is written: "There is no one righteous, not even one; there is no one who understands; there is no one who seeks God. All have turned away, they have together become worthless; there is no one who does good, not even one." - Romans 3:10-12

For all have sinned and fall short of the glory of God, and all are justified freely by his grace through the redemption that came by Christ Jesus. - Romans 3:23-24

But God demonstrates his own love for us in this: While we were still sinners, Christ died for us. - Romans 5:8

"Teacher, which is the greatest commandment in the Law?" Jesus replied: "'Love the Lord your God with all your heart and with all your soul and with all your mind.' This is the first and greatest commandment. And the second is like it: 'Love your neighbor as yourself.' - Matthew 22:36-38

Lord, there are times when I can be a very serious person. The opinions I hold, the beliefs I keep. All of them matter dearly to me. So, I feel compelled to defend them when they are questioned. I can take it personally when they are challenged. Honestly, Lord, I need to lighten up a bit. I need to remember that I am no better than anyone else. I need to remember that I am a sinner saved by grace and not of my own accord. I need to remember that we all remain works in progress. I need to remember that when I was still a rebel. You came for me. It's in that remembering that I will be able to take myself a little less seriously and extend a lot more grace to my fellow man. After all, You've called me to love people. Not change them. The work of Your Holy Spirit will do that. But I need to do my part to create the atmosphere that will welcome You into the space that will make that work possible.

In Your most precious name.

Amen.

WEDNESDAY: Assessment

1. Am I an overly opinionated person? Would others consider me a person who takes themselves perhaps too seriously?
2. How do I react when my beliefs and values are challenged? Do I respond in love, or do I respond to correct or defend?
3. Am I able to laugh at myself? Do I feel secure in how God made me?
4. What am I insecure about? How do my insecurities play out in my interactions with others?
5. Do I seek to win every argument? Or do I instead seek to win people for the Kingdom?

THURSDAY: Battle Plan

1. Where do I feel God would have me "loosen up" a bit? Where do I need to extend grace?
2. How do I remove the insecurities from my life that make me defensive, overly serious, or easily triggered?

3. Has the defense of my beliefs come at the unnecessary expense of my relationships? How do I resolve this?
4. What intake do I need to adjust to avoid becoming overly cynical, critical, or defensive (news feed, social media, etc.)?
5. How do I better root my identity in Christ so as not to be so easily angered by those who think differently than I do?

FRIDAY: *Gut Check*

1. Has my approach to operating or defending my opinions and/or beliefs resulted in becoming an unnecessary barrier to others seeing Christ rightly?
2. Am I a loving, grace-filled person? Do my words and actions show the love the Christ toward others?
3. Am I willing to stop being so serious all the time?
4. Will I resolve to laugh at myself, attempt to find common ground, and overall look to build relationships with those who may not even agree with me even if it costs me?
5. What words or actions do I need to confess as a self-righteous sin in my life? Who do I need to go ask for forgiveness?

SATURDAY: *Baby Steps*

Saying "I'm sorry" can be difficult. Admitting that someone else may actually have a valid point can be hard – especially when it differs from your own. But if the God of Heaven could look at His creation and say, "Come, let us reason together." We certainly should be able to do the same.

Jesus humbled Himself. Left the corridors of heaven. Took on flesh – the form of a bond servant. Walked among us. Endured criticism. Loneliness. Gossip. Hatred. Pain. Suffering. And ultimately, death, and He was right the whole time. Not once did He sin. Not once did He act out in unrighteous anger. Not once did He spew hateful speech toward those who truly deserved it.

How much more do we then, being a broken sinful people, need to take ourselves a whole lot less seriously? And extend a lot more grace and love toward others.

That might start with seeing ourselves correctly. Realizing we don't have full scope or understanding. To humble ourselves and remove the self-righteous and sanctimonious actions and vernacular from our day-to-day activities.

Maybe you need to turn off the newsfeed for a bit. Maybe it's time to unfollow that social media account that does nothing but rail against your "opposition." Heck, maybe it's time to walk away from social media in its totality for a spell.

Whatever it is that is making you so angry. So self-assured. So dug in on the mental construct that "I am right, and they are wrong. I am to be listened to, and they are to be silenced." It's time to put it down.

Everyone is flawed. And that means you are too.

So today, instead of looking to win a fight, maybe find a way to extend a hand. Relax a bit. This life is hard enough. Lighten up…and try and have some fun while you are at it.

SUNDAY: *Reflect and Rest*

Lord, what did I learn this week? What practices do I need to implement to take myself a little less seriously? How can I add levity and life to those around me? How can I make life more fun and enjoyable?

Lord, I can't wait to hear You laugh when I meet you face-to-face. I cannot begin to imagine what hearing that will sound like. The joy that it will bring me. The life will spring up inside of me. Lord, You are the Creator of laughter. You are the One who put me in community with others so that I could both experience and offer the love of Your Son, Jesus, to all those I encounter. You do not desire me to be an overly serious person. An argumentative person. A cynical and critical person. Help me to be reminded moving forward that it is better to build relationships than build platforms. That people are more important than winning arguments. And that ultimately, the only One that should be taken seriously is You.

Thank You, Father, for Your grace. Amen.

April 20, 2006

Dear Bailey,

I didn't realize it had been 4 months since I last wrote. We finally moved into 7130 37th. But a week later we got broken into, your dad + I split up for a while, we have decided to sell the house, we got back together, found a buyer + a new house to put a contract on, plus I had to reconcile w/ Grandpa. Kim. So now we are awaiting the results of the apprasial, + I get to pick out flooring for the new house. You are big. Wearing 4T at 21 months. You can talk a lot. You are great at puzzles. You love shoes + clothes. You still suck on a binky. You like sushi + salmon. You are starting to eat meat. You love mimi + ask for her everyday.

Steve is getting ready to go to SERE school for 2 weeks in May. Vacave + mimi are coming to visit. You are going to be a flower girl in July; + me + Jacque will be bridesmaids.

It's getting warmer here so I think we might try the beach soon. I love you a lot! You are very cute + good. Getting a little asshole through!!

♡

Mom.

June 1, 2006

Bailey,

The appraisal price, so we been trying to strip we want to way we ge neighborhood now - "ye You love the house tur You still try and

Our is good this sum again

Dad in legal to HC- Two and I my lap

Big alice

WRITE IT DOWN AND REMEMBER

MONDAY: *What She Taught Me*

"...your dad and I split up for a while..." - Excerpt from Bailey's Baby Book from April 2006

Bai was appalled. She burst out of her bedroom and bellowed her accusation. "You never told me that!" At first, I didn't know what she was talking about. Then she explained, it was in what she had just read. "You never told me that you and Mom split up!"

I couldn't help but laugh. "Oh yeah," I replied. Looking down. Lost in a memory. "Only for about a week though...quite a story, to be honest."

What followed was a long conversation at the dining room table. Recounting the tale of "us." Soup to nuts. After all. They were gonna learn about it at some point. It was all in those darn "baby books."

The good. The bad. And the ugly.

Since birth. Nik wrote to our kids. Scribing periodically over the years. About everything. A record of sorts. So they could look back at their lives. Our life together. And in so doing. See God's faithfulness through it all.

Out of 150. David wrote about half. And to read them. You can get the impression that the man seemed a bit unhinged. All over the map. Untethered even. His psalms vacillate from praise to pondering. Celebrating triumph to questioning tragedy.

It's all in there. The good. The bad. And the ugly.

But David wasn't unhinged. His feet were fixed firmly on the Rock. He wasn't all over the map. He was secure, in his Strong Tower. He was hardly untethered. His soul was anchored in his trust for his King.

In his honesty. In his willingness to be real. David left us prayers for every season of life. Purposeful. Deliberate. And Thoughtful. Passages, so effective, Jesus Himself quoted them constantly.

It's easy to share our highlight reels. It's preferred to filter our feeds. But I believe there is power in choosing to capture and remember all of it. To give cause and credence to the battle wounds and winnings we've witnessed along the way. When done rightly. Purposefully. It displays God's ever-present faithfulness. Often despite ourselves. Through it all.

Write it down and remember.

TUESDAY: *Commitment*

My God, my God, why have you forsaken me? Why are you so far from saving me, so far from my cries of anguish? My God, I cry out by day, but you do not answer, by night, but I find no rest. - Psalm 22:1-2

I will exalt you, Lord, for you lifted me out of the depths and did not let my enemies gloat over me. Lord my God, I called to you for help, and you healed me. You, Lord, brought me up from the realm of the dead; you spared me from going down to the pit. Sing the praises of the Lord, you his faithful people; praise his holy name. For his anger lasts only a moment, but his favor lasts a lifetime; weeping may stay for the night, but rejoicing comes in the morning. - Psalm 30:1-5

Thank You, Father God! Thank You for the model which you have given me. The example Your servant David left me. In his outpouring and honesty, each psalm he penned gives me a glimpse into his relationship with You. The bond You shared.

Moreover, while likely not understood at the time, when looked at collectively, I can see Your faithfulness to him in every season. Distance creates perspective, Lord. Sometimes I am too close to my circumstances to see the forest through the trees. But with the gift of time. If I go back. If I go back and remember what happened. I can see the movement of Your sovereign hand in my life. I must keep an account. I must write it down. I cannot relegate my experiences to my memory.

With time, like all things, memories fade. If I am to truly remember all of Your activity in my life. I must be diligent to record it. It will serve me someday. It will likely serve others as well.

Thank You Father for the charge to keep a record of all of it.
Amen

WEDNESDAY: Assessment

1. Do I have a system in place to record my life's happenings? Do I journal? Do I blog? Do I keep old photographs? If so, what is that system? If not, why not?
2. Do I find my archived memories helpful? Do I find how I journal about my experiences helpful?
3. How often do I go back and review my journals, scrapbooks, photos, etc.?
4. Do others, such as my children or close friends, know that I journal/ maintain a photo archive/etc.? How do I intend to pass this information along?
5. What keeps me from being intentional with archiving my life? Have I yet to find a system that works for me? Do I have trouble finding the time?

THURSDAY: Battle Plan

1. Ideally, what is the best manner to archive my life – in words, by photo, blog, video, etc.?
2. Ideally, how often should I record my experiences – daily, weekly, each month?
3. When is the best time for me to prioritize this practice? How can I build this time into my schedule?
4. Where do I intend to keep these records?
5. Who do I need to inform about this so that I can pass these records along after I am gone?

FRIDAY: Gut Check

1. What excuses do I need to remove to make archiving my life a priority?
2. Am I willing to honestly give an accurate account of my experiences and seasons of life?
3. Will I be willing to share these experiences when they could be helpful to others? If not, why not?
4. Do I think my life's story matters? If so, why? If not, why not?
5. Will I go back and visit the challenging seasons and/or experiences in my life in the hopes that I can grow from them, see God in them, and potentially help others who will endure similar circumstances in the future?

SATURDAY: Baby Steps

Sometimes that which is most important is pushed out by the tyranny of the urgent. There just isn't enough time in the day. We don't make it that deep on our "to-do" list. Something always comes up.

The enemy is crafty. And often, his preferred tactic is his most subtle. Sometimes distraction is more effective than sinful temptation. Sometimes business is more effective than evil enticements.

Life moves at a thousand miles an hour, and we all have a million and one things that need our attention. Bills need to be paid. Kids need rides to practice. The work deadline is always looming. Regardless of that, if we don't slow down. If we don't take stock of ourselves, our people, and our situations, we will have lived a whole lifetime and forgotten about most of it.

The times we were happy.

The times we felt lost.

The times we were so certain.

The times we were so confused.

And God's faithfulness through it all.

You cannot know where you are going unless you know where you are. And you cannot know where you are unless you know how you got there in the first place. God calls us to remember, to chronicle our lives, to put His majesty on display. Not only for ourselves but for those that will follow.

So go write it down. Go start the scrapbook. Take the photos off the camera reel in your phone and put them in an album. You'll thank yourself for it one day. And so will those who love you most.

Important things are like that. They always leave a lasting impact. Seldom does the urgent do the same.

SUNDAY: Reflect and Rest

Father, what was my biggest takeaway this week? What did I learn about myself when it comes to chronicling this gift You have given me? Have I felt convicted to start a new practice/discipline? Did I realize I need to tweak a system I already have in place?

Father, what a gift this life is! And through all of it – despite my lack of understanding and all of my fitful emotions – You remain faithful! Hindsight truly is 20/20. Only by looking back do I gain the confidence I need to move forward. You loved me too much to leave me where You found me, but You also love me too much to leave me where I currently remain. Lord, You are writing a story through my life. And like any good story. It will be worth being retold. The ability to retell it would depend on whether or not I take the time necessary to slow down, and to archive all.

Thank You for all that You have done and will continue to do throughout my life.

Amen.

THE BEST "I'M SORRY" IS CHANGED BEHAVIOR

MONDAY: What She Taught Me

"Don't tell me you are sorry. Show me." - Nik's "Make It Right" mantra

Our kids hate that phrase. It has been so brow-beaten into them. They could finish that sentence before she was done speaking it.

Talk was cheap to Nik. Often words indicated intention alone. It was conduct that revealed one's true constitution.

After years of being manipulated by a false gospel, one that inextricably intertwined prosperity with His promises, we became wise to the schemes to which we had succumbed, and the horrible relational wake our decisions had created.

What followed were months. Years even. Of contacting. Calling. And messaging those we had wronged in our ignorance. People we had advised badly in our naivete. To admit fault. To admit failure. And to ask for forgiveness.

Those to whom she spoke were surprised by the content. Admitting fault without couching it with circumstance or excuse. Even more astonishing was the work that came after. Years were spent rebuilding the relationships that had been marred by missteps. For Nik, the activity authenticated the apology.

Long after that fateful day on the road to Damascus. Paul wrote his apprentice. Reflecting upon the years spent in His service. In this letter. He owned his previous ignorance and gave premise for a life poured out for the Good News.

Even though once a blasphemer and a persecutor. A violent man full of ignorance and unbelief. He was shown mercy and the grace of Christ. The chief of sinners. Used mightily by the King of Kings.

He didn't waste his second chance. To which the evidence can attest. We gather thousands of years later – in no small part – due to a man's decision to own his wrongs and follow that admission with an activity that sought to make it right.

Saying "I'm sorry" is easy. Walking it out can be hard. Expressing remorse is one thing. Setting out on a corrected course is quite another. God does not want our grand commitments to change. He desires behaviors of a repentant spirit.

After all, talk is cheap. And actions always speak louder than words.

The best "I'm sorry" is changed behavior.

TUESDAY: Commitment

Meanwhile, Saul was still breathing out murderous threats against the Lord's disciples. He went to the high priest and asked him for letters to the synagogues in Damascus, so that if he found any there who belonged to the Way, whether men or women, he might take them as prisoners to Jerusalem. As he neared Damascus on his journey, suddenly a light from heaven flashed around him. He fell to the ground and heard a voice say to him, "Saul, Saul, why do you persecute me?"
"Who are you, Lord?" Saul asked.
"I am Jesus, whom you are persecuting," he replied. "Now get up and go into the city, and you will be told what you must do." - Acts 9:1-6

I thank Christ Jesus our Lord, who has given me strength, that he considered me trustworthy, appointing me to his service. Even though I was once a blasphemer and a persecutor and a violent man, I was shown mercy because I acted in ignorance and unbelief. The grace of our Lord was poured out on me abundantly, along with the faith and love that are in Christ Jesus. - 1 Timothy 1:12-14

Then Peter came to Jesus and asked, "Lord, how many times shall I forgive my brother or sister who sins against me? Up to seven times?" Jesus answered, "I tell you, not seven times, but seventy-seven times. - Matthew 18:21-22

My King Jesus, not only are You the God of second chances. You are the God of third, fourth, fifth, and beyond. Your love is so abundant. So lavish. So incredibly bottomless. That You extend grace when none is deserved. Forgiveness when none is earned. Yet there is an expectation – when I am forgiven – that I truly repent. I am "metanoia." I change my mind and associated activities to walk out the forgiveness You have so freely bestowed. This can be difficult. Or seemingly so. I want the forgiveness, but I don't necessarily want to pursue the righteous course You have laid out before me. Sometimes that is due to convenience. Sometimes that is because I know it will cost me something. Regardless of my motivations, I know that an apology without action is only empty words. Lord, please quicken the spirit within me not only to be a person who rightfully owns that which a screw up, but to also to be a person of resolve. To put activity behind my commitments. It may be hard at times. But with You with me, I know that I can do it.

Thank You, Jesus.

Amen.

WEDNESDAY: Assessment

1. Am I a defensive person? Do I readily make excuses for my behavior(s)?
2. Do I prioritize Kingdom principles over my preferences?
3. Am I an accountable person? When I realize that my actions are out of alignment with God's word, do I repent both in word and deed?
4. Is there an activity in which I am currently participating that I know is out of the will of God? What is it?
5. Is there someone from whom I need to seek forgiveness due to my sin? Who is it?

THURSDAY: Battle Plan

1. Now that I have identified the activity or habit that I need to change, how can I actively walk out this change? What are the practical steps that are involved?

2. Now that I have identified the person/people with whom I need to seek forgiveness, how can I actively ask for and walk out that forgiveness? What are the practical steps involved?
3. If I am uncertain how best to move forward, whose help can I enlist and/or whose wise counsel can I seek out to begin to make things right?
4. Do I need to forgive myself for my actions, activities, or words to break the enemy's chains of guilt and shame? How can I practically do that?
5. What does a healthier version of myself look like after breaking the cycle of bad behavior/sin in 30 days? How about 90 days? How about 6 months?

FRIDAY: Gut Check

1. Am I truly going to trust God through this process knowing that seeking forgiveness and/or changing behavior can be difficult?
2. No one likes feeling exposed. Yet true freedom can only come in coming clean. Am I willing to do what is necessary?
3. What happens if I continue in my unrepentant ways? How does that affect my relationships? How does that affect the way I view myself?
4. Do I truly believe that prioritizing God's Word in my conduct rather than my own preferences will lead to life to the full?
5. Why do I believe God would have me walk out true repentance?

SATURDAY: Baby Steps

Man oh man. Never seems to get easier, does it? Been that way since we were kids. Seems a lot better to keep it hidden. Seems to make more sense if we just did things the way we wanted. But that joy is short lived. And while sin has its pleasure for a season, quickly it turns to ash. Quickly it comes with consequences. Yet even when we know the gig is up, even when we know that altering course is what is best. Not only for those around us, but for ourselves. We can still be slow to move.

Sometimes that is born out of fear. Fear of being discovered. Fear of being found out. Fear of the damage the truth will cause.

Sometimes it's born out of pride. We don't want to admit we are wrong. We don't want to be seen as wrong. We don't want to admit that what we want and what we did wasn't in the best interest of others and/or ourselves.

Regardless of our motivations, it's killing us. It's killing the relationships we cherish. It's killing our closeness with God. We may not see it. We may not even realize it. But slowly but surely. It's stealing our lives away.

So we have to do something about it. You have to do something about it. It's time to face your fear. It's time to lay down your pride. Admit the fault. Own the wrong. Commit to doing better.

And then do something about it.

Don't let it just be words. Back it up. Put in the work and do the activity that proves you mean what you say and you say what you mean. It likely won't be a "one and done" decision. We all have a bent to return to our old ways. But with time, accountability, and the equipping of the Holy Spirit. You will change.

And so will your world, for the better.

>>>>———————

SUNDAY: Reflect and Rest

King Jesus, what did you refine in me this week? What area of my life did You highlight where I know you are working? How do I derive the necessary strength to choose the narrow path of being a person of constant repentance?

Jesus, You are my savior. But You are also my Lord. I am so grateful that You came for me. That You redeemed me. That You bought me by the power of Your blood. Part of my expressing my gratitude for this – the most amazing of undeserved gifts – is to honor You. To honor Your precepts. To honor Your people. To honor Your creation. And to honor myself. Walking in true repentance is how this is done. Owning my mistakes and changing my behavior is so very important. It brings You honor and glory, Lord. Honor and glory that is immeasurably deserved. Help me to remember this frame, Lord. All the days of my life.

Until I see You face-to-face.

Amen.

...not his.

Cancer is such a mind F̶U̶C̶K̶ - Did I cause this? Could I have prevented this? Is God allowing this? Is satan doing this on purpose? Is this b/c of the sin in the world? Is God making an example out of me? Everyone dies - is this my end? Will I be healed and move on? How do you live

NOT EVERYONE GETS ACCESS TO EVERYTHING

MONDAY: What She Taught Me

"Cancer is such a mind f---. Did I cause this? Could I have prevented this? Is Satan doing this on purpose? Is this because the sin in the world? Is God making an example out of me? Everyone dies – is this my end?" - Excerpt from Nik's journal from June 2021

Back in 2019. It just seemed like the only play. Two indisputable facts which led to a singular presumption. First. Nik was a young. Beautiful. Seemingly healthy woman. Just diagnosed with an extremely embarrassing disease. Second. Her husband had a public presence. And a lot of eyes would be on her now. Conclusion: she would likely not be afforded the privacy most would prefer in such circumstances.

So she decided to put her situation on blast. Her thinking. "Better to write your own narrative than spend time dealing with the rumors surrounding it."

And the lion's share of the responses to that strategy were incredible. Nothing short of humbling. At the same time. The outpouring of inquiries often became overwhelming. For all sorts of reasons – many just wanted more. To be in the know. To be privileged with greater detail. To have all the inside baseball.

If you look for it, you can't miss it. We see how many times Jesus slipped away from the crowds to reset with His Father and His dearest friends. To recharge after returning from the hard work of the ministry. To quietly grieve the death of His harbinger. To pray in solitude in the garden before heading off to Golgotha.

Jesus valued His privacy. To be alone with the select few who knew Him best. Even Jesus needed space to process. Because leadership is lonely. So even Jesus had His 12. And amongst His 12. He had His three. And amongst His three. Jesus had His one.

We all need a trusted cohort with whom we can be real. To be honest. And to be raw. To counsel us. To console us. To reassure us. And even rebuke us when required.

But we must be wise as to who gets that influence. We must be mindful of who we allow to guide our course. We are the keeper of the keys to our hearts and minds. And we need to remember that. We need to remember that we all need somebody. But it can't be everybody. Nor can it be just anybody.

Not everyone gets access to everything.

>>>————————

TUESDAY: Commitment

The apostles gathered around Jesus and reported to him all they had done and taught. Then, because so many people were coming and going that they did not even have a chance to eat, he said to them, "Come with me by yourselves to a quiet place and get some rest." So they went away by themselves in a boat to a solitary place. - Mark 6:30-32

Now Herod had arrested John and bound him and put him in prison because of Herodias, his brother Philip's wife, for John had been saying to him: "It is not lawful for you to have her." Herod wanted to kill John, but he was afraid of the people, because they considered John a prophet.

On Herod's birthday the daughter of Herodias danced for the guests and pleased Herod so much that he promised with an oath to give her whatever she asked. Prompted by her mother, she said, "Give me here on a platter the head of John the Baptist." The king was distressed, but because of his oaths and his dinner guests, he ordered that her request be granted and had John beheaded in the prison. His head was brought in on a platter and given to the girl, who carried it to her mother. John's disciples came and took his body and buried it. Then they went and told Jesus.

When Jesus heard what had happened, he withdrew by boat privately to a solitary place... - Matthew 14:3-13a

After six days Jesus took Peter, James and John with him and led them up a high mountain, where they were all alone. There he was transfigured before them. - Mark 9:2

"Then Jesus went with his disciples to a place called Gethsemane, and he said to them, "Sit here while I go over there and pray." He took Peter and the two sons of Zebedee along with him, and he began to be sorrowful and troubled. Then he said to them, "My soul is overwhelmed with sorrow to the point of death. Stay here and keep watch with me." - Matthew 26:36-38

Holy Spirit, I live in the age of access. With a few keystrokes, I have the world at my disposal. I can get insight into matters that truly have little to no concern or influence over my day-to-day life: politicians, celebrities, gossip, news, stories. All of it is readily available to me in an instant. If I am not careful. I can carry the same paradigm and mindset into my own personal life, through a multitude of venues and platforms available to me. I can get an inside look into the private lives of those surrounding me. Conversely, I can equally give access to almost anyone who inquires of me regardless of their relational proximity to me. If I am not careful, I can weigh in on matters that I should not. If I am not careful, I can be influenced by those who do not have my best interests at heart. Lord, help me to be wise and discerning as to when and where I should speak. Similarly, guide me as to which voices I allow to influence my activity and actions. Thank You, Lord, in advance for helping me in this area of my life.

I love You, God.

Amen.

WEDNESDAY: Assessment

1. Who are the people who have access into my life? Do these people provide sound biblical counsel and advice?
2. Are there individuals who have access to my life that should not? Who are they? Why have I allowed them such influence?
3. Am I a "people pleaser"? Am I unduly influenced for fear of disappointing the expectation of others?
4. Am I a stubborn person? Do I seldom listen to the counsel of others because I feel that I know what the best course of action usually will be?
5. What area of my life am I most susceptible to being influenced, either positively or negatively (spiritually, emotionally, relationally, financially, etc.)?

THURSDAY: Battle Plan

1. Who do I know who is wise, experienced, and biblically sound that currently does not have access into my life that, if they did, would be a true asset to me? How do I enlist this person's support?
2. Practically speaking, how can I remove the negative voices from my life?

3. How can I practically not "overshare" to the wrong audience? What safeguards can I put in place to prevent this from happening?

4. How can I practically keep from being too private for fear of embarrassment, judgment, or harm to my pride/ego? What safeguards can I put in place to allow access to those who need it?

5. Who is the ideal cohort of men and/or women that I need around me to help me become the best version of myself?

FRIDAY: *Gut Check*

1. Am I going to be open and honest with those who should have access into my life despite any apprehension I may have due to my ego, embarrassment, pride, etc.?

2. Am I going to cut off the negative voices and influences from my life? When?

3. Am I going to do the work necessary to build a trusted tribe to become the best version of myself? What does that look like six months from now? One year from now?

4. Do I value the assessment and council of the Holy Spirit over those of my friends, family, acquaintances, and strangers? Do my actions validate this?

5. Will I commit to seeking and abiding by wise biblical counsel even when I think I know what is best and even if that course will be judged harshly by the outside world?

SATURDAY: *Baby Steps*

There are a thousand reasons to be so private that we don't let people in. We are embarrassed. We are ashamed. We are insecure. We are worried that we will be judged.

So we don't share with anyone.

There are just as many reasons to seek out approval from those who barely know us. We will spend money we don't have on things we do not need to impress people we will never meet. We want to be liked. We want to be accepted. We want to be respected. We desire for people to hold us in high esteem.

So we overshare with everyone.

There is a middle path. It's narrow but needed. It can be difficult to attain, but it is so indispensable when it comes to living a life lived well.

Having a few trusted friends who are always at the ready and who always have our best interest in mind.

If you have these people. Don't take them for granted. Call them today just to thank them for always being there. Send them a personalized note expressing your gratitude for them in your life.

If you don't have these people, resolve to find them. If someone comes to mind who could fill this gap in your life. Contact them. Ask them out for coffee. Ask them if you could pick their brain. See how they tick. If it works out. Great! Plan to meet again. If it doesn't, try again with someone new.

If you don't have these people in your immediate sphere right now. Change your environment. Join a small group at church. Join a ministry team that serves at the weekend services. Do something that gets you in front of high-caliber people.

Simply resolve to build your team. You will need them someday. And they will likely need you.

>>> ———

SUNDAY: Reflect and Rest

Holy Spirit, what did I learn this week about those who surround me? Do I have the right people influencing my actions and decisions? Who do I need to add to my roster of trusted agents? Who do I need to remove?

Wonderful Counselor, thank You for what You taught me this week. I recognize the need for quality companionship in my life. I should not allow influence where there hasn't been sound relational investment. Just because someone is related to me does not necessarily mean that they should have access into my life. Just because I have always allowed a certain individual to advise me does not mean I should allow that to continue. Wisdom comes from a multitude of counsel. And those counselors need to be wise themselves. Spirit, help me to continue to grow in my own wisdom and discernment as to who I should and should not allow to guide me as I seek to glorify Your precious name.

I love You, and I thank You.

Amen.

spot. I want clear direction
I feel so sad. I just want
it to be over. I want
the reversal. I'm worried
the new covid spikes will
interfere.

So many things I do
not have control over anyth
I'm wondering if the lesson
+ Nikki - supposed to learn is
zero - you have zero control,
zero guarantees, no matter what
you have to trust God.

My body is stiff and
re - so I need to stretch.
etch.

LET GO

MONDAY: What She Taught Me

"I'm wondering if the lesson I'm supposed to learn is 'Nikki – you have zero control, zero guarantees, no matter what you have to trust God.'" - Excerpt from Nik's journal from June 2020

Honestly. This is what she struggled with the most. Realizing her lack of control.

She knew that bad things happened to good people. But this. To be cut down in the prime of her life. With so much left to do. So much left to give. It didn't make sense. So she asked Him questions all the time. "Why God?" and "What could I have done?"

Honestly. Questions that remain unresolved for those of us still here. On this side of heaven.

A long time ago. A righteous man asked similar questions. A man who – despite his obedience and faithfulness to God – was struck down in his prime. Livelihood ruined. Family decimated. And health taken. As a result. Even his own wife said he should curse God and die. But rather than do that. He pondered. And asked. "Why God?" and "What could I have done?"

Job got an answer. An answer so profound it serves all of us as we traverse the uncertain and seemingly unfair. An answer from the Source Himself.

God answered Job with a question of His own – "Where were you?"

Where was Job when God set the foundations of the earth? Did God consult with Job when He hung the stars in the heavens? When He set the limits of the oceans' tide?

God reminded Job who was ultimately in control. And that He was weaving a tapestry throughout the ages incapable of being fathomed by any finite mind. Beyond the understanding of Job then. Beyond our understanding now.

The best Job could do. The best we can do. Is steward that which has been given. And to do so for as long as we have it in our charge. For the glory of God and the joy of those in our stead. Despite the length of our stay here. This life proves fleeting. And our time here is short.

The ability to fully control any aspect is an illusion. We will be crushed under the load of that lie. But there is freedom found in coming under the yoke of the One who can bear the weight. In trusting in the goodness of God as we pass through this precarious place.

There is One who is in control. And it is not us. And He is still working. On our behalf. Even when we do not understand it.

Let go.

TUESDAY: *Commitment*

"I cry out to you, God, but you do not answer; I stand up, but you merely look at me…" - Job 30:20

"Brace yourself like a man; I will question you, and you shall answer me. 'Where were you when I laid the earth's foundation? Tell me, if you understand. Who marked off its dimensions? Surely you know! Who stretched a measuring line across it?

On what were its footings set, or who laid its cornerstone, while the morning stars sang together and all the angels shouted for joy. 'Who shut up the sea behind doors when it burst forth from the womb, when I made the clouds its garment and wrapped it in thick darkness, when I fixed limits for it and set its doors and bars in place, when I said, 'This far you may come and no farther; here is where your proud waves halt'?..." - Job 38:2-11

"I know that you can do all things; no purpose of yours can be thwarted. You asked, 'Who is this that obscures my plans without knowledge? Surely I spoke of things I did not understand, things too wonderful for me to know…" - Job 42:2-3

Almighty Father – Forgive me! Forgive me for being so foolish as to make so much of my life about me. My wants. My desires. My hopes. And my expectations. In and of themselves, those are not bad things. In fact, many of them are good things. Dreams. Desires. And hopes that

You Yourself have given me as unwarranted gifts of Your grace. You are a good Father who pours out good gifts on His children. But, like an immature child, I can lose perspective on these things. I turn my dreams into demands. I want my expectations to become certainties. I want all my hopes to happen. And I will twist and turn. Maneuver and manipulate. Ultimately trying to control the very life You would see me give back to You. If I attempt to save my life by my means. I will lose it. Only in submitting to You will I find the peace and comfort I so readily desire. Help me, Father, to relinquish my illusion of control. Help me come into greater alignment with Your path for me. Even when I do not understand it.

Thank, You, Lord.

Amen.

WEDNESDAY: Assessment

1. How do I react when God says "yes" to my prayers? Do I adequately express gratitude?
2. How do I react when God says "no" to my prayers? Do I become resentful? Angry? Moody?
3. How do I react when I feel called to pray fervently, yet all I perceive is God's silence?
4. How do I react when God is seemingly silent when I seek Him in prayer? Do I feel neglected? Disconnected?
5. How do I handle tragedy? How has tragedy affected my relationship with God?

THURSDAY: Battle Plan

1. What aspect of my life am I attempting to control that needs to be given over to God? What does relinquishing control look like?
2. Who is the person in my life who I am attempting to control, manipulate, or cajole in an attempt to get what I want? What would God have me do about it?

3. What traumatic moment or season do I need to revisit with Jesus because it has affected my relationship with Him? How do I do that? Who do I need to invite into this process to help me?

4. What unmet expectations do I need to revisit with Jesus because it has affected my relationship with Him? How do I do that? Who do I need to invite into this process to help me?

5. With whom do I process the "silent seasons?" The times when I feel disconnected from God and His presence as I am diligently seeking Him?

FRIDAY: Gut Check

1. Am I finally willing to let go of the illusion of control?

2. Do I believe that God is ultimately in control of my life? Do my mindset and actions affirm that belief?

3. Will I repent of being a manipulator? Will I seek forgiveness from those who I have tried to control for my comfort or benefit? When?

4. Do I believe that God works ALL things together for the good of those called according to His purposes that love Him? If not, why not?

5. Do I believe that God is good and that His goodness is not contingent upon my experiences? If not, why not?

SATURDAY: Baby Steps

As a man thinketh so is he.

Our minds are powerful. As His image bearers we have been given the gift of imagination and innovation. We are able to dream lofty dreams and aspire to unimaginable heights. Our ingenuity seems almost limitless. The world is at our fingertips to mold, shape, and maneuver. And, to an extent, our efforts are in keeping with our original design and commission. To take dominion of this place. To be fruitful and multiply.

But we had barely got out the gate when our first ancestors broke it all. We thought we knew better. We thought the system needed tweaking. So we raised our aspirations over those of the One who empowered us in the first place. And in so doing, we fell prey to the lie that we could control all of this, including ourselves, better than the One who built us in the first place.

We all believe that lie in one way or another. We all look to establish our little Kingdoms and courts. But in attempting to do so...haven't you become weary? Haven't you become worn out? Even if you are going strong in your pursuits...how are your relationships doing? Have they become more transactional than transformative? Are you moving your agenda forward while everything that truly matters, your interactions with God and those in your circle, are slipping into the background?

It doesn't have to be this way.

God is beckoning you to lay it down. All of it. Your dreams. Your desires. Your fears of "what if" and "If I don't, who will?" He calls to you to Be still and know. Know that He is God, and He will guide you to a place of rest and true peace. All while building a life of real worth.

So start fresh, friend. Go to Jesus and commit to submit. Do it every day if you have to...in fact...do it when you think you don't, just to be sure.

Give up the illusion of control.

You never had it, anyway.

SUNDAY: *Reflect and Rest*

Father, what did You teach me about my propensity to control certain aspects of my life? What areas of my life are easy to relinquish control to You? Which are more difficult? What changes did You reveal to me that I need to make?

Thank You, Father, for this week. Parts of this week were difficult to be honest. You designed me to lead; to build, to create, and to manage. But the overarching commission You gave me was one of stewardship, not ownership. I want to do better in this aspect of my life, Lord. But I recognize this may be more difficult than I realize. I am so easily distracted by the enemy, the world, and my own nature that sometimes, I don't even realize I am operating in an unhealthy manner regarding my desire to control my circumstances. Thank You, Father, for all that You revealed. I know You do this because You love me and You want me to be healthy – a healthy steward of Your precious creation. I am honored to be used by You in such a way.

I love You, Lord.

Amen.

PEOPLE SUCK

MONDAY: *What She Taught Me*

"On top of all this, there are things you don't realize – keeping up with people, thank you cards, staying away from germs, trying not to be selfish, people disappointing you – strangers being beyond kind and generous, cleaning, laundry…" - Excerpt from Nik's journal from January 2020

The crazy thing about a personally cataclysmic event is that the rest of the world just keeps on truckin'.

There are certain moments that arrest an entire populace. Pearl Harbor. JFK. 9/11. But for the most part. The tragedies we endure are acute and private. Seemingly custom-tailored in their design. The pain unique. Others simply do not experience our plight.

So during her fight. When people said insensitive things. When individuals weighed in on matters above their pay grade or incongruous with our acquaintance. In our battle fatigue and annoyance. On more than one occasion. We wanted to flip out. Flip them off. And get the flip out of Dodge. And occasionally. We did. True story.

In retrospect. I can see now how easy it is to fall prey to spite. To judge others according to their actions. While conveniently adjudicated ourselves by intent.

I love that the Gospels capture the humanity of Jesus. That the Holy Spirit deemed it appropriate to chronicle the accounts that feature His frustration. Such as when an exacerbated Jesus muttered. "How much longer do I need to be with you? How much longer do I need to bear your company?"

But make no mistake. Jesus never sinned. So being irritated is one thing. Reacting unkindly is another.

People aren't the Magi. Sure there are a few gems out there that thrive at overreaching. Some that are fluent in the language of inappropriate commentary or unsolicited counsel. But for the most part – people just want to help. To provide comfort. At least as much as they are able. Despite their limited scope of understanding.

So most of the time. It's best to choose to be patient. To offer grace when not an ounce is deserved. To extend the same unmerited gift that has been given so abundantly to me.

At the end of the day. People are always going to disappoint and fall short. But guess what…I'm a "people" too.

People suck.

TUESDAY: Commitment

And when they came to the crowd, a man came up to him and, kneeling before him, said, "Lord, have mercy on my son, for he has seizures and he suffers terribly. For often he falls into the fire, and often into the water. And I brought him to your disciples, and they could not heal him." And Jesus answered, "O faithless and twisted generation, how long am I to be with you? How long am I to bear with you? Bring him here to me." And Jesus rebuked the demon, and it came out of him, and the boy was healed instantly. - Matthew 17:14-18

If I speak in the tongues of men and of angels, but have not love, I am a noisy gong or a clanging cymbal. And if I have prophetic powers, and understand all mysteries and all knowledge, and if I have all faith, so as to remove mountains, but have not love, I am nothing. If I give away all I have, and if I deliver up my body to be burned, but have not love, I gain nothing.

Love is patient and kind; love does not envy or boast; it is not arrogant or rude. It does not insist on its own way; it is not irritable or resentful; it does not rejoice at wrongdoing, but rejoices with the truth. Love bears all things, believes all things, hopes all things, endures all things. - 1 Corinthians 13:7

Jesus – You are so righteous and so worthy of my praise and adoration. You alone could reconcile me back to my Heavenly Father. The price paid at Calvary secured my eternity. You are my Savior, and You are my Lord. To that end, I display my submission to Your Lordship by hearkening to Your commands. Commands such as: love thy neighbor. Commands like forgive as I have been forgiven.

Yet often, I can be sanctimonious in my dealings with people. Projecting upon them what I believed would be the proper response or action. Expecting them to meet my need adequately without having experienced my circumstances for themselves.

Then there are those who, whether knowingly or not, say the absolute wrong thing or take absolutely the wrong action at what seems like the most inopportune time.

In either case, Lord, I know Your desire is to meet them with love and grace. To offer forgiveness when warranted and seek reconciliation, if at all possible.

My Lord, help me find the humble courage it takes to stay on the narrow path when I am wounded or offended by others. You walked that path for me. I want to follow in Your holy steps.

Amen.

WEDNESDAY: Assessment

1. Am I a person who is easily offended by others' words and actions? Would those closest to me agree with my sentiment?
2. Do I hold high expectations as to what I believe are the right and wrong ways to speak and act toward others? What are those expectations?
3. Am I a gracious person? Do I give the benefit of the doubt when I believe others misstep or say something I deem inappropriate or ill-timed?
4. Would others consider me sanctimonious or self-righteous?
5. Do I judge others by their actions while judging myself by my intentions?

THURSDAY: Battle Plan

1. What is a specific incidence in which another's actions or words have wounded me? Was that wounding intentional or not? Have I forgiven that person? If not, why not?
2. If I have not offered forgiveness yet, what does forgiveness look like practically?
3. What is a specific incidence in which my actions or words have wounded another? Was that wounding intentional or not? Have I sought forgiveness from that person? If not, why not?
4. If I have yet to seek forgiveness, what does seeking forgiveness look like practically?
5. Who can I enlist to talk out difficult or disappointing situations concerning interactions with others? Who do I respect enough that will keep me from becoming self-righteous and, at the same time, help avoid me being overly passive?

FRIDAY: Gut Check

1. Will I commit to love others as Jesus has shown His love for me?
2. Will I accept that my reaction to unkind or insensitive comments and actions is my responsibility? That a bad reaction serves no one?
3. Will I finally forgive that person for hurting me?
4. Will I finally lay down my pride and seek forgiveness for hurting that person?
5. What is Jesus telling me right now as it pertains to handling either a current or past hurtful situation?

SATURDAY: Baby Steps

I once read a shirt that said, "I don't want to go outside today…it's too 'people-ly' out there". There's a reason a company designed that shirt. Likely made thousands of them and sold them at a premium. It's because that message resonates. That message sells. It communicates succinctly and clearly (and a bit comically) how we all feel about the masses – that people really do suck sometimes.

But no man is an island unto himself. We aren't called to be alone. We are called to be in community. And community is messy. It's full of emotions and expectations. And, at times those in that community end up hurting us greatly. And let's be honest. We do our fair share of hurting people too.

So, a good place to start is recognizing that none of us are perfect. Including ourselves. To take a long look in the mirror and repent of our self-righteous attitudes. To recognize the pride in our hearts that has taken hold. To acknowledge the bitterness that is strangling our day-to-day.

So, today, start there. Admit your part in it. Own what you need to. Forgive who needs to be forgiven. And seek forgiveness where you have screwed up. Practice in the mirror first if you have to…but get out there and share your newfound perspective with the rest of us.

We need you.

SUNDAY: *Reflect and Rest*

Jesus, what did I discover about myself this week regarding to my interactions with others during difficult times? What areas do I need to work on to better radiate Your Spirit in me?

Jesus, thank You for all that you revealed this week. I recognize how hard I can be on people; how much I can put on them in expecting them to fulfill my expectations when they have not undergone what I have experienced. I fully admit that there are times when I judge their words and actions harshly rather than extend grace and understanding.

Moving forward, Lord, I ask that You keep my heart soft and sensitive. That my words and my actions are gracious, loving, and kind at all times. That my responses are not dependent upon the actions of another. I understand that my response will always be my responsibility.

Lord Jesus, I want to be as wise as a serpent but harmless as a dove. I want to be salt and light. I want to be seen as a city on a hill whose light, Your light, shines for all to see. Help me to love others well.

Thank You, Lord, for all that You are doing in me.
Amen.

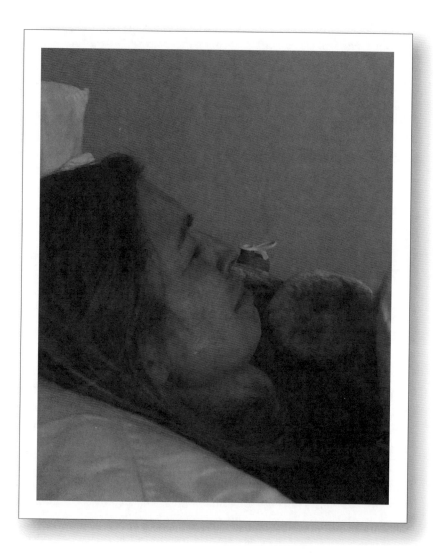

IT'S OKAY TO CRY

MONDAY: What She Taught Me

"I felt so helpless in that moment, and she just brought me hope and wasn't afraid of my tears, or hyperventilating, or pain, or begging God..." - Excerpt from Nik's journal from May 2020

For the first year or so. She hated crying. Losing her emotional footing. She wanted to be strong. Mostly for us. Me and the kids.

Sure she was scared. But she kept that private. Wept mostly in solitude. But as time passed. That changed. As her physical condition weakened. Her ability to hold back the tears waned.

She learned what it was to truly lament. To be in the moment and feel all the feels. And by the end. She was crying daily. Over the effects on our children. Over the passing of friends. Over the loss of her future.

It just wasn't supposed to be this way.

It's the shortest verse in the Book. John 11:35. "Jesus wept." Only two words. Yet the entirety of His cause here surmised. Upon seeing Lazarus laying in the tomb. Upon watching his friends cry out in agony and loss. Jesus indignantly stared at the grave. And He wept.

It wasn't supposed to be this way...so He was going to make it right.

And He did.

Suffering and sorrow were never part of the original plan. But in our longing to rule and reign. To elevate our desires over His Deity. In our dismissal of God and His perfect precepts. We broke the beautiful. Shattered the once superb. And got evicted from Eden. Paradise lost. Heaven forfeit.

Our plight, to daily traverse that which is now torn and tattered. To experience great heights. But never fully reaching the summits originally intended. While now suffering the deep valleys that were not a premeditated part of the path. All this. With no way back home.

Until He came.

Now. Because of His accomplished work. Those that claim His name as Savior and Lord. For us. One day. All pain will end. All suffering will be silenced.

But until then. We must endure our difficulties down here. While holding onto the hope. One day it'll all be made right again. Just not yet. So for now…

It's okay to cry.

TUESDAY: *Commitment*

When Mary reached the place where Jesus was and saw him, she fell at his feet and said, "Lord, if you had been here, my brother would not have died."
When Jesus saw her weeping, and the Jews who had come along with her also weeping, he was deeply moved in spirit and troubled. "Where have you laid him?" he asked. "Come and see, Lord," they replied.
Jesus wept. - John 11:32-35

The Lord is close to the brokenhearted and saves those who are crushed in spirit. - Psalm 34:18

Father God, because of Your Son, I am promised eternity. Because of Your Son, I know one day there will be no more pain and no more suffering. Father, because of Your Son, not even the sting of death will have a lasting effect on those that claim the name of Christ as Lord and King. Yet, Father, my fickle heart is broken at times. Lord, I ache and writhe in my loss. I desire to remain eternally minded. Yet I feel so heavy-laden and, at times, hopeless when my circumstances and situations seem so dire. Father, help me find the pathway that honors You, Your sacrifice, and Your promise. While at the same time, honoring my humanness and the normalcy that is mourning. Lord, You do not desire me to be so heavenly minded that I am no earthly good. You did not design me to be a callous robot devoid of feeling. Help me use my sorrow and grief to lament that it was never meant to be this way. That our sin, my sin, ushered in all the evil that plagues this world. Help me to use my pain to push me closer to You and understand the power found in the cross and the promise symbolized by the empty tomb. Amen.

WEDNESDAY: Assessment

1. How do I deal with loss or trauma? What is my perspective when things go poorly? Do I hold onto my eternal hope when temporal circumstances go poorly?
2. Where do I find my comfort in times of sorrow? Do I self-medicate? Do I avoid processing the pain? Do I turn to Jesus?
3. Do I feel comfortable expressing my honest emotions? Do I have someone in my life that I feel comfortable being honest with when I struggle to understand difficult, unexpected, and/or horrific circumstances?
4. Am I honest with God about my emotions and processing while enduring traumatic events? Do I avoid God? Do I blame God? Does God get the "real me?"
5. Do I strike a balance between being raw and real while at the same time holding onto hope? Would others consider me a "fair-weather Christian?" Holding too closely to my faith when things are going my way but quickly falling away in times of difficulty?

THURSDAY: Battle Plan

1. Is there a specific traumatic event(s) that has shaped me that, if I were honest, I have not processed in a healthy way? If so, what is it?
2. What does healthy processing of this event(s) look like?
3. Who do I need to invite into this process so that I can be a healthier person on the other side?

4.   Do I need to enlist professional services in order to process this event(s) in a healthy way (counselor, pastor, etc.)? Who are they? How can I go about getting this scheduled?

5.   What third party can keep me accountable? To do the work, feel all the emotions, and commit to getting healthy?

FRIDAY: Gut Check

1.   Am I willing to step into the difficult work of healthy processing? If not, why not?

2.   Do I believe that God's love for me is big enough for me not to be okay, even if that means not being okay with Him?

3.   Do I believe God is for me?

4.   What excuses and/or reasons do I need to remove to prioritize dealing with the traumas in my life?

5.   Would I prefer to remain unhealthy rather than do the difficult work necessary to get healthy? If so, why?

SATURDAY: Baby Steps

People are a lot like water. We seek the path of least resistance. We avoid difficulty if possible. Sidestepping struggle when and if at all possible.

The problem is difficulty is unavoidable. Struggles are part and parcel of living in a broken world. As the old saying goes, you are either coming out of a crisis, enduring a crisis, or about to enter a crisis. No one gets a hall pass from pain.

And since it is inevitable that we will have to endure trauma. It's best that we have a battle plan to deal with it rightly.

Some of us will avoid processing the pain. Choosing to self-medicate. Choosing to numb ourselves from all the feelings that are inextricably tied to the damage.

Some of us will try to soldier on with a stiff upper lip. Choosing to dismiss our raw human emotions. Discounting our humanness and demeaning our very nature.

Neither of those approaches are helpful in the long-term. We must choose the narrow path. We must choose to traverse the hard road. To allow ourselves to feel all the feelings. To be raw and real. While at the same time doing so with the only Source who can give us any semblance of comfort and peace. Spending time with the One who understands all things when we understand nothing.

Its okay to cry. But don't waste your tears. Take them to the One who can gather them all up. He can take your honesty. He can shoulder your burden.

He is here for you.

It's okay to cry. But come and cry to your loving Father. Start the conversation with Him today. He is waiting for you.

>>>————

SUNDAY: Reflect and Rest

Father God, what deep truths did you reveal to me this week? Both about myself and Your nature? What work remains to be done to process my emotions in a healthy way?

Father God, this is tough! Choosing to enter into my pain and process it is hard and laborious work. It is like a CrossFit workout for my soul! Yet, like a physical workout, I know in the long run, if I stay at it, I will be a healthier individual. I know You want that for me, Lord. I know You desire me to find purpose in my pain, to perhaps even find a ministry in my misery. You waste nothing, Lord. Even that which the enemy has conspired to destroy me, You will use to magnify Your glory. Help me to remember that on the hard days, Lord. Help me to remember as I cry tears of sorrow and suffering that those feelings need not be wasted; that if I am bold enough to stay in the process, that I will gain a greater understanding of Your sovereignty and faithfulness in my life.

Thank You, Father. I love You.

Amen.

HAVE THE HARD CONVERSATION

MONDAY: What She Taught Me

"…and that's what happens when you have a baby." - Nik explaining childbirth to our girls in Spring 2010

The girls were mortified. Completely. Utterly. Mortified. How could they not be? They weren't even out of elementary school yet.

Nik could barely catch her breath she was laughing so hard. She had dropped a truth bomb on them. And they were left reeling. They thought it was just gonna be another normal day. Just a ride home from school. They weren't expecting that speech. But man on man. They weren't going to be the same after it.

She loved doing that kinda stuff. Cutting through the crap. Saying it like it really was. Remaining sensitive while still being sincere. Honoring the atmosphere without forgoing honesty.

Her girls needed to know the truth. So why not have a little fun with it.

That poor lady never saw it coming. I bet at first she was mortified. How could she not be? She thought it was just gonna be another normal day. Just a quick midday run to draw water from the well. But man oh man. She wasn't the same after He spoke.

"You are right when you say you have no husband. The fact is, you have had 5 husbands, and the man you now have is not your husband…"

The fact was she needed to know the Truth. Maybe He was just having a little fun with how He wanted to reveal Himself.

I so appreciated the way Nik was when it came to real talk. Never fake. Never phony. Head-on. No holding back.

Don't get me wrong. It put me in some awkward positions at times. Some strained moments. But at the end of the day she modeled what she saw in her Savior.

Often the last thing people need is caged conversations masquerading as kindness. Concentrating on the inconsequential while avoiding the elephant in the room. At the end of the day. That approach serves no one.

Including ourselves. Withholding speaking truth in love is as dishonoring as it is exhausting.

We all need honesty. We all need a lot less fake. And when we muster the 15 seconds of courage it takes to start the discussion, it's then that iron can truly sharpen iron.

Have the hard conversation.

TUESDAY: *Commitment*

Jesus answered, "Everyone who drinks this water will be thirsty again, but whoever drinks the water I give them will never thirst. Indeed, the water I give them will become in them a spring of water welling up to eternal life."

The woman said to him, "Sir, give me this water so that I won't get thirsty and have to keep coming here to draw water." He told her, "Go, call your husband and come back." "I have no husband," she replied.

Jesus said to her, "You are right when you say you have no husband. The fact is, you have had five husbands, and the man you now have is not your husband. What you have just said is quite true."

"Sir," the woman said, "I can see that you are a prophet. Our ancestors worshiped on this mountain, but you Jews claim that the place where we must worship is in Jerusalem."

"Woman," Jesus replied, "believe me, a time is coming when you will worship the Father neither on this mountain nor in Jerusalem. You Samaritans worship what you do not know; we worship what we do know, for salvation is from the Jews. Yet a time is coming and has now come when the true worshipers will worship the Father in the Spirit and in truth, for they are the kind of worshipers the Father seeks. God is spirit, and his worshipers must worship in the Spirit and in truth."

The woman said, "I know that Messiah" (called Christ) "is coming. When he comes, he will explain everything to us." Then Jesus declared, "I, the one speaking to you, I am he." - John 4:13-2

Wounds from a friend can be trusted, but an enemy multiplies kisses. - Proverbs 27:6

As iron sharpens iron, so one person sharpens another. - Proverbs 27:17

Holy Spirit, I readily admit that, at times, I fail to speak up when I know I should. I remain silent when my voice is necessary. I do not sound the alarm when danger is imminent; a course correction is needed; or an alternative perspective would be helpful. I do not muster the courage required to act when I know further inaction is unhelpful. I choose to hold onto the immediate convenience and comfort of the "leave it as-is" at the cost of long-term "what it should be."

I do this for a multitude of reasons. I do not want to create an awkward tension in the relationship. I do not want to appear judgmental or mean. I have a myriad of my own issues that need my attention. And sometimes, Lord. I'm just scared.

Lord, help me to trust Your Spirit that resides within me when I am prompted to speak; to take the bold action and start the difficult conversation when need be. I know that You will not force my obedience. Yet, You call me to submit to Your righteously inspired convictions. I trust You will see me through it, Lord. But it remains my responsibility to start the dialogue.

It's in Your precious name, I pray. Amen.

WEDNESDAY: Assessment

1. Do I avoid conflict at all costs? Am I a people-pleaser? If so, why?
2. Edmund Burke once said, "The only thing necessary for the triumph of evil is for good men to do nothing." Do I believe that? Do I have a part to play in the conflict around me? If so, what part? If not, why not?
3. Am I intimidated by the opinions of others about me? Do I consider it easier just to "go along to get along"?
4. Do I have principles for which I am willing to explain/defend despite the resistance I may receive or the relational damage that may occur in standing by them?
5. Do I overextend grace and, subsequently, what I am willing to tolerate at the cost of violating truth?

THURSDAY: Battle Plan

1. Do I need to have a hard conversation? With whom? What is the subject matter?
2. What makes the matter needing to be discussed difficult or sensitive? Is there anything I can do to alleviate those sensitivities to make the conversation more palatable?

3. Should I consult with a third-party prior to having the difficult discussion to gain perspective, which I may not have? Who is it? How could they help me?
4. How can I be sure to have a discussion that is truth-based, not one that is anchored in opinion or feeling?
5. Timing and tone matter. Where and when should this discussion occur so that the message's content has the maximum potential of being received well?

FRIDAY: Gut Check

1. What is holding me back from having this discussion?
2. What lies am I believing as it pertains to this matter?
3. Do I believe Jesus will give me the wisdom and discernment necessary to say what needs to be said in an appropriate and respectful way? If not, why not?
4. Even if this discussion comes at a relational cost, am I willing to stand for truth? If not, why not?
5. What is my biggest fear concerning having this difficult discussion? Am I willing to push past that fear?

SATURDAY: Baby Steps

Goodness gracious it can be so awkward. Sometimes, it really, really is. Like really awkward. Because that has been our experience in the past, we can lock up and avoid having the hard conversation altogether.

At least not with the one with whom we should be having it.

We practice it plenty, though, don't we. We rehearse what we would say in the shower. We play out the conversation during our commute to work. We gesture to emphasize our point to the phantom that is occupying the empty seat where our would-be target would otherwise be sitting. Except they aren't there. They aren't in the shower, the car, or the kitchen table with us. They are far away. Likely completely unaware of the burning desire we have within ourselves to unburden from the message we are carrying for them.

Yet we balk at the premise, the very notion, that we ACTUALLY would have this conversation with them. We worry about how they will receive our words. If they will push back on us. Get offended. Be hurt.

Or maybe we don't want to approach them for fear of them having a perspective that would dismantle our whole paradigm, making us look foolish.

Whatever our motivations for avoiding it, we spend countless hours, perhaps weeks, perhaps years, avoiding the discussion because we fear how it will go and the aftermath that will follow.

We are so concerned about the future status of our relationship that we are robbing its health in the present state.

It's time to face the music. It's time to say what needs to be said. Real relationships are built on trust and integrity. And trust and integrity can only be maintained if we are honest with one another.

While maintaining that honesty may come at a cost, the best kind of relationships can afford such a price. They come out better and stronger on the other side. The alternative rings true, too. A relationship that is devoid of honesty is no real relationship at all. And while maintaining the calm status quo right now may be appealing in the moment, the cost eventually comes due. And that delayed payment may result in the direst of destinations for the relationship and for those that comprise it.

Knuckle up. It's time to put on your big-boy (or girl) pants and start talking it out. With His wisdom and guidance, He promises to lead you.

But, that first step is yours. Take it.

>>>———

SUNDAY: Reflect and Rest

Holy Spirit, what did I learn about myself this week being bold enough to have the hard conversations? Do I espouse and defend the principles that I say I stand for? Where are You calling me to grow in this area?

Holy Spirit, thank You for enlightening me. Thank You for charging me to be bold, to be brave, to trust in the unction of your promptings and be a change agent for good. I know to do this I will need to find my voice. I will need to speak up when it may feel uncomfortable to do so. But I know You are with me. I know You will guide me. The results of these conversations are beyond my responsibility alone. I must trust that the same Spirit that is doing a work in me will be present in these discussions and do the necessary heart work for all that will be involved, myself included. My greatest responsibility is bring this burden to light. To start the conversation. And to ask for Your leading and guidance and grace through it. Thank You Lord in advance for what You will do through me.

For Your glory. And my joy. Amen.

I am believing that you are
on the way. The end of
suffering in near. The time
to sit in front of the
ocean is close.
Joy comes in the
Morning.

DREAM AGAIN

MONDAY: *What She Taught Me*

"I am believing that you are on the way. The end of suffering is near. The time to sit in front of the ocean is close…Joy comes in the morning." - Excerpt from Nik's journal from February 2022

She never made it back to the ocean. By spring the disease had taken its toll. It became too difficult to trek out. Too laborious to do more than required. We had begun the long slow march to her departure. And it all seemed so incomprehensible. So upside-down and wrong.

How could this be the end?

I'm sure those women felt the same as they approached that tomb. Still in shock that Life Himself was lying dead in a crypt.

Except He wasn't.

Bewildered and astonished they ran from that place. Off to report what they had seen and what they had heard. An empty grave. And an angelic commission – "Go tell the others to wait for Him. He is going before them. This isn't the end. He is just getting started."

A few weeks after Nik had passed. As I sat on her beach. Lamenting my loss. I received a message from someone I did not know. Neither did she know me. But she did know about Nik. Her public fight. And her deep faith.

Her father had endured his own terminal battle. One that had left him bitter and broken. Desperate to console him – the woman shared Nik's story and through it – her unshakeable trust in Christ. Eventually. Amazingly. The daughter's desperate efforts broke through. Nik's story inspired the man to find hope – for the first time – in Jesus. The woman had written to express her gratitude. To tell me that because of the steadfastness of my wife. She was certain that, though her father had passed, he was now at rest. In heaven. In the King's presence.

Cancer took my person. But death did not win. Nik's legacy is having an impact beyond that which I could ever comprehend. And I have no doubt her faithfulness is being rewarded. Perhaps to include an unrivaled view from His celestial beach. A spectacle far superior to any I could witness this side of Glory.

As for us. We are still running our race. Our hammocks in heaven will need to wait. So what is it that He has set before us to do? What is left undone that beckons our movement? Because this isn't the end. He is just getting started.

Dream again.

TUESDAY: Commitment

"Now Mary stood outside the tomb crying. As she wept, she bent over to look into the tomb and saw two angels in white, seated where Jesus' body had been, one at the head and the other at the foot.

They asked her, "Woman, why are you crying?"

"They have taken my Lord away," she said, "and I don't know where they have put him." At this, she turned around and saw Jesus standing there, but she did not realize that it was Jesus.

He asked her, "Woman, why are you crying? Who is it you are looking for?"

Thinking he was the gardener, she said, "Sir, if you have carried him away, tell me where you have put him, and I will get him."

Jesus said to her, "Mary."

She turned toward him and cried out in Aramaic, "Rabboni!" (which means "Teacher").

Jesus said, "Do not hold on to me, for I have not yet ascended to the Father. Go instead to my brothers and tell them, 'I am ascending to my Father and your Father, to my God and your God.'"

Mary Magdalene went to the disciples with the news: "I have seen the Lord!" And she told them that he had said these things to her." - John 20:11-18

"Therefore, since we are surrounded by such a great cloud of witnesses, let us throw off everything that hinders and the sin that so easily entangles. And let us run with perseverance the race marked out for us, fixing our eyes on Jesus, the pioneer and perfecter of faith. For the joy set before him he endured the cross, scorning its shame, and sat down at the right hand of the throne of God. Consider him who endured such opposition from sinners, so that you will not grow weary and lose heart." - Hebrews 12:1-3

My King Jesus, as a result of living in a broken world. As a result of my own sin. As a result of the attacks of the enemy. I have suffered losses in my life. Grievous losses. Some which were not my doing. Some which were. Some which I had a part to play. Some which I am merely the innocent victim who was caught in the crossfire. Regardless of the circumstances surrounding these defeats, they have in part (or perhaps in total) caused me to lose hope. Hope for redemption. Hope for a future that is bright and not marred by my past. Yet my King, I know this is not the paradigm to which You would have me keep. Help me lift my gaze again. Remind me again that if Your divine love had any other preferred place for me, surely, I would be there. I am not dead. So I am not done. There is work left unfinished. There are future victories to claim. Would You give me a vision for my future Lord. One spent in the glorious service of You. Help me Lord. I desire to dream again. Amen.

>>>——————→

WEDNESDAY: Assessment

1. What are the significant events/losses in my life that have robbed me of hope for my future?
2. Was I a hopeful/optimistic person prior to the event(s) that robbed me of my optimism? What did I think about having hope or being optimistic after that event(s)? How have those events shaped my paradigm?
3. Looking back, can I see God's activity in those circumstances? Do I believe He was present?
4. Has my past made me more resilient and hopeful or has it made me more bitter and pessimistic?
5. What is my preferred future? What are my dreams? Why are they so important to me?

>>>——————→

THURSDAY: Battle Plan

1. Where is the area in my life that God is calling me to dream again? Does that make me excited? Scared? Both? Why?
2. What past trauma do I need to unburden myself from so that I can move towards the dream God would have for me? What does unburdening look like specifically?
3. Have I taken my dreams to God? If so, what do I feel He would have me do about them?

4. Do I have the time, energy, and resources available to me to begin to chase down the dreams of my heart? If so, when can I start? If not, how can I gain access to those things?

5. Who can I share my dream with that will both encourage me and hold me accountable?

FRIDAY: Gut Check

1. Do I trust God with my dreams? If not, why not?

2. When it comes to failed dreams, who do I blame? Myself? God? Circumstances beyond my control? Have I owned my part in the failure and/or forgiven those persons and circumstances which either partially or fully caused my pursuits to fail?

3. Do I believe God has a preferred future for me? If not, why not?

4. Do I believe that because of His Son, Jesus, I am part of the royal priesthood commissioned to bring His Good News to His creation? Do I believe I am part of God's redemptive plan? If not, why not?

5. What is the greatest challenge to chasing my dream? Am I willing to face it? If so, how? If not, why not?

SATURDAY: Baby Steps

Ask any group of 5 year olds what they want to be when they grow up and you will get no shortage of outlandishly bombastic responses. Policeman. Pilot. Princess. President. And their certainty of seeing such a dream realized is as certain as the ground they find themselves standing.

Ask that same question to a middle schooler. You'll get a bit more of a reserved response. And by high school, most kids are uncertain at best. At worst, some have stopped dreaming of a preferred future all together.

And by 18. Life's disappointments have already taken their toll. Sometime, somewhere down the line either circumstances or some person in authority said, "you can't do that." And the dream was dashed. Along with it. At least in part. So was the dreamer.

We learn to settle. We learn to compromise. We learn to relegate dreaming to the wide-eyed kindergartners and choose to be far more "realistic" in our approach to life.

We do it in our jobs. We do it with our relationships. We do it with our finances. We do it with ourselves. We adopt a "well it is what it is" mentality and begrudgingly drag on day after day just hoping to get through it rather than march our way towards something grand. Something worth actually pursuing: a God-given dream. Born in our hearts. Perfectly personalized just for us.

But all that can change with a single step. The trajectory of our entire lives can be altered. Right now. By taking the first actionable move towards that dream. It can all change. Right now.

So what is it? What's the first move? Is it finally signing up for the college course? Is it applying for that job you have been pondering? Is it going up to that person you see every week at the coffee shop and starting a conversation?

What is the first step toward running down your dream? Are you bold enough to take it? Who cares how it turns out?!?! The important thing is that you take the step. Because once you take that first step. You can take another. Then another. Then another. Not every step will be a step forward. But it will be a step in your process.

It's a wild ride, baby...but you gotta get on board to see all that it has to offer.

Take the first step. Dream again.

>>>> —

SUNDAY: Reflect and Rest

Jesus, Lord what did You reveal to me as it pertains to my future, my desires, and my dreams? What are the hindrances that stopped me from dreaming? Where are You calling me into deeper trust as it pertains to my future?

Jesus, thank You for reminding me this week that You have great plans, hopes, and dreams for me. Thank You for reminding me that You waste nothing and You work all things for my good. Even those things that hurt me in the past. Even those disappointments I still don't fully understand. I am choosing to trust You, Jesus. I am going to continue to submit my hopes and dreams before You and trust that what You have for me in this life is far better than anything I could ever hope for myself. I will choose to do the hard work required to chase down the God-honoring dreams You have given me. I recognize that there will be unanticipated twists and turns along the way. That the plot line will likely not look anything like I could imagine. Still. I know with You with me and guiding me. I will live a life of adventure. Chasing after all You have for me. Lord Jesus. I am choosing to dream again. Amen.

SELFISHNESS IS GROSS

MONDAY: What She Taught Me

"Also praying for other people has helped me not think about me." - Excerpt from Nik's journal from August 2020

Nik had very little tolerance for selfishness. She was more a "you get what you get and you don't throw a fit" kinda gal. Even in her battered state. She hated complaining about her circumstances. Elevating her issues beyond what was necessary. Time was better spent elsewhere. In prayer. In worship. With family. In petitioning for those who needed help and encouragement.

For Nik, having a keen self-awareness was a good thing. To be commended actually. But too much self-focus. Too much prioritization of the "me" was just plain yucky. It always led to an ungrateful, self-centered heart. A heart likened to that of Satan. And that dude is the worst.

James certainly wasn't an early adopter. Can't blame him really. If my brother told me he was God I think him barking mad, too. Except my brother isn't Jesus. And when the Son of Man revealed Himself. Scars and all. It was a bit of a checkmate move.

To his credit, James admitted his ignorance. And turned over his life to become a herald of the Gospel. And in a turn of events so consistent with Christ. Jesus used the foolish things of the world to confound the wise. Turning this man of ignorance into a titan of wisdom.

His penned remarks are considered the Proverbs of the New Testament. Dripping with sage council inspired by the Holy Spirit Himself. In it. God warns us: "What causes quarrels and what causes fights among you? Is it not this, that your passions are at war within you? You desire and do not have, so you murder. You covet and cannot obtain, so you fight and quarrel..."

We are lovingly warned that it is our self-serving ambitions that lead us to ruin. Since the Garden. Our wanton desire to gratify ourselves. Often at the expense of others. Remains our downfall. We would be wise to be on guard from it. To remain circumspect. Ultimately the Enemy seeks to sift us.

To graft his desires into our own. By alluring us with the very thing we desire most. All the while. Destroying us in the process.

Selfishness is gross.

TUESDAY: *Commitment*

"Now the serpent was more crafty than any of the wild animals the Lord God had made. He said to the woman, "Did God really say, 'You must not eat from any tree in the garden'?"

The woman said to the serpent, "We may eat fruit from the trees in the garden, but God did say, 'You must not eat fruit from the tree that is in the middle of the garden, and you must not touch it, or you will die.'"

"You will not certainly die," the serpent said to the woman. "For God knows that when you eat from it your eyes will be opened, and you will be like God, knowing good and evil."

When the woman saw that the fruit of the tree was good for food and pleasing to the eye, and also desirable for gaining wisdom, she took some and ate it. She also gave some to her husband, who was with her, and he ate it." - Genesis 3:1-6

"What causes fights and quarrels among you? Don't they come from your desires that battle within you? You desire but do not have, so you kill. You covet but you cannot get what you want, so you quarrel and fight. You do not have because you do not ask God. When you ask, you do not receive, because you ask with wrong motives, that you may spend what you get on your pleasures." - James 4:1-3

"Death and Destruction are never satisfied, and neither are human eyes." - Proverbs 27:20

Father God, I fully admit I can be an extremely selfish person. Considering my wants. My needs. My desires. My expectations. All well in advance of considering those around me. Let alone what You may desire from me. Lord my first parents were duped into fulfilling their selfish desires and as a result, they lost everything, most importantly, perfect fellowship with You. I recognize and fully acknowledge that I am no better. My desire for self-gratification is strong and makes me a slave to my sin. Help me recognize that Lord. Help me realize this is part of the reason Your Son came. To set the captives free. I need not be selfish any longer! I have been redeemed! Everything that I could hope for or desire is found in You and You alone. Help me to rip the selfish root from my soul. And replace it with the wisdom and understanding You have given me as Your adopted child. In Your most precious name. Amen.

WEDNESDAY: Assessment

1. Am I driven or am I selfish? Am I self-motivated or am I self-gratifying? Do I prioritize my wants and desires at all costs?
2. Would those who know me best consider me a selfish person? Why or why not?
3. What is the area of my life that I struggle with the most as it pertains to not being self-serving or self-gratifying?
4. Do I recognize when I am being selfish? If so, do I do something about it once I recognize it?
5. What triggers my selfish ambitions? In what areas of life do I trust God the least?

THURSDAY: Battle Plan

1. What does being less selfish practically look like in my life?
2. Who can I count on to call me out when I am acting selfishly or in an overly self-serving way? Will I commit to allowing them to speak into my life without becoming offended by their observation/opinion?
3. Are there temptations in my life that I need to remove so that I do not act in an unhealthy self-gratifying manner? What are they specifically? What does removing them look like practically?
4. Is there someone who has been affected by my selfish behavior to whom I need to apologize? Who are they? How do I approach them in a restorative way?
5. Is there someone in my life who has negatively affected me because of their selfish behavior? Who are they? How do I approach them in a restorative way?

FRIDAY: *Gut Check*

1. Am I willing to own how my selfish behavior has negatively affected me and those around me? Am I willing to do something about it?
2. Am I willing to recognize how the selfish behavior of others has hurt me? Am I willing to do something about it?
3. Am I ready to repent of being selfish? Am I ready to commit to submitting to God's best for my life not just what I want in the moment?
4. Am I willing to be held accountable?
5. Do I trust that God desires to redeem me, make me more selfless, and more like His Son?

SATURDAY: *Baby Steps*

Can't get away from this one. It's part of our broken birthright. Ever since Momma Eve and Daddy Adam ate that apple. We have been genetically predisposed to desire that which we don't have while remaining unsatisfied with that which we do.

In part. Our ambition has accomplished great things. Huge cities have been built. Lifesaving technology has been developed. And all the vast creature comforts of this life are readily at our disposal. All because mankind desired "more." Yes sir. From as rudimentary as the invention of the wheel to the modern marvel of the internet. Our kind and our self-ambition has propelled us further and higher than any other species that has ever graced this planet.

But in all of our accomplishment. In all of our daring. We daily destroy our walk with God and with one another. We elevate our wants over what the One would want for us. We metaphorically (and at times through the ages – actually) stand on the necks of our fellow man to get that which we desire.

We are a selfish people.

But we need not be. Christ came and did what we could not. He redeemed us back to our Father by paying for all of our sins. And if we accept Him and His free gift of grace. We can have all of our sins paid for in full – including our selfishness. And we can take hold of the fact that what He wants for our lives is far greater than what we want for ourselves.

So what is that area of your life that you are white-knuckling? What is your Gollum's golden ring that you mutter to daily, "My Precious?" You know what it is. You don't have to think on it too hard. You think about it all the time anyway. It's right there. On the tip of your brain.

Are you finally willing to let it go? To fight with all that is in you to give it to God and trust that He has far better for you? Because He does. Now be on guard. As soon as you make the brave decision to be selfless. The serpent will slither in to give you doubt. So enlist help quickly! Talk to your spouse about it. Talk to a friend. Your pastor. Talk to someone you can trust and ask them to help you. And if you need to. Ask them to forgive you. For being selfish. For not trusting Jesus.

Be brave. There is a way forward. He is with you.

>>>———>

SUNDAY: Reflect and Rest

Father, where do I need to continue to do the deep healing work as it pertains to my selfish behavior? What relationships have been affected that need further repair? What areas of my life do I need to continue to work because they are the areas I tend to be most selfish?

Father God, thank You for the heart work that was done this week. It wasn't easy Lord. To be honest about myself and my proclivity to be selfish. Thank You for the strength to do the hard work of analyzing this aspect of my life. Thank You Lord for enlightening me as to how my behavior has affected those around me. Thank You for showing me how the selfishness of others has hardened me. I know until I see You in Glory I will struggle with my own selfish ambitions. And while I know You would have me be diligent and hardworking, I ask that You guard me against myself when I am tempted to disorder my agenda so that I may gain what I may desire at an unnecessary cost. Thank You Lord for going before me. As You always do.

I love You Lord.
Amen.

I Can Do HARD Things

Which - I Know I can - I've proved that to myself so many times over the years - I've chosen to do the hard thing and survived - if not thrived

That doesn't make the new hard things easier or attractive The new hard things are still hard. And most people in their right mind don't want to do hard things.

BE YOUR HARDEST CRITIC

MONDAY: What She Taught Me

"I can do HARD things…which, I know I can, I've proved it to myself so many times over the years – I've chosen to do the hard thing and survived – if not thrived. That doesn't make the new hard things easier or attractive. The new hard things are still hard. And most people in their right mind don't want to do hard things." - Excerpt from Nik's journal from September 2021

She was married to a helicopter pilot. Concordantly. She adopted a piece of a helicopter pilot's mentality – there is no ejection seat.

Bailing out wasn't an option. Quitting was never a consideration. For better or worse. No matter how it turned out. Her commitment to see it through wasn't negotiable.

So she conducted herself accordingly. Both for the woman she faced in the mirror. And for the King she loved and served. All-in. Always.

Early on in Revelation. Jesus gives a State of the Union. An assessment of His bride prior to His return. For the church at Laodicea. It is a hard word. A warning. Spoken in love. To pull up before it is too late.

It is not an accusation of dormancy. Quite the opposite. Jesus' grievance is not with the activity itself. His concern was the heart behind it. He assesses it is neither hot. Nor cold. Rather lukewarm in nature. Flaccid and weak in zeal.

He goes on to say what He will do with such apathy. Such indifference. Such half-hearted, mundane measures. Being repulsed by them. He will spit them out. Nauseated. Casting the nonsense into oblivion.

Men of feeble constitution serve the world little if at all.

It's a caution to each of us. To take stock. To be sincere. To be candid as to whether we are all-in or simply participants of convenience. Willing to play the part just as long as the road doesn't prove too difficult. Better to judge our actions and intentions now. And course correct accordingly before it's too late.

Because at the end of the day. The verdict will be levied. It will all be weighed and balanced. Our decisions and the motivations behind them. At the end of the day. The final bill comes due.

Be your hardest critic.

TUESDAY: Commitment

"To the angel of the church in Laodicea write:

These are the words of the Amen, the faithful and true witness, the ruler of God's creation. I know your deeds, that you are neither cold nor hot. I wish you were either one or the other! So, because you are lukewarm, neither hot nor cold, I am about to spit you out of my mouth. You say, 'I am rich; I have acquired wealth and do not need a thing.' But you do not realize that you are wretched, pitiful, poor, blind and naked. I counsel you to buy from me gold refined in the fire, so you can become rich; and white clothes to wear, so you can cover your shameful nakedness; and salve to put on your eyes, so you can see.

Those whom I love I rebuke and discipline. So be earnest and repent. Here I am! I stand at the door and knock. If anyone hears my voice and opens the door, I will come in and eat with that person, and they with me." - Revelation 3:14-20

Examine me, O God, and know my mind; test me, and discover my thoughts. Find out if there is any evil in me and guide me in the everlasting way. - Psalm 139:23-24

Holy Spirit, while I am mindful of the critic, I know that it is not he who determines if I am being forthright. Nor is it my most avid supporter who honestly can weigh the authenticity of my efforts. Only You and I truly know when my actions authenticate my beliefs and vice versa. Only You and I know when I am all in. Divine Counselor, stir up a convicting spirit within me. Make me a person who always acts with integrity. Make my desire for accountability strong and end my proclivity to make excuses.

You have called me to be effective for the Kingdom. And while I will never achieve perfection in my effort in that pursuit. It will require an honest assessment of both my intentions and actions. I am not called to be critical. But Your spirit that does reside in me is there to authentically guide me. Give me the courage to follow it. Regardless of the outcome. In Your precious name, I pray. Amen.

WEDNESDAY: Assessment

1. Am I a person who challenges myself? Do I look for areas of weakness and/or growth in my life and look to improve myself in those areas?
2. What is the area of my life that I struggle with the most? Why do I struggle in this area?
3. Am I overly critical of myself? Are my self-assessments constructive and edifying or do they amount to nothing more than negative self-talk?
4. Am I too lenient on myself? Do I make excuses for my mindset and/or activity (or lack thereof)?
5. Do I invite trusted and mature voices into my life to speak into both my mindset and activity, challenging them, and even correcting them when need be? If not, why not?

THURSDAY: Battle Plan

1. What is the area of my life that I have been overly critical of? What does giving grace to myself in this area look like?
2. If I have been overly harsh to myself in a certain area, what does forgiving myself look like?
3. What is the area of my life that I have been overly lenient? What does healthy accountability and course correction look like?
4. Where my leniency has created unnecessary strife or problems, who do I need to ask for forgiveness for my negligence?
5. Who can speak into the blind spots of my life that I know will have my best interest in mind? How can I enlist their help?

FRIDAY: *Gut Check*

1. Will I commit to being honest about my mindset and activity? When I am being either overly critical or too lenient in my approach?
2. What is the primary area I know God is calling me to grow? What is my hesitancy to do it? What is that fear rooted in?
3. Do I trust that God has my best interest at heart when it comes to committing to growth and holding myself accountable to that process? If not, why not?
4. Am I a person of integrity? Do my actions authenticate my espoused beliefs? Am I the same person in public as I am in private? If not, why not?
5. When growing and maturing inevitability becomes difficult, will I still commit to the process, honestly assess my efforts, and take the necessary steps to continue to improve? What will I do when the road gets hard?

>>>———

SATURDAY: *Baby Steps*

Let's be honest. We would rather be comfortable. We would rather not do the hard things. Sleeping in sounds a lot more appealing than setting an alarm for the gym. Keeping the peace sounds a lot better than confronting our loved one. Giving generously to charity can lose its luster when it costs us our new plaything. Do the hard stuff is exactly that…hard.

But choosing to do the hard stuff matters. It makes us more resilient. More dependable. More compassionate. More tenacious. More loving. And more selfless.

We need to do the hard stuff. We gotta do it. Not only for ourselves but for those we love.

But the only way we are going to gauge as to whether or not we are actually doing the hard stuff is to be our own authentic critic. Only we truly know if we have committed to the cause or not. If our efforts are matching our voiced intent.

So start taking stock. Are you actually taking your health seriously? Are you actually doing what you can physically as often as you can to ensure you are around for your wife, for your husband, and your kids? Are you actually taking your finances seriously? Are you actually keeping your credit card and your frivolous spending in check? Are you actually taking your time to spend with Jesus? Are you actually taking time out of your day – each day – to pray, meditate, and listen to Him?

Each of us has an area of our life that we aren't taking seriously enough. And the truth is we know what that area is. It's time to be honest. To be our own hardest critic and call it what it is. To own poor stewardship and put a plan in place to get it back on track.

Today is that day. Identify it. Commit to fixing it. Lay out a plan. And get to work.

There is nothing wrong with a little constructive criticism.

>>>⟶

SUNDAY: Reflect and Rest

Beloved Counselor, what were my biggest takeaways from this week? Where am I overly critical of myself? What areas of my life have I allowed to grow stagnant? How can I grow and become more like my King, Jesus?

Holy Spirit, You inspired Your servant to pen the words that state You discipline those that You love. A good parent does not allow a child to do whatever he wants whenever he wants. You have placed limits and boundaries on our lives that, when we operate within them, we grow and thrive in a healthy way. It is when we operate outside of those boundaries that we falter, fail, and often wound ourselves and others. Thank You, Lord, for quickening the Spirit within me, the same Spirit that rose Jesus from the grave, to serve as a Guide as to when I am, and when I am not, operating in accordance to Your will. I now pray for boldness. Boldness both to acknowledge that prodding when correction is needed and to choose to do the hard work necessary to steward this life You have given me to the best of my ability. It is hard work. But with You, I know it can be done. Thank You for keeping me honest with myself, with You, and with those You have placed in my stead.

I love You, Lord,
Amen.

247

Dec 18 2021

Nikki, you have the faith of
Jesus within you. Therefore,
break any spirit of doubt
that would cause you to stumble
or be unstable. You are bold
and stout and your faith in
Jesus moves mountains. You
have the backing of heaven
and the Father's love gives you
courage. Your prayers are big
and bold and you ask
according to the unction of
the Holy Spirit. You are in
alignment with Him, therefore,
whatever you ask for, you are
confident in His answer for
you. You and the Father are one.
You hear Him and you feel His Holy
prompts. You are filled with his
authority and walk in the
fullness of it. There is no mt. big
enough to keep you from your Divine
purpose.

"Be still, and know that I am God!"

Ps. 46:10

EXTEND GRACE TO EVERYONE (ESPECIALLY YOURSELF)

MONDAY: What She Taught Me

"Your prayers are big and bold and you ask according to the unction of the Holy Spirit. You are in alignment with Him, therefore, whatever you ask for, you are confident in His answer for you. You and the Father are one. You hear Him and you feel His holy prompts. You are filled with His authority and walk in the fullness of it. There is no mountain too big enough to keep you from your divine path and purpose." - Excerpt from Nik's journal from December 2021

She had to write them down.

His promises. Because. Candidly. She struggled to hold onto them at times. Often she would beat herself up that she wasn't doing enough. That her situation was somehow her doing.

She struggled to break the narrative that the enemy wanted her to believe:

This is your fault. This is your error. You are culpable.

Jesus alone could crush the condemnation. He alone could provide her comfort. And while not His exact words. She found peace and joy in the meaning found in "The Message" by Eugene H. Peterson:

"Are you tired? Worn out? Burned out on religion? Come to Me. Get away with Me and you'll recover your life. I'll show you how to take a real rest. Walk with Me and work with Me, watch how I do it. Learn the unforced rhythms of grace. I won't lay anything heavy or ill-fitting on you. Keep company with Me and you'll learn to live freely and lightly."

So she wrote them down. His assurances. And she read them daily. That she was not to blame. That she was not condemned. That she was redeemed.

That He was speaking to her. That He was using her. That she was walking in His will.

We are not called to be perfect. Because Perfection has already come. We need not move forward in our own might. Because the Almighty has already preceded us.

We are certain to falter as we traverse life's path. Yet we find solace that His love will cover the multitude of our missteps. Our mishandlings. And our misfortunes. We take comfort in what He has called us to. He will see us through.

So you just keep walking. Keep pushing on. And be sure to be kind to yourself along the way. He loves you. You should love you, too.

Extend grace to everyone (especially yourself).

TUESDAY: Commitment

"Come to me, all you who are weary and burdened, and I will give you rest. Take my yoke upon you and learn from me, for I am gentle and humble in heart, and you will find rest for your souls. For my yoke is easy and my burden is light." - Matthew 11:28-30

"Are you tired? Worn out? Burned out on religion? Come to me. Get away with me and you'll recover your life. I'll show you how to take a real rest. Walk with me and work with me, watch how I do it. Learn the unforced rhythms of grace. I won't lay anything heavy or ill-fitting on you. Keep company with me and you'll learn to live freely and lightly." - Matthew 11: 28-30 (The Message)

The Lord is close to the brokenhearted and saves those who are crushed in spirit. - Psalm 34:18

For a righteous man may fall seven times and rise again, but the wicked shall fall by calamity. - Proverbs 24:16

Lord Jesus, I need You. I need You more than I need the air I breathe. Yours truly are the words of eternal life. Lord, I can become so discouraged sometimes. I feel as though I should be farther along than I find myself. I think I shouldn't struggle with the same temptations that continue to overtake me. God, I lost confidence in myself. I feel so unworthy at times. Yet for reasons I will never understand on this side of glory, You saw me as worthy, worthy enough to die for. When I was still far off, You came for me. When I was still a traitor to the King, You bore my burden and reconciled me back into right relationship with You and my heavenly Father. Help me Jesus, to hold onto this truth. Help me to see myself rightly. Thank You, Jesus. For all that You have done for me and all that You continue to do in me and through me.

Thank You for Your grace.

Amen.

WEDNESDAY: Assessment

1. Am I hard on myself? Am I overly critical? What lies do I believe about my need to get it right all the time? When did those lies take root? Why?
2. Am I hard on others? Am I overly critical of their actions? Do I extend grace or do I withhold it? If so, why?
3. What is the area in my life that I extend myself the least amount of grace? Why is that?
4. What is the area in my life where I extend the least amount of grace toward others? Why?
5. What is my paradigm as it pertains to the relationship between pursuing reconciliation vs. extending grace/forgiveness? Are they the same thing? Are they different in any way? If so, how?

THURSDAY: Battle Plan

1. What is the one thing for which I continually condemn myself?
2. What is the result of withholding forgiveness and grace to myself? How do I perceive myself? How do I perceive others?

3. To whom is God calling me to extend grace? Why am I withholding it? What must be done (by both them and myself) to make this happen?

4. What am I going to do when thoughts of self-condemnation creep in? Who can I talk to about it?

5. What am I going to do when I find myself becoming overly critical towards others? What boundaries and triggers can I put in place to prevent this from happening?

FRIDAY: Gut Check

1. If Jesus has forgiven me, why haven't I forgiven myself for some things?
2. What lies have I believed in regard to receiving complete forgiveness in Christ?
3. Do I count myself worthy of His offered grace? If not, why not?
4. Am I willing to let go of the bitterness I have felt and exchange it with extending grace to the one who has hurt me? If not, why?
5. Do I trust Jesus' final words – "It is finished?" That all has been paid for and that, because of Christ, He sees me as righteous before Him now? Do my thoughts and actions validate this belief?

SATURDAY: Baby Steps

In this day and age, accountability is a rare quality. From the governments that run the land to the big corporations that run our economy. Responsibility and culpability are often avoided like the plague. It's refreshing when you see someone actually own their part. To say, "I'm sorry" without adding a "but" to the end. Finding people who don't offer lengthy explanations as to why their actions are always understandable if not justified and righteous. Yes, accountability is a quality that is rarely seen, but it remains of deep value in the King's economy despite falling out of favor in our modern times.

But there is a bastardized version of the virtue that is equally as dangerous. If not more so. It creeps in when, under the guise of "being accountable," we choose to become overly critical and overly judgmental. Of both others and of ourselves. Leading us into feeling the necrotic emotions of shame, guilt, and bitterness.

Quick fact check for you, you are not God. And neither is anyone else for that matter.

As such, you, and everyone you will come into contact with, will make mistakes from time to time. Some will have trivial and temporary effects. Others will be significant and lasting. In either case, the only salve that will soothe will be to extend grace.

So after a long week spent analyzing and planning. Finding and removing excuses. Who is it that you need to extend grace to today? Whom do you need to forgive? From whom do you need to seek forgiveness?

The enemy will tell you that you are not deserving of such love. Nor is the person who hurt you. But that is a lie.

For God so loved the world...

He loved you when you were yet far off. And He desires to rid you from the bonds of shame and bitterness today.

What is the step you need to take today towards freedom? Be brave... choose to extend grace.

>>>———➤

SUNDAY: Reflect and Rest

My King, what lies did I need to face this week as it pertains to the grace you offer? Do I find myself worthy of this grace? Do I accept it freely? Do I extend the same grace You offer me towards those around me?

Jesus, thank you so much for all that you unearthed in me this week. I must be mindful not to buy Satan's counterfeit of accountability, and harbor a critical spirit. I need to be kind to myself and kind to others. To extend grace often and keep short accounts. There are wounds that I have in my life that sometimes make it hard for me to be gracious, both to myself and to others. Lord, as it pertains to those deep wounds, would You help me to continue to do the deep heart work necessary to heal, to restore relationships, and to see myself and others rightly, as holy, righteous, and blameless before my Father in heaven. All of that is possible because of You and You alone Lord.

Thank You. I am eternally grateful.

Amen.

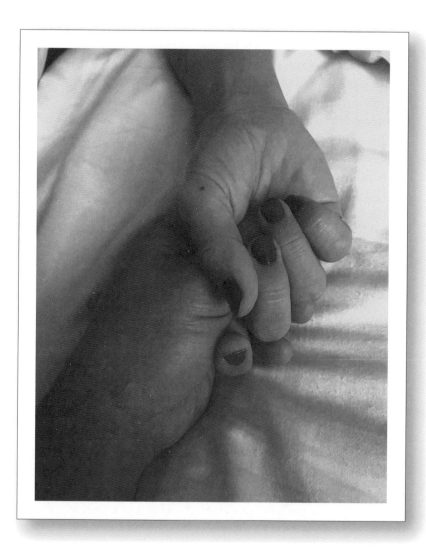

HOLD HANDS

MONDAY: What She Taught Me

*"Praying that because Steve can sit with me and hold my hand...
I'll be okay."* - Excerpt from Nik's Journal from September 2021

She was a tough chick. Don't think He makes them any tougher. Me on the other hand. I stub my toe and I want a narcotic and a nap.

Despite that. There were still times when the situation got to her. Its enormity. And the uncertainty surrounding it. In those moments. It wasn't the assuaging effect of sedative she desired. More often than not. She wanted to grasp my readily available hand. That simple practice provided her comfort.

It made her feel supported. It made her feel less alone.

In my opinion. Old Pete gets a lot of undeserved flack for that whole botched "walking on water" situation. At least he had enough audacity to step out of the boat in the first place. No one else did. Yet I can't argue. That despite his initial courage. Amidst the wind and the waves. His gaze eventually drifted from his Savior and sank towards his circumstances.

The imminent threat of drowning in the deep became all too real. Pete lost confidence in his unsteady footing upon an uncertain sea. Subsequently. He lost his poise. His mojo gave way. And he began to sink.

In that moment. When all seemed lost. Christ grasped him. Graciously giving support where the waters would not.

Some of us are tougher than others. Some of us are like a Nik. Seemingly able to weather more than seems humanly possible. Some of us are so bold as to step out of the boat. Despite the doubt surrounding the situation.

But even the stoutest among us. Amidst the uncertainty. Begin to sink at some point. In those moments. When our confidence will convey us no further. We need those that love us. To reach out and to catch us. And carry us if need be. For a time.

Conversely. We must keep a vigilant watch. For those in our stead. To be diligent. And avoid becoming myopic. So self-centered that we miss the opportunities to be the refuge needed in the tempest. The safe harbor required during the storm.

We must have those that we can hold onto. And those that can hold onto us. After all. We are all in this together.

Hold hands.

TUESDAY: Commitment

"Immediately Jesus made the disciples get into the boat and go on ahead of him to the other side, while he dismissed the crowd. After he had dismissed them, he went up on a mountainside by himself to pray. Later that night, he was there alone, and the boat was already a considerable distance from land, buffeted by the waves because the wind was against it.

Shortly before dawn Jesus went out to them, walking on the lake. When the disciples saw him walking on the lake, they were terrified. "It's a ghost," they said, and cried out in fear.

But Jesus immediately said to them: "Take courage! It is I. Don't be afraid."

"Lord, if it's you," Peter replied, "tell me to come to you on the water."

"Come," he said.

Then Peter got down out of the boat, walked on the water and came toward Jesus. But when he saw the wind, he was afraid and, beginning to sink, cried out, "Lord, save me!"

Immediately Jesus reached out his hand and caught him. "You of little faith," he said, "why did you doubt?"

And when they climbed into the boat, the wind died down. Then those who were in the boat worshiped him, saying, "Truly you are the Son of God." - Matthew 14:22-33

"My command is this: Love each other as I have loved you. Greater love has no one than this: to lay down one's life for one's friends." - John 15:12-13

Holy Spirit, it is easy to begin something. It is much harder to finish. It is easy to take the first few steps toward You. But often the winds and waves of this life quickly pull my gaze from Your majesty. I am overcome and I am overwhelmed. Where I once had full confidence, I am left with only doubt and dismay. If it is not my response to my own circumstances, it tends to be my reaction when those I care for most are met with chaos and uncertainty. God it is my desire to be sure-footed. Both in my own life and in the lives of others. I want to be steadfast. I want to be strong. Yet I know that it is in my weakness You show Yourself mighty. Lord, please grant me the humble strength that comes from drawing my confidence from You. Allow me to be a person that points others to You. Let my life be a testimony of Your amazing grace. Let my life be a life marked by supporting others and allowing others to support me.

For Your glory. And for my joy.

Amen.

WEDNESDAY: Assessment

1. Am I a dependable person? Am I someone who is steadfast despite my circumstances? Do others look to me to draw spiritual strength. If not, why not?
2. Do I have dependable people in my life? Do I have someone (or others) whom I can call upon when I have lost my confidence or have become despondent? Who are they? Why can I depend upon them?
3. Am I vulnerable and honest with those closest to me when I am going through a difficult season? Am I someone who others can trust to be vulnerable with when they find themselves in time of difficulty?
4. Where do I draw my strength in time of difficulty? Do I tend to be self-reliant? Do I rely upon my faith? Do I rely upon others?
5. Do I "step out of the boat" when I am called? Am I obedient to follow Jesus through the storms of life?

THURSDAY: Battle Plan

1. What is the current storm in my life that I am having difficulty keeping my eyes fixed upon Jesus? Why am I having such difficulty?
2. Who can hold my hand through this storm? What does that look like practically?
3. Who do I know that is currently enduring a difficult and uncertain time? Have I connected with them about it? If not, why not?

4. How can I practically help them through this time? What does "hand holding" look like in this season?

5. What is the next right step to take in this season of difficulty (for myself or for someone I love)?

FRIDAY: *Gut Check*

1. Do I trust God with this difficult matter or in this hard season? If not, why not?

2. Am I relying upon my own strength to see me through this time? If so, why?

3. Why am I afraid to be honest and vulnerable with people who can help me through this difficult time?

4. Why am I hesitant to help a friend who is experiencing difficulty? Why do I feel inadequate or out of place? What lie have I believed?

5. What is the excuse I need to remove (for myself or for others) in taking the next right step? Why haven't I removed it yet?

SATURDAY: *Baby Steps*

To paraphrase the great theologian Mike Tyson, "everyone has a plan until they get hit." We all can walk around with such confidence, such bravado, such swagger when the seas are calm, the hay is in the barn, the ledger is fat, and our bodies are in tip-top shape. But how quickly we can crumble with one bad phone call, one horrible discovery, one tragic moment. And as if our lives were not fragile enough, there is the constant bombardment that seemingly happens on the daily to those whom we love.

For all of us, we find ourselves in a crisis, coming out of a crisis, or going into a crisis. Oh, ain't life grand.

But we have a choice in how to endure it. We can try to run from it, but eventually it will catch up with you. We can try to ignore it, but eventually it will become unignorable. We can attempt to cage it, but eventually, it will become uncontrollable. Or we can face it.

But we need not face it alone. While there is always another in the fire who will never leave you or forsake you. Our gracious King has also put people in our lives to help us weather the worst of storms and vice versa.

Moses needed Aaron. David needed Jonathan. Paul needed Silas. You need someone, too. And someone needs you.

Maybe you have already identified that individual. Maybe they already know who they are intuitively, but perhaps they don't. You don't want to wait until you are in the foxhole to start identifying who is in there with you.

So as awkward as the conversation may be. As vulnerable as you may need to become. Reach out and tell them that they are your person, when things go awry (as they most certain will), that you will be depending upon them to help you keep your eyes fixed on Jesus and to practically hold your hand through your worst days. Promise to extend the same to them.

We all need a battle buddy in this life. Best to identify them before the dark clouds gather if possible.

Make the call. Send the text. Have the discussion.

Eventually the storm is coming. Don't face it alone.

SUNDAY: Reflect and Rest

Holy Spirit, who is the person (or people) in my life that I need to cultivate a deeper relationship with so that I can depend upon them when life becomes difficult? Who is it that I need to commit to stand beside when their life endures difficulty? Where do I need to grow in my trust of You as it pertains to enduring difficult seasons?

Holy Spirit, Your instruction for me is clear. I am called to stand firm, even on the darkest of days. I am reminded that no matter what it is I endure on this side of glory, it will pale in comparison to the joy I will experience once I am in Your eternal presence. Yet I fully admit Lord that often I am overwhelmed by my temporal circumstances. My gaze falters and I see only the difficulty I am enduring. The same rings true when I hear of those I care for and love. When I hear of the pain they are experiencing, my confidence and hope can wane. Lord, thank You for reminding me yet again, that You are my strong tower. The place where my hope comes from. Thank You for reminding me that I can withstand the storms because You are in them with me. Thank You for the people in my life who are Your hands and feet and help me through my difficult hours. Thank You for the opportunity to do the same for those whom I love. Lord, I know that in this world we will have trouble. But You have overcome the world. And we will prevail. Together. Thank You, Lord! Amen.

READ THE BIBLE AT LEAST ONCE A DAY

MONDAY: *What She Taught Me*

"This Book will keep you from sin. Or sin will keep you from this Book" - Nik's father's inscription from the inside cover of her personal NKJV Bible from June 1998

Just because I am a pastor. By no means did I get a pass. A pat "because I said so" never would suffice. She wanted to know what the WORD said. Especially in light of the times. Where once trusted truths were constantly being called into question. When mindsets once presumed wicked had become welcome. She needed to understand the assignment.

Because. She took her enemy quite seriously. And at the same time. Viewed herself very circumspectly. She knew she could not win the day with sheer wit or will. With what a Google search said or the latest poll deemed suitable. Even her own fickle heart wasn't to be trusted. Her victory would need to come from elsewhere. In her ability to wield His Word rightly.

After 40 long days. And 40 long nights. The tempter showed up. That's when evil incarnate took his shot. To depose the King of Glory. But not with an overt approach. Satan's tactic was much more subtle. More subdued.

He chose the weapons with which he was most fond and familiar – Deceptions. Duplicities. And lies. Malicious manipulations of the Sacred Scriptures. An attempt to contrive. Twist. And turn. The very Instructions that stood against him. For his gain.

The most dangerous lies are often the ones that seem so righteous.

But Christ saw right through the ruse. And he crushed the serpent's efforts. Not through fancy parlance. Not with skillful debate. He simply levied God's Word. He stuck to the Script. As inspired by the Holy Spirit Himself. And as a result. He sent the deceiver packing. Tail tucked. Forked tongue and all.

The enemy will always come to sell us altered truths. Believable ones, too. Ones that are soft and sweet and so enticing. Nonetheless always leading to captivity. Bondage. And eventually. Death.

Our best defense will always be a good offense. Wield your sword rightly. Resist the devil with God's truth. And he will flee from you. Eat this Book. You will need it.

Read the Bible at least once a day.

TUESDAY: Commitment

"Then Jesus was led by the Spirit into the wilderness to be tempted by the devil. After fasting forty days and forty nights, he was hungry. The tempter came to him and said, "If you are the Son of God, tell these stones to become bread."

Jesus answered, "It is written: 'Man shall not live on bread alone, but on every word that comes from the mouth of God.'"

Then the devil took him to the holy city and had him stand on the highest point of the temple. "If you are the Son of God," he said, "throw yourself down. For it is written:

"'He will command his angels concerning you, and they will lift you up in their hands, so that you will not strike your foot against a stone.'"

Jesus answered him, "It is also written: 'Do not put the Lord your God to the test.'"

Again, the devil took him to a very high mountain and showed him all the Kingdoms of the world and their splendor. "All this I will give you," he said, "if you will bow down and worship me."

Jesus said to him, "Away from me, Satan! For it is written: 'Worship the Lord your God, and serve him only.'"

Then the devil left him, and angels came and attended him." - Matthew 4:1-11

"The heart is deceitful above all things and beyond cure. Who can understand it?" - Jeremiah 17:9

"Create in me a pure heart, O God, and renew a steadfast spirit within me. Do not cast me from your presence or take your Holy Spirit from me.

Restore to me the joy of your salvation and grant me a willing spirit, to sustain me. Then I will teach transgressors your ways, so that sinners will turn back to you." - Psalm 51:10-13

Father God, Your Word says that my enemy, the devil, prowls about like a roaring lion seeking for someone to devour. Yet Your Word describes me as a sheep. Candidly Lord – sheep are dumb. They are stubborn. They are weak. And they are vulnerable. Sheep need protection. From the world. From the enemy. And from themselves. Sheep need a shepherd. You are the Good Shepherd. And Your sheep know Your voice. You lead them and guide them. You protect them and provide for them. Lord, I desperately need to know Your voice. Because the enemy seeks to mimic Your voice. To manipulate it and counterfeit it so as to destroy me. Knowing Your voice comes from knowing Your Word. Give me a fresh hunger to consume Your Holy Scriptures. Through them, You will serve as my front and rear guard. I need not fight. You will fight for me. I need only sit in the presence of Your Word and be still.

Thank You, Father.

Amen.

WEDNESDAY: Assessment

1. Do I have a daily Bible reading plan? What does it look like? How do I develop it/choose it?
2. Do I anchor my prayer life in God's Word? Do I make it a practice to memorize Scripture?
3. What do I do when I come across a portion of Scripture that I do not understand or necessarily agree with? Do I seek further understanding of its meaning?
4. Do I tend to champion the Scriptures that affirm my actions and beliefs and neglect those that challenge my position? What do I do when I determine I am operating outside of the guidelines given in God's Holy Word?
5. Do I consider God's Word a weapon? Do I treat it as such? If not, why not?

THURSDAY: *Battle Plan*

1. What does a practical 90-day Bible study look like for me? When can I commit time in my schedule to develop this/protect this practice? How about 6 months? 1 year?
2. Outside of my daily devotional time I already have in place, can I commit to reading the entirety of the Bible in 1 year? If not, why not?
3. What is the area of the Bible with which I know the least? How can I practically bolster my knowledge of this area?
4. How can I practically sanction a place of silence and solitude for my study? Where will I do it? At what time?
5. Who can hold me accountable to this new practice?

FRIDAY: *Gut Check*

1. What excuses do I need to remove when it comes to committing to reading God's Word?
2. What lies have I believed as it pertains to God's Word? Why have I bought those lies?
3. Do I place my preferred beliefs over God's righteous Word? Why? What am I going to do about it?
4. Do I believe that God desires to build a relationship with me through His Word? If not, why not?
5. Do I believe that the Bible, both Old and New Testaments, were supernaturally inspired by God, inerrant, and authoritative in all matters? If not, why not?

SATURDAY: *Baby Steps*

You should never bring a knife to a gunfight.

Often in life, we tend to rely on pithy "Christianese" one-liners in hopes that God will see us through the difficult days we traverse. Statements like:

"We shouldn't judge."

"God never closes a door without opening a window."

"He will never give you more than you can handle."

Meanwhile all of those statements (and many more like them), are, at best, barely anchored in any semblance of truth at all, and at worse, in outright opposition to what God's Word really says and means.

So we bring these dull butterknife paradigms onto the battlefield of life and we wonder why we are getting our tails handed to us. We are outmatched and outgunned at every turn.

Sweet friend. You have an ancient enemy armed to the teeth with demonic, yet proven, tactics that have sifted men like wheat for millennia. You need to take this fight seriously.

Yes – Your God will fight for you, but one of the primary means in which He does that is by getting His Word deep into your soul so that you can depend upon it, rely on it, and wield it when it is necessary.

Yes – Our enemy is ancient, but God's Word is eternal.

It is sharper than any two-edged sword, piercing the very soul and spirit, and discerning the thoughts and intentions of the heart.

And it is there and available for you. God intended it that way. God has given you a mighty weapon.

So start your training. Start reading. Start journaling. Start spending time in deep devotion to grasp, understand, and rightly divide His eternal Word. Stop putting it off. Because don't look now…

You are in a gunfight.

>>>———

SUNDAY: Reflect and Rest

Father God, after examining it this week, how healthy is my practice of studying Scripture? What lies have I believed about God's Word? Where do I need to take the Bible and its precepts more seriously?

Eternal Father, thank You for the gift of Your Holy Scriptures. Thank You for the guidance You have given me through them. Thank You for the soft comfort it provides. Thank You for the necessary rebukes it gives. Thank You for the constant correction it dispenses. Truly Lord, life and life to the full is found on its pages. Let me never again take the Holy Bible for granted. Never again Lord, let me manipulate its eternal truths for my benefit. It is Your most precious gift to me. I pray for the humble conviction to always treat it as such. Thank You, Father, for Your guidance. Thank You, Father, for Your love. Thank You, Father, for Your kindness. Thank You, Father, for Your Word. In Your great and powerful name I pray. Amen.

DON'T BURY FEELINGS ALIVE

MONDAY: What She Taught Me

"I was so happy she started talking! And I just tried to encourage her that all her feelings are totally normal – just press into them and ask God to show Himself and prove Himself to her..." - Excerpt from Nik's Journal from December 2019

Happy. Sad. Joyful. Mad. Whatever it was. She just wanted you to be honest about it. She hated when people feigned indifference when they were obviously unnerved. Saying "I'm fine" when clearly that wasn't the case.

Sure, being driven by emotions is unhealthy. But denying their effect altogether is equally destructive. For Nik. The best move was to face the feelings. Head on. To acknowledge our condition, human beings having human reactions. Head AND heart. Mind AND soul.

After His assessment. The father asked the Teacher if He could help his tormented son. Jesus quickly corrected the man. "If I can?... Anything is possible for one who believes."

Instantly. The man cried out. "I do believe. But HELP ME overcome my unbelief."

We are His most precious handiwork. Created to feel and be felt. To deny that is to deny our humanity. To deny that is to deny the gift that is the human heart.

In our broken world. Good things still happen. But most assuredly. Bad things do, too. We are revered. And we are rejected. We are wanted. And we are wounded.

And as we go. We experience the plethora of emotions caused by all of it. The highest of highs. The lowest of lows. Seldom feeling one emotion independent of the presence of another. Joy mixed with mourning. Grief intertwined with gratitude. And so on.

It can be a lot. All those feelings. And it can be tempting to avoid dealing with them. Perhaps to endeavor to be strong and steadfast for others. Perhaps to avoid experiencing embarrassment or inadequacy for ourselves. We have a million reasons to evade our need to process.

But whatever the reason. Being candid about our state remains our only hope. Whatever the reason. It is better to be forthright with our feelings. Emotions will always have their effect. But in facing them – like the frantic father before Jesus – we find our miracle often lies on the other side of our honesty.

Don't bury feelings alive.

TUESDAY: *Commitment*

"When they came to the other disciples, they saw a large crowd around them and the teachers of the law arguing with them. As soon as all the people saw Jesus, they were overwhelmed with wonder and ran to greet him.

"What are you arguing with them about?" he asked.

A man in the crowd answered, "Teacher, I brought you my son, who is possessed by a spirit that has robbed him of speech. Whenever it seizes him, it throws him to the ground. He foams at the mouth, gnashes his teeth and becomes rigid. I asked your disciples to drive out the spirit, but they could not."

"You unbelieving generation," Jesus replied, "how long shall I stay with you? How long shall I put up with you? Bring the boy to me."

So they brought him. When the spirit saw Jesus, it immediately threw the boy into a convulsion. He fell to the ground and rolled around, foaming at the mouth.

Jesus asked the boy's father, "How long has he been like this?"

"From childhood," he answered. "It has often thrown him into fire or water to kill him. But if you can do anything, take pity on us and help us."

"'If you can'?" said Jesus. "Everything is possible for one who believes."

Immediately the boy's father exclaimed, "I do believe; help me overcome my unbelief!"

When Jesus saw that a crowd was running to the scene, he rebuked the impure spirit. "You deaf and mute spirit," he said, "I command you, come out of him and never enter him again."

The spirit shrieked, convulsed him violently and came out. The boy looked so much like a corpse that many said, "He's dead." But Jesus took him by the hand and lifted him to his feet, and he stood up." - Mark 9:14-27

Lord Jesus, I know your desire for me to remain steadfast. I know You wish for me to stand firm in my faith. But at the same time Lord,

You do not desire for me to feign emotional health when I am hurting. You do not want me to discount my feelings. You want me to process my emotional response in a healthy way. So Lord give me the wisdom as how to do exactly that. To acknowledge my feelings but not be overwhelmed by them. Make me like that of a skyscraper, whose foundation is solid, anchored deep, uncracked, and certain, yet whose heights are able to flex and bend under the force of the changing winds of circumstance. My desire is Your desire my King. To be healthy in every way – including mentally and emotionally. Help me to be authentic and honest with my feelings and experiences. So as I can be fit to perform the work You have for me to do. In Your name I pray. Amen.

WEDNESDAY: Assessment

1. Am I an emotionally healthy person? Do I process my feelings in a healthy way? Would those closest to me agree with that assessment?

2. Am I overly emotional? Am I easily triggered? Are my emotional responses congruent with my experiences? Are they often exaggerated, extreme, or unnecessary?

3. Am I emotionally unavailable? Do I easily shutdown emotionally? Do I dislike "being emotional" or being around others who I deem to be "too emotional?" Why?

4. Am I controlled by my emotions? Do I let my emotions dictate my actions or responses toward others? How has this effected my relationships?

5. Are their difficult emotional experiences that I have buried and chosen not to process? Why? How has this neglect affected me and my relationships with others?

THURSDAY: Battle Plan

1. Who can I talk to in order to process my emotions associated with a difficulty I experienced? Should it be a friend, pastor, or certified counselor?

2. What unhealthy behaviors must I address as a result of unprocessed emotional baggage?

3. Who do I need to seek forgiveness from as a result of my unhealthy and/or unprocessed emotional state?

4. Who do I need to confront that has contributed to my unhealthy emotional state? What does that discussion look like? Where and when should it be done? Should this be done alone or do I need to enlist the help of other(s)?

5. Who can hold me accountable when I am acting triggered, overly emotional, or emotionally unavailable? Who will I allow to speak truth into my life when I am in a difficult emotional state?

FRIDAY: Gut Check

1. Have I made excuses for my unhealthy emotional state? If so, why?

2. Am I willing to go back and process difficult experiences or seasons in order to become healthy, both mentally and emotionally? If not, why not?

3. Why am I scared to process my emotions? Why do I choose to bury them rather than face them?

4. Why am I afraid to open up emotionally toward others? What lies am I believing? Why am I afraid to be vulnerable?

5. Do I trust that God wants to redeem my mental and emotional pain? If not, why not?

SATURDAY: Baby Steps

Suck it up. Put on a brave face. Rub some dirt on it.

Perhaps this is the mantra you grew up under. That feelings are wrong. They are bad. Experiencing them and giving in to them makes you weak and childish. That a strong person is never overwhelmed by their emotions.

That is a lie.

Conversely, perhaps this is your experience:

Feelings equals truth. All feelings should be validated. Follow your heart.

Perhaps this is the paradigm to which you hold. They are all good and therefore that our feelings should serve as our compass. To use reason or time-tested paradigms is folly. That only the individual gets to determine their own truth. That a strong person is obedient to their feelings and would never dictate to another anything that would be received as unwelcome or unwanted.

Sweet friend, that is also a lie.

Feelings are important. Very important. They are the barometers of our kind. They give us real time information as to how we are affected by other people and outside circumstances. They also give us a keen insight as to how we view ourselves.

But feelings are not the end-all-be-all. They give us a proper diagnostic on our psyche but by no means serve as an adequate guide as we go along. That provision comes from the council of our King Jesus.

And He tells us, "In this world, you will have trouble…but I have overcome the world."

In that simple statement lies wonderful news. First and foremost, that He promises to see us through. While at the same time, acknowledging, that this life will prove difficult at times.

So for each of us as we go, to do so effectively, we must process all that we feel in a healthy way. If we do not, it is only a matter of time that all of those unprocessed emotions will result in action and activity that will harm not only ourselves – but all those with whom we come into contact.

It's time to take our emotions seriously. It's time to do the work necessary to determine what we feel that is valid and that which has led us to believe a lie. It's time to face your dragon. He can never be slain if you do not face him.

Draw the Sword of Truth. Enlist the help of a trusted confidant. And start to do the work. He promises to help you…even in your unbelief.

SUNDAY: Reflect and Rest

King Jesus, what has been the result of unprocessed emotions in my life? What steps can I take now to become more emotionally and mentally healthy? Who can help me process both my past difficulties and the ones I have yet to experience?

Lord Jesus, thank You. It has not been easy to go back to all these emotionally triggering events in my life. Reliving those moments brought back so much pain and hurt. However, Lord, the fact remains, in leaving those moments unprocessed, I was unhealthy as were some of my relationships. While the work is just starting, I know this process will lead me to becoming a healthy person, operating in the freedom You have given me through Your sacrifice on the cross. I pray for the courage to continue to do the difficult but necessary work. Help me find and enlist those that can help me in this endeavor. I am excited to see the redemptive work that You are going to do through me. I love You, Lord. Amen.

SPEND THE MONEY

MONDAY: What She Taught Me

"…the fact that all of our friends came out and spent so much money and time with us – we feel so loved and special. It was a perfect break in the middle of this long treatment." - Excerpt from Nik's Journal from February 2021

By February 2021 Nik's regimen was something out of the surreal. At a specialty treament center in Arizona. Treatment was 5 days a week. 4 to 8 hours a day. And the constant bombardment was taking its toll.

In this place of deep sorrow. Came a source of incalculable comfort. An oasis in the desert. A shelter in the storm. A few days reprieve and rest with those who knew us best. Our closest packed up their crews and joined us. To celebrate us. To laugh with us. To cry with us. And to pray with us.

It cost them a pretty penny to do it. A lot of sacrifice was made. But the impact – not only on Nik – but on my whole family. Was nothing short of profound.

These friends of ours put their money where their mouths were. These friends of ours showed up. And in so doing. Proved that they were more than friends. They were family.

The Samaritan acted far differently than the men that had gone before him. The priest had passed by. The Levite had left him. But the Samaritan stopped. He bound up the broken man and tended to his wounds. Gave him wine and oil. Transportation and lodging. And prior to departing. Ensured the bill was paid in full so as not burden the patient any further.

He put his money where his mouth was. And in so doing. Proved that he was more than just a friend. He was family.

That week in Arizona has forever changed me. I tip a little more now. I'm quicker to buy flowers for no reason at all. I'll pick up a tab unexpectedly. And travel with my kids on a whim.

I don't do these things to be boastful. I don't do these things for praise. I do them because I learned all too well the power of blessing others with what God has graciously given me.

We are stewards. Nothing more. It was never ours in the first place. And besides. Hearses don't come with luggage racks. So. Be sure to give to God. Save a little too. But my goodness. Never be stingy. We are blessed to be a blessing.

Spend the money.

TUESDAY: Commitment

On one occasion an expert in the law stood up to test Jesus. "Teacher," he asked, "what must I do to inherit eternal life?" "What is written in the Law?" he replied. "How do you read it?"

He answered, "'Love the Lord your God with all your heart and with all your soul and with all your strength and with all your mind'; and, 'Love your neighbor as yourself.'" "You have answered correctly," Jesus replied. "Do this and you will live." But he wanted to justify himself, so he asked Jesus, "And who is my neighbor?"

In reply Jesus said: "A man was going down from Jerusalem to Jericho, when he was attacked by robbers. They stripped him of his clothes, beat him and went away, leaving him half dead. A priest happened to be going down the same road, and when he saw the man, he passed by on the other side. So too, a Levite, when he came to the place and saw him, passed by on the other side. But a Samaritan, as he traveled, came where the man was; and when he saw him, he took pity on him. He went to him and bandaged his wounds, pouring on oil and wine. Then he put the man on his own donkey, brought him to an inn and took care of him. The next day he took out two denarii and gave them to the innkeeper. 'Look after him,' he said, 'and when I return, I will reimburse you for any extra expense you may have.'

"Which of these three do you think was a neighbor to the man who fell into the hands of robbers?"

The expert in the law replied, "The one who had mercy on him." Jesus told him, "Go and do likewise." - Luke 10:25-37

"No one can serve two masters. Either you will hate the one and love the other, or you will be devoted to the one and despise the other. You cannot serve both God and money." - Matthew 6:24

Holy Spirit, thank You for blessing me so abundantly. Despite how I may view my situation, and though it may not feel like it from time to time, the fact remains I live as one of the wealthiest people in the wealthiest era of human existence. I have access to comforts and conveniences that my ancestors could never dream of embracing. Yet despite my abundance, I crave more. Despite all that I have at my disposal, I tend to use it primarily for my gain and desire. Help me to see me for what I am, that I am called to be a generous steward, not a miserly owner when it comes to the money and resources I have at my command. Help me look for opportunities to bless others even if it comes at the cost of my own personal comfort. Help me, Lord, to seek to be a blessing with that which You have blessed me. Thank You, Lord, for the work You promise to do in me. For Your glory and my joy. Amen.

WEDNESDAY: Assessment

1. In general, how do I approach my personal finances? Am I generous, or am I stingy? Am I a spender, or am I a saver? Where did I learn this behavior? Why do I approach personal finances in the manner I do?
2. Do I have a budget? Do I stick to it? What are the line items on that budget? Do I budget in a way so that I can be generous should I see a need arise for another?
3. Do I consistently make charitable donations? Do I tithe? If not, why not?
4. When was the last time I went out of my way to help someone in need with my resources? What prompted that action?
5. Do I expect recognition, gratitude, or praise when I am generous? If so, why?

THURSDAY: Battle Plan

1. If I do not tithe (10%), what amount can I start contributing now to start working towards that amount? How can I grow that amount over time to reach 10%? What does that look like from a calendar/timeline perspective?
2. Apart from my tithe, what amount of money can I set aside each month to bless someone spontaneously should I see a need arise?

3. Based on my finances, what amount of money should I save monthly?
4. Where am I overextended in my discretionary spending that is inhibiting my ability to be generous? How can I eliminate these costs?
5. Who do I know that could use my help right now? How can I employ either my finances and/or my resources to help them in a tangible way?

FRIDAY: *Gut Check*

1. Do I believe in God's command to be generous to His church and His people? Do my actions reflect that belief? If not, why not?
2. What selfish motives and actions do I need to remove in order to be more generous? Will I remove them? If so, how and when?
3. Will I commit to being more generous with my money and resources towards others? If so, how?
4. Will I commit to being more generous with my time and schedule towards others? If so, how?
5. Do I trust God's plan for my finances and resources more than I trust my own? If not, why not? If so, what do I need to change to reflect that belief?

SATURDAY: *Baby Steps*

Jesus taught a lot using parables. In one in particular, He tells the tale of a man who had amassed much wealth. So much so, that the man planned to tear down his storehouses in order to build bigger ones. More space for more stuff. It sounded like a good plan, until he died that night, and God counted him a fool.

To be clear, God did not count him as reckless for the wealth he had accrued. God has no more issue with the concept of money than He does the height of a mountain or the depth of a sea. God's issue was the man's heart. The man had created an idol out of his abundance, looking only to hoard his resources for himself. At the end of the day – God is always after our heart. And He is clear: where your money lies, your heart will lie also.

Our God has been graciously lavish with us, pouring out blessings both big and small. We are blessed with everything from the food on our tables to the promise assured of the glory of heaven. As His image bearers, we are called to be the same – graciously lavish in our stewardship of His resources at our disposal.

What is the sacred space you have sanctioned off in your life? The part of your schedule for which you sacrifice everything, including those things that, in the right order, should take greater precedence?

It isn't hard to find. You need only look at your checkbook ledger and your calendar. Where your time and money go – that is what matters to you most.

It's time for an audit, friend. To sit down and get honest about what God has given you. Perhaps it is indeed time to build bigger barns. But more than likely, there are matters that need to be addressed first.

Time to get honest. None of us are promised tomorrow. And no one wants to be counted as a fool.

>>>———————

SUNDAY: *Reflect and Rest*

Gracious Spirit, what did I learn about myself this week regarding my generosity or lack thereof? What area do I need to work on the most, my finances or my schedule? What changes do I need to implement and how do I implement them effectively?

Holy Spirit, thank You for blessing me so deeply. Thank You for the gift of time. Thank You for the resources that are at my disposal. You are so so good to me. Yet, Lord, I know that Your desire for me is to pour out of my abundance so that I can be a blessing to others. I ask for Your guidance and discernment as it pertains to handling my finances. I ask for Your help in the management of my time. Lord, help me be known as a generous person. Not for my ego, Lord. And not for my pride. Rather that I may be seen as a city shining on a hill that burns bright with the light of Christ. That I am seen as a person motivated by their deep faith in their Author and King. I want the desires of my heart to be Your desires, Lord. To bring You the honor and glory You so rightfully deserve. In Your holy name, I pray. Amen.

DON'T BE DRIVEN BY FEAR

MONDAY: What She Taught Me

"These doctors tell me I'm terminal and it just doesn't compute. But in reality. We are all terminal – nobody lives forever. I don't feel scared – I feel incredibly blessed and lucky." - Excerpt from Nik's journal from February 2021

One of Nik's greatest regrets was that she found her voice so late. As a kid. She was timid. As an adult. She was quiet. Some thought her reserved. Some may have even thought her rude.

Neither of those assessments hit the mark.

Truth be told. Often she held her tongue for fear of reprisal. Often she kept her sentiments hidden for fear of being caught up in the fray.

Eventually she found it. Her voice. The shift caused a lot of people to be caught off-guard. Dumbfounded. And confused. It was so unlike Nik. But apparently. When you stare death in the face. You don't mind so much about the fallout that will ensue after speaking up and holding the line.

One must wonder what the Sanhedrin was thinking. As those two fisherman stood boldly before them. When just days ago. One was rumored to have denied even knowing Him. Not once. But three times. All before a rooster had crowed.

Now here were these men. Disciples of Jesus. Refusing to give ground. Refusing to fold under relentless threat. Eventually. Surprised. Dumbfounded. And confused. They let them go. Commanding at minimum. They never speak the name of Christ again.

Even at this – Peter and John refused. Promising never to recant Christ nor His truth. They found their voice. They cast off all fear and restraint. Apparently in staring Life Incarnate in the face. They didn't mind so much about the fallout that would ensue. They chose their faith over fear. They decided to speak up. And hold the line.

In the end. It all boils down to a few distinct facts. Life is short. And by contrast. Eternity is not. And of the two potential ends – heaven is magnificent. And hell is hot.

We are all motivated by something. Glory. Fame. Acceptance. Applause. But in the end. All fades into oblivion. In the end. All that will remain. Is us. Before Him. All that will remain. Is an account to give. And a destination to be given.

Don't be driven by fear.

TUESDAY: Commitment

Then they seized him and led him away, bringing him into the high priest's house, and Peter was following at a distance. And when they had kindled a fire in the middle of the courtyard and sat down together, Peter sat down among them. Then a servant girl, seeing him as he sat in the light and looking closely at him, said, "This man also was with him." But he denied it, saying, "Woman, I do not know him." And a little later someone else saw him and said, "You also are one of them." But Peter said, "Man, I am not." And after an interval of about an hour still another insisted, saying, "Certainly this man also was with him, for he too is a Galilean." But Peter said, "Man, I do not know what you are talking about." And immediately, while he was still speaking, the rooster crowed. And the Lord turned and looked at Peter. And Peter remembered the saying of the Lord, how he had said to him, "Before the rooster crows today, you will deny me three times." And he went out and wept bitterly. - Luke 22:54-62

When they saw the courage of Peter and John and realized that they were unschooled, ordinary men, they were astonished and they took note that these men had been with Jesus. But since they could see the man who had been healed standing there with them, there was nothing they could say. So they ordered them to withdraw from the Sanhedrin and then conferred together. "What are we going to do with these men?" they asked. "Everyone living in Jerusalem knows they have performed a notable sign, and we cannot deny it. But to stop this thing from spreading any further among the people, we must warn them to speak no longer to anyone in this name."

Then they called them in again and commanded them not to speak or teach at all in the name of Jesus. But Peter and John replied, "Which is right in God's eyes: to listen to you, or to him? You be the judges! As for us, we cannot help speaking about what we have seen and heard."

After further threats they let them go. They could not decide how to punish them, because all the people were praising God for what had happened. - Acts 4:13-21

Lord Jesus, You never once backed down. You never once cowered in fear. You always stood on truth. You never were swayed by the unmerited opinions of men. You are bold and fierce, and righteous. As Your disciple, I am called to be the same. I am called to be courageous and audacious and confident. Yet I do not need to muster this mindset on my own. The source is not found in my own bravado. I need only fix my eyes on You and Your love for me. Your perfect love casts out all fear. God, let me see how You see. Let my hands and feet and mouth be strengthened by Your Spirit within me. The same Spirit, Lord, that raised You from the dead. Lord, I want my life to be one that is spent doing the good work You would have me do. Not one that is wasted catering to the crowd's flippant concerns and trivial opinions. Lord, I want to be bold. For Your Glory, Lord. And my joy. Amen.

WEDNESDAY: Assessment

1. Where are my core beliefs rooted? In Christ and His Word, or in the opinions of the crowd? Why do I believe what I believe?
2. Am I easily swayed by the preferences of others? How do I react when my beliefs are challenged or unpopular?
3. Do I espouse my beliefs, or do I hold them to myself in silence? Do I "go along to get along," or do I stand my ground when the prevailing opinion begins moving in another direction?
4. Am I bold? Am I courageous? Do my actions reflect this? If so, how? If not, why not?
5. What is the primary area I struggle with being brave and holding to my beliefs? Why do I struggle in this area?

THURSDAY: Battle Plan

1. Where is Christ beckoning to be bolder? What does bravery look like in this area of my life?

2. Is there an aspect of my life I have acted or failed to act due to a motivation of fear? Do I need to repent for this mindset? What does repentance look like?
3. With whom can I discuss my fears? How could they help me and/ or hold me more accountable when it comes to operating in God-honoring boldness?
4. Who do I need to stand up to? Who has bullied me or belittled my beliefs? What does standing up for myself look like, practically speaking?
5. Who do I need to stand up for? Who is depending upon me to be bold for them? What does standing up for them look like, practically speaking?

FRIDAY: *Gut Check*

1. Why am I afraid? Why do I not trust God in this area of my life?
2. Do I believe His promises over me? Do I believe that no matter what, He will never leave me or forsake me?
3. What lies do I believe that are causing me to operate in fear? Why do I believe these lies?
4. Am I ready to act boldly for Christ? Am I committed to standing up for my beliefs despite the fallout that may arise? If not, why not?
5. What step of boldness am I going to take today? What area of my life will I start taking back from fear?

SATURDAY: *Baby Steps*

When my son was just a toddler, he had the strangest fear. He was deathly afraid of dryer sheets. I don't know if it was the look. I don't know if it was the texture. But the sheer sight of one would send him into an unrecoverable panic. I found it comical – he did not.

The truth was, though – it was just a dryer sheet. Nothing to be afraid of. At the end of the day, it could not cause him lasting harm.

I sometimes wonder, from His eternal perspective, if our Heavenly Father looks at His sons and daughters the same way I looked at my toddler

– comically wondering why we are so raptured in fear when so much of what concerns us is trivial and temporal.

Even the weightier matters of our lives – our health, our finances, our relationship – all the worries about those things pale in comparison to the magnitude of God's promises. God cares more about us and our condition far more than we ever could imagine. And God wants to use all of those matters to bring glory to Himself. But to do so, He wants to partner with us, see us step up in boldness, and show a watching world that we trust Him, in all things, at all times.

So where is God beckoning you to lay down your fear? Where is God daring you to step out in courage? Not everyone will agree with it. Some people may even hate you for it. But if God be with you, who could stand against you?

Stop living safely. Stop being boring. Stop hiding. Choose to be bold. Choose to be brave. Choose the adventure of following Christ.

Lay down the fear. And chase after all that He has for you.

It promises to be a heck of a ride.

SUNDAY: Reflect and Rest

King Jesus, where are You calling me to step out in boldness? What fearful lies have I been operating under? What concerns have I allowed to crowd out my belief in Your promises over me?

Lord, Jesus, thank You for Your patience with me. Thank You for Your longsuffering kindness towards me. I know there are times and areas of my life that I am fearful. There are times I have allowed the lies of the enemy and the opinions of others to dictate my actions rather than standing on the truth of Your Word. God, I do not want to be a fearful person. Lord, I do not wish to be passive any longer. Embolden me by Your Spirit. You have not given me a spirit of fear. You have promised me a spirit of love, power, and a sound mind. You promise that You will complete the good work You have started in me. You have promised me that You will never leave me or forsake me. God, let me choose courage today. Not because I can trust in my own ability. But because You have already gone before me. I trust You, Lord. And I love You. Thank You for choosing me. Amen.

You are worth Love and Respect
Dear Bails,
I'm very very sorry the conclusion has came to this, your mom, Mrs.Niki will always be in our hearts.
You have her smile, her humor, you are your mom. You were so strong for your mom, did everything
you could to make … even with all the weird moments. The time you have spent with her,
meant the world … You are one of a kind during these past couple years you've
been through, … on your shoulders, know one would ever know because you
always have a … keeps others the priority.
Your mom

BE INTENTIONAL

MONDAY: What She Taught Me

*"**You are worth love and respect ♥.**"* - Nik's written message left on Bailey's bedroom whiteboard in February 2022

Nik saw the absolute best in her kids. Often when they could not see it in themselves. When they would lose confidence. She provided comfort. When they were confused. She provided counsel. When they would crash and burn. She provided consolement and correction.

She was almost militant about it. In the deliberate way she raised them. But that was intentional too. For Nik. She saw the potential for growth in every gap. An opportunity to improve in every instance. Nothing was to be wasted. Opportunity was everywhere. You just had to look for it.

When it was over. A few of his disciples tried to seek solace in what they knew best. Returning to the past. The pointless place they plodded about prior to meeting the One that upended everything. Back to the sea. Back to the boat. Back to fishing.

They fared poorly though. No catch at all. That is until the Figure called out from the shoreline. And encouraged them to lower their nets once more – specifically on the right side this time. "Surely," He told them, "They would find some there."

And some they did. 153 to be exact.

It would have been completely understandable if Jesus had scolded those men instead of choosing to comfort them. Rather than seeing them restored. Berating them for their abandonment. In His hour of deepest need no less. Instead. He purposefully chose words of life and actions anchored in reconciliation. Preferring to rebuild a future full of promise rather than feed into the ruin of the past.

Each situation calls for a unique tactic. Each relational dynamic demands a different approach. So often it's best to slow down and size up a situation before moving in haste.

Because each of us holds the ability to either inspire or to eviscerate. To encourage or to deaden. To lift up or to tear down. Our ways and our words with our people matter. We would be wise not to forget that. To be mindful of the approach. We would be wise not to lose the war for the sake of the battle that could be won. Remember, there is a golden opportunity in every crippling crisis. We just need look for it.

Be intentional.

TUESDAY: Commitment

Afterward Jesus appeared again to his disciples, by the Sea of Galilee. It happened this way: Simon Peter, Thomas (also known as Didymus), Nathanael from Cana in Galilee, the sons of Zebedee, and two other disciples were together. "I'm going out to fish," Simon Peter told them, and they said, "We'll go with you." So they went out and got into the boat, but that night they caught nothing.

Early in the morning, Jesus stood on the shore, but the disciples did not realize that it was Jesus.

He called out to them, "Friends, haven't you any fish?"

"No," they answered.

He said, "Throw your net on the right side of the boat and you will find some." When they did, they were unable to haul the net in because of the large number of fish.

Then the disciple whom Jesus loved said to Peter, "It is the Lord!" As soon as Simon Peter heard him say, "It is the Lord," he wrapped his outer garment around him (for he had taken it off) and jumped into the water. The other disciples followed in the boat, towing the net full of fish, for they were not far from shore, about a hundred yards. When they landed, they saw a fire of burning coals there with fish on it, and some bread.

Jesus said to them, "Bring some of the fish you have just caught." So Simon Peter climbed back into the boat and dragged the net ashore. It was full of large fish, 153, but even with so many the net was not torn. Jesus said to them, "Come and have breakfast." None of the disciples dared ask him, "Who are you?" They knew it was the Lord. - John 21:1-12

With the tongue we praise our Lord and Father, and with it we curse human beings, who have been made in God's likeness. Out of the same mouth come praise and cursing. My brothers and sisters, this should not be.

Can both fresh water and salt water flow from the same spring? My brothers and sisters, can a fig tree bear olives, or a grapevine bear figs? Neither can a salt spring produce fresh water. - James 3:9-12

Heavenly Father, the power of life and death is found in my words. The capacity to build up or tear down is found in my hands. Father, there are times that I do not count the cost of my actions or my words. I can be flippant and hasty. I can be rash and thoughtless. Remind me, Lord, of the power with which You have entrusted me. Show me where I have been irresponsible in my activity. Give me a repentant spirit and contrite heart to acknowledge my missteps. Also, Lord, allow me to see the opportunity in the mess. The ability to see the good in the crisis. The chance to edify and train and help those who are in my charge when they can only see insufficiency, sorrow, or loss. Lord, I desire to be more intentional. To see Your Kingdom come, and Your will to be done. On earth as it is in heaven. In Your matchless name, I pray. Amen.

WEDNESDAY: Assessment

1. Do I consider my words before speaking? Do I take the time to ensure I have something worthy of being spoken before speaking? Do I consider my timing and my tone?
2. Do I consider the repercussions of my actions before taking them? Do I take the time necessary to determine if my response is warranted and helpful? Do I consider how those will be received by others?
3. Have my words wounded others? What have I done about it?
4. Have my actions caused pain? What have I done about it?
5. With whom do my words and actions carry a great deal of weight? Do I consider that and honor that responsibility rightly? If not, why not?

THURSDAY: Battle Plan

1. Who can I intentionally edify with my words and actions right now? What does that look like practically?
2. Who is it that I need to seek forgiveness from for not being mindful of my words and actions? What does that look like practically?

3. Who do I need to thank who has edified me through their intentional words and actions? What does that look like practically?
4. Who do I need to confront in a loving way who has harmed me with their words and actions? What does that confrontation look like, practically speaking?
5. What is the primary area and/or person I tend to be far too flippant with my words and actions? How can I be more mindful and considerate in this space and/or with that individual?

FRIDAY: *Gut Check*

1. Have I taken responsibility for my missteps with my words and actions? Have I sought forgiveness both from God and those who have been affected? If not, why not?
2. Do I recognize the significance of my words and actions? Does my activity validate my response?
3. Do I trust God can do the redemptive work necessary where I have failed others with my words and actions? If not, why not?
4. Do I trust God can do the redemptive work necessary where others have failed me in word and deed? If not, why not?
5. What lies do I believe about the words spoken over me? How can I replace those lies with God's truth?

SATURDAY: *Baby Steps*

I once heard how an angry manager came out of his office to reprimand an employee who had made a significant error. However, as he stormed down the hallway, his assistant caught him. The assistant said, "Why don't you let me talk to them?" Flustered, the manager asked why he would do such a thing. The assistant further explained, "This definitely needs to be handled, but despite the mistake, the employee in question is a good worker. If I say something, it will be a 25lb corrective criticism. If you say something, it will be a 500lb condemnation. Your words carry far more weight. If this comes from you…it will crush them."

Far too often, we can miss the forest for the trees. In our attempt to deal with the bad hand dealt, the misstep taken, or the poor decision made, we can speak and react out of anger. What follows are words and actions that can maim and mar.

On other occasions, for various reasons, we simply miss the opportunities to edify and encourage those in our lives who so desperately desire our approval and love.

In either case, we discount the significance we have in others' lives. We misjudge the weight of our words. We are flippant in how we treat them with our actions.

Every single interaction, every single conversation, is an opportunity to build up or tear down. Each day we have countless opportunities to make others feel valued – or not. From how we treat the cashier in the grocery store to how we speak to our teenage daughters. From what we say to the fellow coworker we pass in the hallway to how we interact with our spouse when we get home.

Every interaction matters. It could very well be the best part or the worst part of that individual's day.

So, who is it that you need to be more mindful about? Who has God placed on your heart to help today?

He wouldn't prompt you if He didn't want you to do something about it. So do it.

Time to be intentional.

SUNDAY: Reflect and Rest

Everlasting Father, who is it that you are calling me to be more intentional with concerning my words and actions? How can I be more mindful in both word and deed? What was my biggest takeaway from this week?

Father God, thank You so much for opening my eyes this week. For showing me the impact of both my words and my actions. For helping me clearly see the importance of stewarding my interactions in a more intentional and edifying way. You are so patient with me, Lord. I should be the same. You are so careful and mindful of my fragility. I should be the same with those under my care. Lord, please quicken my spirit within me to always be mindful of both my circumstances and my reactions to them. Help me to measure my words, actions, and responses to others in a way that honors You. Thank You, Lord, for the work You continue to do in my heart, for the betterment of not only myself, but others as well. In Your holy name, I pray. Amen.

ENJOY CHRISTMAS

MONDAY: What She Taught Me

"Today is the Monday before Christmas...every day I pray, read my devos, and work on kindness." - Excerpt from Nikki's journal from December 2019

On anybody else, it would have looked ridiculous. But she rocked it. Christmas Eve 2019. She sat in her treatment chair. Getting chemo. Listening to worship. Dressed as festive as she could be. Even brought a little tree with her. She had resolved to still revel in Christmas. Despite her circumstances.

It took her a minute to get there though. A few months prior. When she got her treatment schedule. She cried. She loved Christmas. But this one would be spent being poisoned. Cancer wasn't going to take the holiday off. Which meant she couldn't either.

Therefore she had a choice. She could sit in her situation. Or she could concentrate on her King. Wallow. Understandably so. Or choose joy. The decision was hers. And she made it.

Regardless of where she found herself. It was Christmas. And that meant much more than tinsel and garland. More than carols and cookies.

It meant the God of Heaven had come to redeem His bride. Jesus. "Who, being in very nature God, did not consider equality with God something to be used to His own advantage. Rather He made Himself nothing. Taking the very nature of a servant. Formed in human likeness. And found in appearance as a man. The God of Heaven. Humbled Himself. And became obedient to death – death on a cross." (Philippians 2:6-7) So. One day. We could all go back home.

This is Christmas. The ancient promise was fulfilled. That if we but claim His name. Submit to Him as Lord and Savior. It is all paid for. It is finished. Every wound will be bound up. Every tear will be wiped away.

So this Christmas, whatever you are facing, to the degree you may be suffering I hope you find comfort that no matter how bad it may be, if you walk with our King, the bad thing you are enduring will not last.

And no matter what you have done. The failures you have sustained. I hope you find joy. Because, if you walk with our King, the good thing secured at Calvary can't be taken away.

Because of Christmas and the Cross. The best is yet to come.

Enjoy Christmas.

TUESDAY: Commitment

In those days Caesar Augustus issued a decree that a census should be taken of the entire Roman world. (This was the first census that took place while Quirinius was governor of Syria.) And everyone went to their own town to register.

So Joseph also went up from the town of Nazareth in Galilee to Judea, to Bethlehem the town of David, because he belonged to the house and line of David. He went there to register with Mary, who was pledged to be married to him and was expecting a child. While they were there, the time came for the baby to be born, and she gave birth to her firstborn, a son. She wrapped him in cloths and placed him in a manger, because there was no guest room available for them.

And there were shepherds living out in the fields nearby, keeping watch over their flocks at night. An angel of the Lord appeared to them, and the glory of the Lord shone around them, and they were terrified. But the angel said to them, "Do not be afraid. I bring you good news that will cause great joy for all the people. Today in the town of David a Savior has been born to you; he is the Messiah, the Lord. This will be a sign to you: You will find a baby wrapped in cloths and lying in a manger."

Suddenly a great company of the heavenly host appeared with the angel, praising God and saying,

"Glory to God in the highest heaven, and on earth peace to those on whom his favor rests." - Luke 2:1-14

Who, being in very nature God, did not consider equality with God something to be used to his own advantage; rather, he made himself nothing by taking the very nature of a servant, being made in human likeness. And being found in appearance as a man, he humbled himself by becoming obedient to death, even death on a cross! - Philippians 2:6-8

King Jesus, I am in awe of You. Your majesty. Your magnificence. Your power and Your might. To consider that You left the ivory corridors of heaven. All that was peaceful, harmonious, and good. To come here. To Your beautiful creation that we corrupted. That we had soiled. That we had squandered. Not to destroy it. Not to destroy us. Though we deserved it. We deserve it still. But to come to redeem it. To restore it. To bring us back into a relationship with You. With Your Father. With Your Spirit. Then to consider HOW You did it. How You made a way when there was no way. How You set aside all the glory and honor that should have been and should always be attributed to You so as to pay a price we could never pay. To fulfill a sin debt that would be insurmountable by any human effort. Paid in full. It cost You everything. It cost us nothing. We should be separated from You forever. But because You stood in our place. We will be praising You for all eternity. Thank You, my King! Thank You, my God! Thank You for coming! Thank You for Christmas!

WEDNESDAY: Assessment

1. What do I concentrate on the most during the Christmas season?
2. Have I grown callous to the Christmas narrative? Of Christ's leaving heaven and coming to earth?
3. What is my countenance during Christmas? Joyful? Happy? Content? Sad? Despondent? Depressed? Stressed? Why? What is the root cause for those emotions?
4. Does the Christmas narrative lead me to believe my best is yet to come despite what I have or am currently enduring? If not, why not?
5. Do I need to be more thankful to Christ for His arrival and sacrifice? Would others say that my actions during the Christmas season display a posture of gratitude and thanksgiving?

THURSDAY: *Battle Plan*

1. What are some practical steps I can take during the Christmas season to prepare my heart and create a posture of gratitude?
2. During a season that can be stressful and busy, how can I restructure my schedule in order to remain at peace and remain focused on Christ?
3. What practices or thought processes do I need to eliminate that are either overly stressful, selfish, or self-serving during the Christmas season?
4. Who can I talk to when I become overwhelmed, saddened, or stressed during the Christmas season that will help me refocus on Christ?
5. Who am I called to model peace, joy, gratitude, and grace to during this Christmas season?

FRIDAY: *Gut Check*

1. Have I become a materialistic person? Have I relegated Christmas purely to gift giving and gift receiving?
2. Have I transferred the true focus of this season to the importance of social gatherings, parties, and occasions? Do I care more about my social calendar than the reason for the holiday?
3. Do the implications of Christ's arrival on my eternity overshadow the circumstances I am experiencing temporarily? If not, why not?
4. Am I giving Christ the glory He is due in this season? If not, why not?
5. What practice/habit is God laying on my heart to either give up or take on so as to keep Christmas more reverent? How will I hold myself accountable?

SATURDAY: *Baby Steps*

You've likely heard the narrative countless times. Likely it was told to you as a child. Perhaps you've heard it read by a pastor or a priest during a packed-out Christmas Eve service or mass. You may have even heard Linus recount it as you watched, "A Charlie Brown Christmas." But somewhere along the line, it became commonplace to you. It lost its luster. It lost its brilliance. And as a result, you lost your awe. You lost your wonder and amazement.

Resolve to get it back.

Go somewhere quiet. Shut the door. Open the Gospel of Luke. Read Chapter 2. Verses 1 through 20. Read it slowly. Paint the picture in your mind. Imagine the trek Joseph and Mary had to take. 90 miles on a donkey's back. Place yourself in the field where the heavenly host filled the sky exclaiming His arrival. Think through that Holy Night. Where the King of the Universe was surrounded by nothing but his peasant parents. A few farm animals. And a cold, dark barn.

Be moved by His humility. Be struck by His struggle. Get your awe back. Resolve to find your wonder again. And remember this moment. And choose to never lose it again.

Read the Christmas story.

>>>————

SUNDAY: *Reflect and Rest*

Lord Jesus, what did You reveal to me this week? What paradigm and perspective did I need to have shaken and properly aligned as it pertains to the mystery and majesty of Your arrival? How do I hold fast to my awe of Your coming and never grow callous to it again?

Thank You, Jesus. Thank You for coming. Thank You for making a way when there was no way. Thank You for paying for it all. Every sin. Every misstep. Every broken promise. Every wrong deed done. It cost You everything. It cost me nothing. The Great Exchange. My ruin for Your righteousness. Your glory for my grave. It all started the night You came. The night the angelic host sang to lowly shepherds. The night You resided in a manger instead of a palace. Lord, thank You for reminding me of the majesty of that night, what it started, and what You finished on the cross. Let me never look at Your arrival with a calloused heart again. Thank You, Jesus. Amen.

REST

MONDAY: *What She Taught Me*

"He is in the resting." - Excerpt from Nik's journal from August 2019

I've always considered myself a hard worker. But I couldn't hold a candle to her. That chick had a motor that just wouldn't quit. And she took pride in that. In her ability to get things done.

So when cancer forced her to slow down. She warred against it. She willed herself onward. Frantically moving about. Attempting to redeem the time taken from the days stolen by the disease and its treatment.

But even that became impossible over time. Eventually. She was forced to stop. To sit still. And to hold her peace. She could no longer muster the vigor necessary to tie up all the loose ends.

And though it was not her intended aim. I am convinced it was His. Because in that stillness. In the silence. Nik spent hours alone with Him. Being comforted by the Sovereign of Solace Himself.

The very first place Nik told me to go upon her passing was her beach – to start to seek my own rest. So dutifully. I went. Somewhat begrudgingly to be honest. I thought that there was too much left undone to go away. The tyranny of the urgent grasped for my attention. It attempted to stifle the matter of greatest importance – my need for quiet. My need for rest.

But Nik knew what I really needed was not another task to be accomplished. But rather, what comes only from laying down the agenda. Putting down the to-do list. And stepping back from the itinerary. And giving it all back to God.

What was born out of that time has been what has followed since. Those days spent seaside in seclusion laid this foundation. The bedrock upon all of this has been built. The result, precious time spent chronicling God's faithfulness and provision as witnessed in the life of my late wife.

Productivity is important. Efficiency matters. But there is a spiritual supernova that can be accessed by sitting in solitude. Our effectiveness is not born of our might. Rather. It is derived from the well from which we draw. A well that needs constant replenishment. He is the vine. We are but the branches. Apart from Him. We can do nothing.

So be sure to take the time necessary. Get alone. Get quiet. And listen.

Rest.

TUESDAY: *Commitment*

"I am the true vine, and my Father is the gardener. He cuts off every branch in me that bears no fruit, while every branch that does bear fruit he prunes so that it will be even more fruitful. You are already clean because of the word I have spoken to you. Remain in me, as I also remain in you. No branch can bear fruit by itself; it must remain in the vine. Neither can you bear fruit unless you remain in me.

"I am the vine; you are the branches. If you remain in me and I in you, you will bear much fruit; apart from me you can do nothing. If you do not remain in me, you are like a branch that is thrown away and withers; such branches are picked up, thrown into the fire and burned. If you remain in me and my words remain in you, ask whatever you wish, and it will be done for you. This is to my Father's glory, that you bear much fruit, showing yourselves to be my disciples." - John 15:1-8

Then, because so many people were coming and going that they did not even have a chance to eat, he said to them, "Come with me by yourselves to a quiet place and get some rest." - Mark 6:31

There remains, then, a Sabbath-rest for the people of God; for anyone who enters God's rest also rests from their works, just as God did from his. Let us, therefore, make every effort to enter that rest, so that no one will perish by following their example of disobedience. - Hebrews 4:9-11

Lord Jesus, with so much to do and so little time to do it. I count my effectiveness, largely, in how productive I can be – how many things I can accomplish in a given day. Leaving things undone leaves me feeling anxious. Leaving things unresolved leaves me feeling uneasy. I would rather work myself to the bone than to slow down, let alone stop, and take care of what matters most – cultivating a deeper relationship with You. Yet I know that operating in such a manner has a shelf life. I can only move so fast for so long. And if I am not careful, continuing in such a way for too long can only lead to burnout. It will lead to dropping my guard and giving way to sin. It will lead to me becoming isolated and susceptible to being sifted by the enemy. Lord, please help me! Make me lie down in Your pastures. Lead me to Your still waters. That is where life is found. Because that is where You remain. In the stillness. And in the quiet. Draw me closer to You, Lord. Let me find my rest. I ask this in Your most holy Name. Amen.

WEDNESDAY: Assessment

1. Do I schedule rest into my routine? If not, why not? If so, what does that rest practically look like?
2. Do I equate my worth to my ability to be productive? Do I see resting as laziness? What formed these beliefs?
3. Do I work too much? Would I describe myself as a "workaholic?" What would those closest to me say on this matter?
4. Where do I find rest? Where am I at peace? What environment is the most effective in creating space for me to experience restorative rest?
5. Why do I fear slowing down? Why won't I stop and rest? What is it that I feel solely capable of being responsible for?

THURSDAY: Battle Plan

1. What discretionary decisions are keeping me from rest? How do I alter those to build time into my schedule for rest?

2. Where can I go routinely to find rest? Practically, what does creating a restful space look like?
3. What meetings, calls, events, etc., do I need to alter or eliminate in order to create space for rest?
4. How do I get quiet before God for five minutes a day? Ten minutes? Fifteen minutes? Thirty minutes?
5. With what project, initiative, responsibility, etc., do I need to find support to alleviate my load and create a margin for rest?

FRIDAY: Gut Check

1. Will I commit to prioritizing my rest? If so, how?
2. Will I commit to stopping the habits that keep me from resting (i.e., staying up too late, overcommitting my schedule, poor planning, etc.)? How will I stop these habits, practically speaking?
3. Do I trust that God can do more in my life effectively if I choose to trust Him and rest frequently as He commands? If not, why not?
4. What excuse do I need to remove that is keeping me from seeking rest?
5. What lies do I believe concerning my rest?

SATURDAY: Baby Steps

You can't be serious right? I mean, deep down inside, you gotta know the truth. Even He did it, and He didn't have to. He worked six days and decided to rest on the 7th. He did that for us, you know. To model what we need. We are created in His image, and as such, we are called to operate as He does – even when it comes to rest.

So, what's stopping you from slowing down? What is keeping you from getting quiet? What has you so distracted that you can't spend ten minutes in silence with the King of the Universe?

I promise whatever it is, it can wait.

So, choose to let go. Choose to trust Him. Choose to take control of your life. Choose to manage your schedule in a more sustainable way.

You can't be effective if you are burned out. You can't be effective if you are anxious and overwhelmed. You can't be effective if you are stretched too thin.

Commit to finding time to be alone with Him. Not tomorrow. Not next week. Today. Start with five minutes if that is what you have. Commit to building it over time. Like any relationship worth having, you will have to invest in it. He wants to spend time with you, but He isn't going to force you to spend time with Him.

It takes two to tango.

But if you do, it will be so worth it. You will be lighter, more joyful, and less stressed. Often, it's not that we have to do more. We may very well need to find contentment in doing less.

But one thing you must do is for certain – you need to slow down, get quiet, and listen for Him.

Today.

>>>>———

SUNDAY: *Reflect and Rest*

King Jesus, what did I learn about myself this week concerning my need for rest? Do I take my rest seriously? What adjustments to my life and schedule do I need to make to prioritize my rest?

My Lord Jesus, thank You for our time spent together this week. Thank You for showing up when I slowed down. Lord, I know that You designed me for work. That You would have me take dominion over Your creation in Your stead. But thank You for reminding me this week that that is only part of my commission. Thank You for reminding me that the only way to carry out my assigned duties here in this life is to slow down and spend time with You first. To listen for Your still, small voice. And to abide in the shadow of Your wing. Lord thank You for the reminder that You are the vine, and I am the branch. That my sustainment is found in You and You alone. Please, Jesus, help me to remain mindful of that fact every day. Help me to protect my schedule so that I stay in constant contact with You. Thank You, God, for the gift of rest. I love You, Lord. Thank You for desiring the best for me. Amen.

TRAVEL. BUT AVOID CAMPING IF AT ALL POSSIBLE.

MONDAY: *What She Taught Me*

"Why would I want to spend hundreds of dollars to live like I am homeless?" - Nik's response to my asking if she would like to go camping in Summer of 2014

With only a few weeks to go. I am compelled to share Nik's lighter. Quirky. Humorous side. One more time. I'll save the deeper stuff for the last two weeks.

Upon our return to the East Coast. I took Nik camping. Once. She swore off it after that. Despite the picturesque scenery. The beautiful rippling river. And quaint peaceful surroundings. The accommodations were a bit dilapidated. To put it mildly.

After that trip. Nik encouraged me to continue to camp. Specifically with Everett. Very manly bonding experience. To be certain. She just wouldn't be attending anymore.

She wasn't being pretentious. Uppity. Or bougie. Chick just knew what she wanted. And what she constituted was the right atmosphere for her recreation.

For Nik. Shorelines trumped riverbanks. Every time. Game. Set. Match.

In reflecting upon her approach. I've come to appreciate Nik's "never settle" mentality. The desire to pursue excellence in all things. Both at work. And at play. To live out the mandate that whatever we eat or drink. Whatever we do. To do it all for the glory of the Lord. Resolving not to accept less than is achievable. Daring to take the chance. Committing to what is required. And fighting to see it attained.

Life is a grand gift. And a good portion of my time and my coin should be spent enjoying it. After all. God is the author of fun and frivolity too. All work and no play makes Steve a dull boy. And in a culture of striving and achieving. There is something to be said about allowing time for lounging and laughing. Occasionally slowing down and spending a holiday along the seashore.

So I encourage you to find something you love and go do it. To plan for that trip of a lifetime. Save for it. And go experience it. Heaven's grandeur is inconceivable. And each of us should live this day for that day. That is for certain. But the key is to actually LIVE while we are here. To experience the awe and splendor of His creation. And to praise Him for it along the way.

Travel. But avoid camping if at all possible.

TUESDAY: *Commitment*

"So whether you eat or drink or whatever you do, do it all for the glory of God." - 1 Corinthians 10:31

"This is what I have observed to be good: that it is appropriate for a person to eat, to drink and to find satisfaction in their toilsome labor under the sun during the few days of life God has given them, for this is their lot." - Ecclesiastes 5:18

"The thief comes only to steal and kill and destroy; I have come that they may have life, and have it to the full." - John 10:10

Holy Spirit, I readily admit at times I take life too seriously. I run from project to project. Task to task. Duty to duty. I run so much that I run myself ragged. Even on the days I take "off," I find myself cramming in so much activity that I barely have time to enjoy the rest. Often, I find myself saying that I need a vacation, right after I have returned from vacation. Lord, I want to enjoy the life You have given me. I don't want to strive unnecessarily. Furthermore, deep down, I know the places, experiences, and things that give me that enjoyment. I don't want to settle for less than You have for me in any area of my life – including the pleasurable parts of this existence. Please help me to do that. Thank You, Lord, for such an incredible planet to enjoy. Thank You, Lord, for the people I have to enjoy it with. Thank You for all that this life has to offer. I pray I experience it all to the full. In Your precious Name, I pray. Amen.

WEDNESDAY: Assessment

1. Do I live life to the full? Do I prioritize the people, places, and/or interests that provide me God-honoring enjoyment? Do I schedule "fun?"
2. What destination provides me a sense of peace, joy, and happiness? How often do I go there? Why does that place make me feel so good?
3. What hobby or interest provides me a sense of peace, joy, and happiness? How often do I do it? Why does it make me feel so good?
4. When was my last real vacation (one that was restful and enjoyable)? What made it so enjoyable? Do I have a plan to create another similar experience?
5. Do I plan and save for my vacations and/or hobbies sensibly? Am I considerate of others when doing so? Do I plan for the financial impact of my social calendar?

THURSDAY: Battle Plan

1. Where do I want to go? When can I reasonably go there? How can I financially plan for it? Who do I want to take with me?
2. What are the trips, hobbies, or interests that I am participating in right now that are not providing me an adequate return on my investment of time, money, or resources? What is preventing me from canceling these activities?
3. How can I build a plan to take one enjoyable vacation each year? What needs to shift to make this happen?
4. How can I build an appropriate amount of time into my weekly schedule for fun? Who do I need to inform about this plan? What sacrifices will I need to make to make this a routine?

5. Who can hold me accountable to the plan regarding saving and preparing for these activities so that I do not overextend myself financially? Who do I need to inform as a courtesy about my plan? Whom do I need to include in this planning? Who do I need to seek permission from to approve this plan?

FRIDAY: *Gut Check*

1. What is preventing me from experiencing life to the full? Why am I tolerating it?
2. What excuses am I making that are preventing me from enjoying my life?
3. Am I stewarding my resources poorly, resulting in me not being able to enjoy my life to the full? Why am I doing this?
4. Do I think God desires me to have fun? If not, why not? If so, why aren't I doing it?
5. Do I think I am worthy of enjoying this life? What lies do I believe about fun and enjoyment?

SATURDAY: *Baby Steps*

For the better part of 5 years, I saved money for a beach vacation. Specifically, I saved for a beach house for our 10th anniversary. I did it in secret. With every raise, with every promotion, and with every "cost of living" adjustment, I saved a little more in a secret account for the surprise. I felt a bit like Andy Dufresne in the "Shawshank Redemption," the way he clandestinely tunneled through his prison wall only to hide the rubble pebble-by-pebble, in the prison yard. I took the few meager dollars I had and, day-by-day, month-by-month, year-over-year, added them to the account. And like Dufresne, when the time was just right, I made my move.

On our 10th anniversary, I presented the gift, paid-in-full. A one-week beach vacation right on the sea. A trip of a lifetime.

It took a lot of work, a lot of planning, and a whole lot of explaining once it was presented. But man, was it worth it.

It's amazing what we can accomplish when we put our minds to it. As a man thinketh, so is he. Very little is beyond our grasp if we try. It may take time. Years. Decades even. But if we plan for it and stick to it, we can make it happen. It may take a lot of money to accomplish. More than we can accumulate without significant sacrifice, patience, and discipline. But if we budget for it and stick to it, we can make it happen.

So, what is your dream? What will it take to turn it into a reality?

Get serious for a minute. Don't blow it off as an impossibility. Sit down and put pen to paper. Map it out. Get a plan together and enlist the support you need.

Dream bigger, boys and girls. Don't just dream of the destination. Start to dream up the plan that will get you there.

It'll be so worth it.

>>>————————

SUNDAY: *Reflect and Rest*

Holy Spirit, what did I learn about enjoying life more this week? What do I need to change or plan better in order to make this happen? What are the desires of my heart that bring me joy? How can I prioritize them in a healthy way?

Loving Counselor, You love fun! You love to see Your people laugh! You love to see Your people enjoying the precious gift of the life You have so graciously given us! As the old saying goes, if the devil can't get me to sin, he'll just try and keep me busy. Help me to see that, Lord. To not be so busy with my to-do list that I miss the opportunities that You place before me for the occasional, but much needed, rest and frivolity. At the same time, convict me to be disciplined in my planning and preparing for these opportunities. Not to be flip or inconsiderate. To properly make proper provision for these experiences in my life. God, I wish to enjoy all that You have for me better and more fully. I know You can help me to turn that possibility into a reality. I am ready to do it, Lord. It excites me. Thank You in advance for what I will witness and be a part of because of You and Your leading. I love You. Amen.

THE BEST IS YET TO COME

MONDAY: What She Taught Me

"Hope is expecting the best is yet to come." - Excerpt from Nik's journal from July 2021

A few weeks before her final breath. I was wrestling with the finality of it all. That despite the ferocity with which she fought. Despite the plethora of prayers from the masses. Despite the thousands that stood in the gap. It was apparent. Nik was not going to be healed.

I surmised. It was over.

Then God reminded me that it wasn't. Actually. Far from it. I found it in Paul's first letter to the church at Corinth. In his closing remarks. He reminds the church of the significance of the cross and the resurrection of Christ. The atonement was paid at Golgotha. And the glory gained as revealed by the empty grave. The complete and accomplished work. And the resulting promise therein. That one day. Because of Jesus. All things will be made new.

One day. In the twinkling of an eye. The perishable will put on the imperishable. The mortal will don immortality. That all the torture. All the torment. And all trouble of this broken life will be no more.

One day. We will exchange the terrestrial for the celestial. Demise will be cheated of its victory. Death will lose its sting.

One day. The only tears shed will be those wept in the joy of the Savior we will behold. And the loved ones with whom we are reunited once more. Forever. In Glory.

It is not over. Far from it.

So in the waiting. The Apostle tells us. Stand firm. Always abounding in the work of the Lord.

Nik did just that. I want to do the same. And I want the same for you.

While this instruction has reached its end. And this class has drawn to a close. I hope that you will take these lessons with you. To help you traverse life's assured triumphs and trials.

I hope that you keep pushing on and keep moving forward. You keep being brave and setting boundaries when necessary. That you stand up for yourself and love Jesus with your whole heart. And that you take lots of vacations along the way.

I hope you live this life to the full. Simultaneously. I hope you always stand firm on His promise.

The best is yet to come.

TUESDAY: Commitment

But someone will ask, "How are the dead raised? With what kind of body will they come?" How foolish! What you sow does not come to life unless it dies. When you sow, you do not plant the body that will be, but just a seed, perhaps of wheat or of something else. But God gives it a body as he has determined, and to each kind of seed he gives its own body. Not all flesh is the same: People have one kind of flesh, animals have another, birds another, and fish another. There are also heavenly bodies and there are earthly bodies, but the splendor of the heavenly bodies is one kind, and the splendor of the earthly bodies is another. The sun has one kind of splendor, the moon another, and the stars another; and star differs from star in splendor.

So will it be with the resurrection of the dead. The body that is sown is perishable, it is raised imperishable; it is sown in dishonor, it is raised in glory; it is sown in weakness, it is raised in power; it is sown a natural body, it is raised a spiritual body.

If there is a natural body, there is also a spiritual body. So it is written: "The first man Adam became a living being"; the last Adam, a life-giving spirit. The spiritual did not come first, but the natural, and after that the spiritual. The first man was of the dust of the earth; the second man is of heaven. As was the earthly man, so are those who are of the earth; and as is the heavenly man, so also are those who are of heaven. And just as we have borne the image of the earthly man, so shall we bear the image of the heavenly man.

I declare to you, brothers and sisters, that flesh and blood cannot inherit the Kingdom of God, nor does the perishable inherit the imperishable. Listen, I tell you a mystery: We will not all sleep, but we will all be changed, in a flash, in the twinkling of an eye, at the last trumpet. For the trumpet will sound, the dead will be raised imperishable, and we will be changed. For the perishable must clothe itself with the imperishable, and the mortal with immortality. When the perishable has been clothed with the imperishable, and the mortal with immortality, then the saying that is written will come true: "Death has been swallowed up in victory."

"Where, O death, is your victory? Where, O death, is your sting?"

The sting of death is sin, and the power of sin is the law. But thanks be to God! He gives us the victory through our Lord Jesus Christ.

Therefore, my dear brothers and sisters, stand firm. Let nothing move you. Always give yourselves fully to the work of the Lord because you know that your labor in the Lord is not in vain. - 1 Corinthians 15:35-58

Heavenly Father, You are so faithful. You are always with me. You are always available to me. Because of Your Son, Jesus, and the price He paid on my behalf, I am now reconciled to You. No matter what happens to me in this life. I am assured because I have claimed Him as my Lord and Savior, that one glorious day, I will be in Your presence and enter into Your celestial city for all eternity. That all suffering will be over. Pain will no longer exist. I will be reunited with those who have gone before me. I will be at rest and have an unshakeable peace. So, Lord, with that, let me stand firm in the confidence of Your promise. Let my eyes be fixed on heaven and the crown to be gained. Anchor my soul again, Lord. Renew my confidence. Let me confidently embrace Your banner over me: the best is yet to come! Thank You, Father. Amen.

WEDNESDAY: Assessment

1. Are my eyes fixed on eternity? Do I live this day for that day? Am I confident that my eternal destination is secure?
2. Do I believe that my best is yet to come? Do I trust God's plan for my life?
3. Am I surrounded by a community that spurs me onward? That challenges me to stand firm in my faith despite my circumstances.
4. Am I giving my life to Christ? Am I walking out the Great Commission (Matthew 28:16-20)? If not, why not?

5.   What aspect of my life requires further submission to God's will and authority? Why am I reticent to give it up to Him?

THURSDAY: Battle Plan

1.   What specifically is preventing me from standing firm? What wrong thinking or lie do I believe that is causing me not to operate in this truth?
2.   Practically speaking, in what area of my life is God calling me to be more courageous and stand up for my core beliefs?
3.   What does standing firm look like in this area? What do I need to change?
4.   What do I need to repent of for not standing firm? What does repentance look like, practically speaking?
5.   Who do I need to seek forgiveness from for not standing firm in my faith? How has it negatively affected that individual? How can I restore that relationship, situation, or circumstance?

FRIDAY: Gut Check

1.   No matter what happens – will I stand on God's promise that the best is yet to come?
2.   Do I love my temporal life here more than the eternal one promised me? Do my words and actions validate my response to that question?
3.   Do the misfortunes of this life shake my faith? Am I "hot" and "cold" in my faith based on my feelings or experiences?
4.   Will I commit to being a hopeful person? Will I be counted as someone who can be relied upon to have unwavering faith?
5.   Will I commit to running my race and chasing after Jesus with all that I have? Will I pursue Him at all costs?

SATURDAY: Baby Steps

You have done a lot of work this year, friend. A lot of work. In committing to this process, you have intentionally and diligently done what few dare to attempt – you've committed to becoming the best version of yourself. Now as this year has come to a close, I leave you with this charge:

Don't stop.

Everything you have done has been for a purpose, beyond yourself. There is a community that needs what you have learned. There is a family that needs the wisdom you have obtained. There is a wife or a husband who desperately needs to obtain what you have so diligently sought. There are sons and daughters who need the deeper love that you have grown to have. All of us, we need your help.

So today, reflect on the lessons you learned. Reflect on how Christ has molded you and matured you this past year. How He has given you a greater ability to stand firm. How He has assured you that your best is yet to come.

Reflect on these truths – and commit to passing them along. Share what you have learned. If you think it would help, give them a copy of this devotional to help them along their own journey.

You have obtained this wisdom for a reason, friend. And if you aren't dead, He's not done using you.

For His glory, and for your joy.

Step into a new season today. Commit to helping someone else.

They need you.

SUNDAY: Reflect and Rest

My Father, what must I do now, knowing that the best is yet to come? What perspective needs to shift? What actions need to change? How can I be salt and light to a broken world?

Gracious and Heavenly Father, hallowed be Your Name. Thank You, Lord, so much for all that You have taught me this year. Thank You, Lord, for the intentional time we spent together. Thank You for the wisdom You have given me. Thank You for the help You have provided me. Thank You for the renewed Godly perspective I've gained. Lord, help me find a way to use it. To help others in my stead. To provide hope on the darkest days. To celebrate well on the brightest ones. Help me, Lord, to always stand firm. To always hold to the truth, that because of Jesus, my best is yet to come. Thank You, Lord, for being my King. It is an honor to be Your child. In Your most holy and precious Name, I pray. Amen.

CONCLUSION

"They triumphed over him by the blood of the Lamb and by the word of their testimony; they did not love their lives so much as to shrink from death." - Revelation 12:11

It's no small thing when the God of heaven instructs us on how we slay our ancient enemy, the devil. Three elements in total:

1. The Blood of the Lamb (i.e., the complete and accomplished work of Jesus Christ)
2. The Word of our Testimony (i.e., the way we live our lives)
3. Not Shrinking from Death (i.e., standing firm on the promise that our best is yet to come)

Thankfully, the first matter was fully resolved roughly 2000 years ago when Christ fulfilled all the prophesies and every iota of the law. He conquered Satan, Sin, and Death. All three of those adversaries are now living on borrowed time until His triumphal return.

In the meantime, the second two pieces – those remain securely in our court: living as God would have us live and keeping our eyes fixed on heaven.

Hopefully, this devotional has helped you take hold of that truth. Cementing the fact that every aspect of our lives matters: how we live; how we interact, what we pursue, what we endure, and how we endure it. Most importantly, what we pass along to those that follow us.

For my part – that has been the goal and the aim of this entire exercise, to pass along the wisdom of Christ given to me through the testimony I witnessed in the life of my late wife. To not hold these lessons to myself, but rather, put them on display for anyone who cares to slow down long enough and study them.

It's my way of trying to punch the devil in the mouth I suppose. My attempt to walk out my own Revelation 12:11.

It's my hope that it helped you. Because, after all – you did a lot of work this year, friend. A lot of work. Well done. You are to be commended. It wasn't easy, I know.

So, as we close, my final charge to you is this:

I hope your approach to life will be a little different now, a little more intentional, and a lot more thoughtful. I hope you never look at a beach the same. I hope you give yourself the liberty to laugh harder than you have in the past. I hope you give yourself the grace to cry when you need it. And I hope you are quick to offer a hug to anyone who is hurting. I hope you return to these lessons often and use them as guideposts for traversing all of life's ups and downs.

I hope you are more committed to being a better husband, wife, mother, father, son, daughter, aunt, uncle, grandparent, friend, and coworker. I hope this past year spurs you to continue pursuing being a better human and follower of Christ. I hope you pass these lessons along and learn a few of your own.

After all, your testimony is still being written. So be sure to take note of what He is teaching you. Continue to spend time with Him and meditate on His deep truths. You are still here, which means there is still more for you to do. He is still speaking. You just have to get quiet with Him and listen.

Remember – this life is a beautiful gift. Be sure to live it to the fullest. Don't waste it.

And once again, remember to take lots of vacations. After the work you put in this year, you've certainly earned one.

All the best.

ACKNOWLEDGMENTS

To my **Heavenly Father**, to my **Lord and Savior, Jesus Christ**, and to the **Holy Spirit** that has guided me through this entire process. From the years of joy I spent married to Nik, through her diagnosis and fight, and through her loss, my God has remained the singular constant. Through it all, despite all my questioning and struggle, He has not once left me or forsaken me. He alone remains worthy of praise.

To my late wife, **Nik**. You were my person. It was the greatest honor of my life to love you to the best of my ability before sending you home. I love you. I miss you. And I can't wait to see you again real soon.

To my children, **Bailey**, **Rian**, and **Everett**. Witnessing your collective grace, poise, and resilience in the most difficult season of our lives has been nothing short of inspiring. Thank you for being incredible human beings. I am so proud of you, and I am so excited to see what your futures hold. I really do believe our God wastes nothing and that your best is yet to come.

To my parents, **Richard** and **Amy**. I have no words. I am crying as I write this thank you. I stand in awe of your love for each other and for our family. You two are the epitome of Christ-centered parents. It is an honor to be your son.

To the **Healanderbard Crew**. You are my brothers and my sisters. My nieces and my nephews. I will never be able to repay you for the way you stood in the gap for my family throughout our darkest season. Thank you from the bottom of my heart.

To the **elders, pastors, staff, and congregants of Lighthouse Church**. In ways both great and small, you have proven time and time again what it means to be the hands and feet of Jesus. I am proud to call you my church and I am so grateful to each of you for the years of endless support.

To my assistant, **Abi**. Thanks for making me sound a lot smarter than I am. Without your edits and insight, this book would have fallen woefully short of its potential. Thank you for your tireless efforts to make this devotional the best it could be.

To **Brandon Janous** and the entire crew at **Blue Hat Publishing**. There would be no book without you. You took my content and my vision and brought it to life. Because of you, Nik's wisdom will be available for many, including our future grandchildren. I can never thank you enough for that.

Finally...

To **Rae**. Your boldness to choose to walk faithfully beside me has brought me a depth of healing I will never be able to fully articulate. Prior to her departure, Nik prayed you into my life. And I am so grateful God saw fit to answer that prayer. I love you.